FREEDOM FROM WANT

EDWARD GRESSER

Soft Skull Press
Brooklyn, NY

Library of Congress Cataloging-in-Publication Data

Gresser, Edward.
    Freedom from want/by Edward Gresser.
    p. cm.
    ISBN-13: 978-1-933368-62-7
    ISBN-10: 1-933368-62-4
    1. Globalization—Economic aspects. 2. Globalization—Social aspects.
        3. Human rights. 4. Quality of work life. 5. Environmental
        protection. I. Title.
    JZ1318.G75 2006
    330—dc22   2007028507

Printed in the United States of America

Soft Skull Press
55 Washigton St.
STE 804
Brooklyn, NY 11201
www.softskull.com

10 9 8 7 6 5 4 3 2 1

CONTENTS

Introduction

PART I

I. THE MODERN GLOBAL ECONOMY AND ITS DESIGN

   1. Some Numbers, A Worker, The Rules

   2. An Indictment

II. THE BACKGROUND

   1. Hope, Gloom and Virtue

   2. The American Background

   3. Victorian Globalization and Its Collapse

   4. Liberal Internationalism and the Trading System

   5. Re-Enter China

   6. Happy Ending?

PART II

I. BACKLASH

   1. Loss of Faith

   2. Trade & Labor: The New Whig Argument

   3. Trade & Environment: Interlude with Turtles and Fish

4. Poverty: Why Trade Policies are Toughest on the Poor

5. War and Peace: Middle East as the Blank Spot on the
    Trade Map

II. PROGRAM

1. At Home

2. A Trade Agenda

3. A Concluding Thought

INTRODUCTION

TIME IN THE WILDERNESS, just as it can ease the soul, can revive the political movement. Years in opposition can be time for reflection upon past mistakes, revision of old ideas, or adoption of new ones better fitted to changed times and circumstance.

Often it works out just so. American liberals in 2007 suddenly find their ideas back in fashion and the jagged-edge conservatism of the Bush era in disrepute. With the Committee chairs lost twelve years ago reclaimed, and a Presidential campaign approaching, liberal hopes are high and Congress full of ideas developed in exile: health reform, energy efficiency, climate change, and the like.

But time in the wilderness can be unhealthy too. Time for reflection can be spent nursing and exaggerating grievances. Old principles and ideas are often still good ones, and apparently new ideas are sometimes ideas abandoned long ago, for good reason. Something of the sort has happened as liberals consider trade and the global economy.

A story popular in many liberal assemblies runs roughly as follows: Not long ago, America was a happy and mostly self-sufficient "national" economy. By the 1950s the New Deal and the trade union movement had built an egalitarian, middle-class country, in which jobs were secure and work well-paid. In the 1960s and 1970s, liberal activists and reformist politicians made us decent as well as rich, as they wrote environmental bills, drafted workplace safety regulations, and passed food-safety laws that improved health and the quality of life. The good society seemed within reach—and then it vanished.

Thirty years later, we live in a global economy. Its foundation is a mesh of conservative ideas, evolved during the conservative exile of the 1960s and 1970s. Its architecture, built during the 1980s and 1990s by ascendant right-wing politicians, is a series of trade agreements like the North American Free Trade Agreement, capped by the enforcement mechanisms of the World Trade Organization. Its consequence is a novel and ruinous competition, pitting American labor against the desperate, exploited workers of the third world.

This newly created global economy leaves workers jobless at home and mistreated abroad, as factories escape to poorer countries in which they cut wages and ignore environmental law. Global economic institutions enforce inhumane and profit-obsessed rules, which reduce the nation's ability to protect families from pollution and unsafe food, and permit powerful new competitors to erode American industrial power. Blocked abroad by the WTO and perverted at home by business wealth, the American government has failed to act. But the people understand. One day their government will have to listen.

A 2004 book by the Chairman of the Democratic Party, Howard Dean, illustrates the thinking well. On most pages a standard political tract, it takes on a vivid tone of outrage and betrayal when it turns to the global economy:

> It was incredibly shortsighted to believe that globalizing the advantages of world trade without globalizing protection for workers, human rights and the environment would lead to sustainable economic benefits for workers in the United States or anywhere else . . . Unless we protect workers everywhere, open borders are ultimately unsustainable and probably incompatible with democracy.

The passage is familiar and unsurprising—until we realize that Dean's blast is not at amoral businesses or cold Republican theorists, but at the last Democratic President.

Bill Clinton spoke differently of the global economy—always with nuance, often critically, but never as something to fear or deplore. His speeches portray an opening world as a support for prosperity at home, a chance to reduce poverty abroad, something to reform and improve, a path toward stable peace. A passage from 1997 is typical:

> We do not need to be afraid to trade with the rest of the world. We are the most productive economy in the world. There will always

be changes in this economy. There will always be new jobs being created and some going away. But on balance, we have benefited for sixty years by leading the way to integrate the world's economies. And that will promote peace; it will promote freedom; it will promote stability; it will raise the level of living standards in other parts of the world even as it maintains America as the world's most prosperous nation.

Dean's "incredibly short-sighted" policies, it turns out, are neither inheritances from the age of Reagan nor innovations of the younger George Bush. (So far, except for raising farm subsidies in 2002, Mr. Bush has left the American trade regime much as he found it.) Instead they are Clinton's legacies. All—passage of NAFTA, creation of the WTO, re-opening of trade with Cambodia and Vietnam, preferences for Africa, elimination of trade barriers on computers and semiconductor chips, permanent Normal Trade Relations for China—came between the spring of 1993 and the autumn of 2000.

As I write in the late spring of 2007, many or most liberals see the Clintonian ideas as an aberration, a capitulation to business, or even a betrayal. Their view is not universal; as I write in the late spring of 2007, Harlem's Congressman Charles Rangel is attempting to revive and build upon the Clinton-era record, using relatively small agreements with Peru and Panama as a starting point. But even a figure as reassuring as Rangel—and even when joined in the effort by Sander Levin and Nancy Pelosi—finds the venerable *Nation* magazine jeering his effort as a "sellout" to business and denounced by more leftish colleagues as a coalition of "foxes and wolves."[1] Evidently, for most American liberals Dean's is the principled and natural position.

But in fact, Clinton's record was the authentic tradition of American liberalism. The great liberal Presidencies of the century—Wilson, Roosevelt, Truman, and Kennedy; Carter and Johnson too—all based their view of trade and the global economy on a premise much like Clinton's. Defined best by Roosevelt as the Second World War approached its end, it is simple: freedom from fear depends upon freedom from want; and an open world economy is a guarantor of freedom from want.

These presidents, not later conservatives, created America's open-market policies. To the extent politicians from any single country can claim credit, they also built the WTO. Their vision fused permanent liberal causes: foreign policy based upon mutual interest and the rule of law as well as military deterrence, special concern for the poor, policy-making based upon empiricism and close study of issues. And though their vision remains incomplete, it has helped to create a happier and more peaceful world.

Their 21st-century critics are right, of course, to say that the opening world exacts a price. Intense competitive pressures arrive along with cheap goods and easier relations among the great powers. Domestic policies to ease the pressures often come later, and sometimes not at all.

But the pressures are not novelties. Almost every generation of Americans has encountered them. Every generation has debated the response, often in eerily similar terms. Fears of low-wage competition were as powerful one, two, and even three centuries ago as they are now. Solutions bright politicians with claim to liberal values suggested in the 18th and early centuries remain appropriate, in general terms, today.

The genuinely new element in the debate is that liberal politicians have the gloomy and fearful view. For most of American history, from the Napoleonic wars to the 1950s, this was the theme of the right. Its essence—a lost golden age, an elite betrayal, the destruction of good and stable ways of life—is a conservative trope. Its particular fear, competition from low-wage countries, was the basis of conservative policy for a century. Born with the 19th-century Whig Party of Daniel Webster and Henry Clay, stoked by business lobbies, passed on to the century by the Gilded Age Republicanism of William McKinley, the case against competition with poor countries ("pauper labor," as they called it) was an article of faith for five generations of conservatives. It survived well into the century, to die only in the general debacle of the Hoover administration.

Its adoption by liberals is full of risk for liberal causes: sympathy for the poor abroad, progressive taxation at home, international law and foreign policies based upon more than military power. An activist on behalf of the poor, sympathetic to the Haitian farmer and the Phnom Penh seamstress, cannot help either by keeping out of American stores the mangoes he picks and the sweaters she sews. An idealist in foreign affairs, committed to collective security and international law through the United Nations, cannot abandon these principles in trade and finance. Dr. Dean's fear that letting American buy cheap, high-quality TV sets, clothes, and spoons from abroad threatens democracy is a bit silly.

Supporters of the older approach need not, of course, pretend it is perfect and complete. Trade policies and institutions are imperfect and incomplete. They can be much better. But even as they are, they are not conservative plots but irreplaceable parts of the liberal internationalist system developed after the Second World War. And this system is the best yet devised to manage a troubled world: fairer and more equitable than any before it, more realistic about power and conflict than any alternative its critics on left or right can offer today.

The -century liberals who designed this system were far-sighted, optimistic, rational, and right. Their thinking has lasting power, because it organizes complex policies around simple values and coherent theories of economics and foreign affairs. Their work needs updating, but its intellectual foundations remain relevant to the compelling problems of the modern world—the question of poverty, the threat of environmental degradation, the struggles of the Muslim world—and the world's best hope for freedom from want and freedom from fear.

My hope in writing this book is not simply to complain about the loss of a valuable and honorable old liberal tradition. Neither is it an effort to bash American's 21st century liberals—there are already too many bashers—or to improve upon the good primers on trade theory available from academic economists. It is instead an attempt to explain the political origins of trade policy in Roosevelt's design for the postwar system, suggest the continuing relevance of his vision in the modern world, and offer some moral support and a few ideas to those trying to preserve and build upon it.

I.
THE MODERN GLOBAL ECONOMY AND ITS DESIGN

Some Numbers,
A Worker, The Rules

LET US START WITH A PENCIL-SKETCH of the trading world, drawn with a few numbers, an individual, and a country; and then an outline of its rules.

By the Numbers: The Global Economy Today

Numbers first. In 2006 the world's population reached 6.5 billion. Four billion men and women worked on farms and in factories, in offices and on street-corners, in restaurants and schools and barbershops, on boats and at construction sites. Together, according to the statisticians at the International Monetary Fund, they produced sixty trillion dollars worth of goods and services.

Twelve trillion, a fifth of the total, crossed a border (often more than one border) to find a foreign customer. Each dollar's worth finds a buyer. To borrow a phrase from a Chinese writer whom we will meet in a few pages:

> When all work willingly at their occupations, just as water flows ceaselessly downhill day and night, things will appear unsought and people will produce them without being asked.

If trade resembles the flow of water, manufacturing trade is the metaphorical Amazon. About two hundred million people work in factories, sweaty elbow to gleaming elbow-joint with a million industrial robots. Their daily collaboration work accounts for eight of the twelve trillion dollars in exports: planes, cameras, sweaters, cars, baseballs, copper ingots, medicines, paint, semiconductor chips, chemicals, medicine, toys, television sets, and the like. The figure approaches half the world's manufacturing production.

Farmers—many more, well over a billion, joined by about thirty-eight million fishermen—produce a bit less than a trillion dollars in food exports. These are sixty-kilo bags of Jamaican coffee beans, shiploads of Australian grain, refrigerated containers filled with Argentine beef and Norwegian salmon fillets, planes packed with winter-grown Chilean raspberries, boxes of prawns bred in salty Thai ponds. In all, a third of the world's annual farm and ranch produce, and a third of its fish, cross borders.

Mining products—oil and gas especially, but also coal, wood, metal ores, and minerals like salt and sulfur—accounted for another trillion dollars of trade. Like the Nile, in some years they flood the world and in other years they run dry. Two trillion dollars' worth of services makes up the balance, in the form of international shipping and air fees, architectural blueprints, analysis of X-rays, music and news, and telephone calls, beamed from satellites or slipping through fiber-optic cables.

The numbers suggest the world crowding in on us, and rightly so. Trade is intimate and personal as well as abstract and global. Most of the things Americans buy in shops, wear on our skins, and put in our houses have traveled long distances. Almost all the energy that drives our cars, and much of the metal that makes them, come from abroad. So too, does a fair chunk of the food and fish on American tables; so a relatively small, but rapidly growing fraction of our services, arriving almost instantaneously by satellite or fiber-optic cable.

Nor are we wholly wrong to think this is something new. The perception of radical change rests on fact: The 2.5 billion people of 1950 billion people produced five trillion dollars' worth of goods and services. They sent $125 billion, or only a fortieth of the total, across borders as exports. More than half of it was natural resources and bulk farm commodities—not the television sets, clothes, cars, movies, and bank-loans of the modern "globalized" world, but rice, corn, tin, lead, iron, oil, coffee, cocoa, and tea.

Six decades is less than a lifetime. A man in late middle age has seen the world's population triple, the value of the global economy grow ten-fold[2] and trade grow eighty-fold. If he has paid close attention, he has seen trade in manufactured goods and services shoot past older commerce in grains, coffee, tea, fuel, and minerals. He has seen something change fundamentally and quickly.

Meet a Worker:

Numbers are flat and impersonal, of course. They are only a place to start. But if we look carefully, we can see through them—foggily, as if through a clouded pane of glass—to find machines, transactions, and humanity. Flat-decked container ships, some as big as aircraft carriers, arrive at berths under the shadows of seventy-foot cranes. Robots jerk back and forth on assembly lines. Retail clerks pile up clothes and television sets in stores. Shoppers take them away.

Clothes are among the largest—also the most controversial and best-known—fields of trade. The World Trade Organization reports that clothes accounted for about $300 billion worth of exports in 2005 and 2006. Nearly two hundred nations make clothes, and nearly one piece in three eventually comes to America.

To spread the garment industry out on a map is to see an empire as large as Victoria's—one which, like hers, never sees the sunset. An army of young women, thirteen million strong, works each hour of the day and night to make the world's shirts, socks, dresses, and pants.

If you are reading this book in the evening, a corps of fifteen thousand is taking lunch in Maseru, capital of the hilltop kingdom of Lesotho in southern Africa. More than a million are awakening in Guangzhou. Fifty thousand are climbing onto buses bound for home in San Pedro Sula, the commercial capital of Honduras. Three hundred thousand are preparing for work in Phnom Penh, the capital of Cambodia. We can meet one now.

✧

CAMBODIA, THOUGH A NEW ENTRY in the modern global economy, is not new to trade. The kingdom has been part of at least four earlier "global economies." In the 19th century it was part of the French empire, shipping pepper and cardamom to Paris restaurants. Much earlier, it conducted a shadowy trade with Rome and India. In between, during the 13th century, a young Chinese diplomat found its capital a busy commercial center and a promising partner for the Chinese empire.

His report, filed after a stay of six months and preserved in the Yuan Dynasty's diplomatic archives as *Report on the Customs of Cambodia,* describes the kingdom as a promising source for industrial raw materials. The diplomat, Zhou Daguan, thought China's luxury manufacturers could buy lacquer, cardamoms, ivory, and pepper from Cambodia's mines and farms, and that the court at Angkor might be in return be a buyer for Chinese silks, umbrellas, jewelry, needles, and silverware.[3]

Modern Cambodia, though, is one of Asia's simplest and poorest economies, still struggling to recover from the extraordinary years between 1970 and 1990. It has only three big roads—one south from Phnom Penh to its port at Sihanoukville, another east to Vietnam, and a third northwest to the archaeological park at Angkor. Cambodia has no chemical industry, no paper plant, no television or computer factories. But it is busy nonetheless, and its businesses and diplomats watch the American shopper as closely as those of any nation on earth.

Cambodia's 300,000 garment workers are young rural women between eighteen and twenty-five years old. They make almost everything the country sells abroad. One is a 23-year-old named Srei, with a round face and a slight wave in her jet-black hair. As she talks with a foreign writer—the first westerner she has ever met—her expression mixes puzzlement over his interest with obvious confidence born from personal achievement.

Srei arrived in the capital from a village outside Kampong Cham two years ago. Her memory of the first day is vivid: she suffered a bout of terrified paralysis at a busy intersection. No cars would stop for her. Motor-scooters weaved in and out and sometimes veered straight at her, buses honked their horns. Kampong Cham itself is a small town— 64,000 people by the latest census—and the villages around get no traffic at all. Srei needed almost an hour to summon the courage for a sprint through a gap in the traffic to make it across the street.

Now she is used to the traffic, and walks to work six days a week through fresh morning air. Phnom Penh has little of the smoke of near-by Bangkok or Saigon—its buildings are low and its factories are low-polluting light industry. She passes street-vendors selling steaming bowls of noodles and fried frogs on a stick, a corner market filled with stacked piles of fruit and vegetables, an English-language school, pools of standing water that steam a bit, dry-goods stores carrying pots, toys, and religious posters.

A few minutes before eight, Srei arrives at her factory. The building, which employs five thousand young women, is something like an oversized metal barn, lightly air-conditioned, with a corrugated roof, white-painted walls to reflect the afternoon sun and keep the air-conditioning bills down, and pipes painted sky blue. Outside the main building, the managers have placed a row of pepper-trees in ceramic pots, each about three feet high and about twenty feet apart. It looks much like the garment factories elsewhere in the world—Honduras, China, Lesotho, Madagascar, El Salvador, Bangladesh, Peru—and its Malaysian owner runs similar plants in Thailand and mainland China, too. Dr. Muhammad Yunus, the 2006 Nobel Peace Prize Laureate, believes that the jobs they create are one of the two reliable paths out of poverty—along with micro-credit programs like the one he pioneered in Bangladesh twenty years ago—for rural women in developing countries.[4]

Srei takes her seat, tenth in a row of forty young women in yellow T-shirts. Like her neighbors, she will work a ten-hour day and leave at six. Cambodia's labor law, written in 1999 and still overseen by the International Labor Organization (ILO), requires an eight-hour day with an hour for lunch, but allows the factory managers to ask for two hours of optional overtime.[5] Almost all factory workers take it for the extra pay.

Factories like this are often the first big building a rural girl has ever entered. A manager explains that the adjustment can be difficult—at home, village girls often work hard, but walk around as they please. To sit all day in a chair is unfamiliar and uncomfortable. The skill takes time to develop. But they adjust, learn to operate a sewing machine, and within three weeks are ready to put on a yellow T-shirt, sit down, and start to sew.

Each production worker gets a task and works at it all day. Today, Srei's production line is filling an order of light brown long-sleeved pullover blouses. She and her neighbors to the right and left sew the cuffs onto the sleeves. As each cuff is done, she puts the shirt aside into a cardboard box. When the box is full, she pushes it up to the next row.

The next set of women add small lacy flourishes to the shirtfronts, over the heart. Earlier teams have cut out front and back panels and added sleeves. Later teams will put on the collars and buttons. The shirt is a twenty-step operation—the shirts begin at the middle of the line and move outward to the ends—and each step has a specialist. When they are done, a quality-control officer inspects the shirt and folds it up for shipping. The quality-control people are slightly more senior employees. Each wears a red T-shirt. Until the order is filled, Srei's production line will make a thousand blouses just like this one every day.

Srei's factory is one of Cambodia's larger plants. The average plant has about a thousand production workers; the biggest in the country, named Ocean Garments, has eight thousand. Altogether, Phnom Penh had 278 of these factories in 2006, and their workers made up a fifth of the capital's 1.5 million people. Joining tourism as one of Cambodia's two major industries, the plants sent two billion dollars worth of clothes to the United States in 2006.

Each factory has satellites—clusters of noodle shops, truckers, messengers, real estate firms. Each, also, is not only a clothing-maker but a training ground for Cambodia's future elite. Depending upon its size, a factory will employ twenty to forty young Phnom Penh college graduates in human resources, accounting, security, and other mid-level jobs. If the industry survives another decade, it will train five or ten thousand educated young Cambodians to buy and sell on the international markets, deal with demanding customers, and meet payrolls. As they move up, or start their own firms, they will become a local business class to replace the one the wars and the Khmers Rouge destroyed.

☙

AMERICAN TRADE POLICY created this industry from nothing, mainly by accident. As late as 1996, Cambodia's export trade amounted to $10 million in miscellaneous junk—a million dollars' worth of crude rubber, ten tons of cork, a few old radio antennas—and Phnom Penh's big employers were international humanitarian groups distributing medicine and artificial limbs to war victims.

But in 1996, Congress lifted the trade embargo imposed in 1975, when the Khmers Rouges entered Phnom Penh, and granted Cambodia "Normal Trade Relations" status. Three years after NAFTA, the decision drew little attention. No protesters attended the Senate Finance Committee's hearings. Only John McCain and the bill's actual author, Alaska Republican Frank Murkowski, bothered to comment when Senate voted on the bill in the autumn.

Some careful observers did, however, take notice. Weeks after the vote, Hong Kong and Taiwanese clothing entrepreneurs were flying into Phnom Penh to interview aspiring seamstresses. Forty factories had sprouted up by the middle of 1997. They shipped ten million dollars' worth of clothes to the United States every month by the end of the year. Ten years later, the monthly total is about $200 million.

But the industry's future is uncertain. Foreigners own and operate all but one of Cambodia's garment factories. They are Koreans and Chinese from Taiwan, Hong Kong, and Malaysia. A factory like Srei's is large, elaborate and well-maintained—but takes only two months to set up. If the faraway owners find they can earn more money in China or Vietnam, they can dismantle and move it in two weeks. The two larger countries have lower electricity prices, better roads and larger ports than Cambodia. In 2006, though, temporary American quota limits were holding Chinese and Vietnamese clothing exports down. Next year, who knows?

☙

AFTER PASSING QUALITY CONTROL, the pullovers go into sealed boxes. Young men move them onto a conveyor belt, and then to a loading dock. Another team of young men then packs the shirts into a twenty-foot steel container fixed to the bed of a truck. The truck rolls for six hours over a bumpy road, patrolled occasionally by soldiers and bandits, to Cambodia's Sihanoukville port. The town's white-sand beach, advertised by the Cambodian Ministry of Antiquities and Tourism, is beginning to attract European backpackers as the port attracts the shippers.

A crane takes the container holding Srei's shirt and stacks it alongside a hundred more containers. There it lies for a day, until a flat-topped container ship arrives from Singapore. Its deck is already stacked with steel boxes, at the standard size of forty feet, by eight feet, by eight and a half-filled with clothes, toys, furniture, and television sets. A crane moves the Cambodian containers on board. Three thousand ships like this one circulate around the world constantly. Some carry a few hundred containers. The biggest, made in Korea, carry over eight thousand. A busy port like Singapore's (or those of Hong Kong, Los Angeles, Rotterdam, Shanghai, Hamburg, and New York) see dozens of ships and a hundred thousand containers daily. Sihanoukville is a small stop; each day, it will berth one or two ships and load 150 containers.[6]

Srei and her neighbors make Cambodia a small player in the pullover blouse business. Its factories produce a few more blouses than their competitors in Sri Lanka, and a few less than Nicaragua. Last year the Cambodian factories sent about twenty million shirts to American retail outlets, which is a noticeable, but not huge, part of the larger stream of eighty million Southeast Asian blouses. The four Chinese dragon heads—the Pearl River Delta, Shanghai, Xiamen, Tianjin—add another eighty million blouses. At the American ports they join seven million a year from Africa, forty million from Central America, and ten million from the Middle East.

The blouses in their turn are only one part of a much larger flow of shirts. The champion in the business, incongruously and a bit unsteadily, is the small Central American republic of Honduras. Its T-shirt sales alone raise $600 million a year, which is a tenth of the Honduran GDP. A hundred garment factories, fed by twelve textile mills, employ a hundred thousand Hondurans. Like their counterparts in Cambodia, the employees are mostly young women. Honduran factory owners, union chiefs and diplomats, also like their counterparts in Cambodia, look anxiously at the Chinese flood and wonder about their future.

The shirts then separate again at the Port of Long Beach. Seventy-foot cranes pluck the containers off the deck and attach them to waiting trucks. Computers have electronically registered their arrival already. Ten thousand Cambodian blouses sell at the border for $20,000, or $2 per shirt on average. The customer—most likely the Gap chain, which buys a third of Cambodia's exports; Wal-Mart or JC Penney are also big buyers—has paid a tariff of 16.5 percent, or $3,300, on the transaction.

The trucks leave the port in a long slow line and scatter onto the American roads. A few days later, you will buy Srei's shirt for ten or twenty dollars. From her soft hand at her sewing machine to yours at the store checkout, the trip takes about twenty days.

⚜

AS A FIRST-YEAR FACTORY WORKER, Srei earned $45 a month. She received a five-dollar monthly bonus for good attendance, and over-time pay of two dollars an hour when orders were heavy.[7] Each year she can earn a small raise.

The pay sounds trivial, maybe even unjust. It is nothing of the sort. In 2006, a Phnom Penh policeman earned a base salary of $20 per month, and a doctor at a local health clinic started at $60. (Though both policemen and clinic workers often earn more than their salaries, by charging fees and soliciting small bribes.) Even without the bonus and overtime pay, Srei's $600 per year is nearly twice Cambodia's per capita income.

Srei shares a room with three village friends—Nuon, Rith, and Sar—in a nearby apartment building. All four roommates are garment-workers. Their room costs $20 a month and food runs about $30. If Srei gets overtime work, therefore, she can save $10 a month. (Seamstresses in their fourth year on the job, whose pay has risen to $60 per month, can save half their income.) Because they are paid cash and rural ID card systems are spotty, they have trouble opening bank accounts. Like most workers, Srei therefore wears her savings on her body, in the form of cheap silver earrings, necklaces, rings, and bracelets. When a holi-day approaches—the Southeast Asian New Year festival in April, Cam-bodia's Independence Day in the autumn, a wedding or a funeral in the village—she joins young women all over Phnom Penh in selling a few bangles, and tens of thousands of return together to the countryside with cash for their families.

The money is welcome, as rural Cambodia is almost destitute. Phnom Penh's lively markets and restaurants are full of colorful tropical produce—hot pink and snow-white dragon-fruit, dull and bright yellow mangoes and lemons, crimson rembutan, lime-green vegetables—but local farmers supply almost none of it. The provincial roads are primi-tive, and few Cambodian farmers have money for fertilizer, irrigation, or mechanized equipment anyway. Most simply grow food to eat and sell in local markets. The capital's fresh produce arrives each morning on the highway on a long line of morning trucks from southern Vietnam, or by boat from Thailand.

Lacking cash, a rural family typically has two months of food security. With a daughter in a garment-factory job, they have a year of food security. Two daughters in a factory mean a motor-scooter, a set of metal farm implements and fertilizer, or a television. The jobs are prized for good reason; the holidays are not simply occasions to return home to deliver savings to family. A factory girl will usually return from the village to the capital with a few relatives and friends eager to apply.

⚜

THE ALTERNATIVES TO FACTORY work are less appealing.

Cambodia's government faces a stark demographic challenge. Cham Prasidh, an intense hawk-faced man who has served as Commerce Minister for the past decade, explains it over a bowl of spicy soup. When the Vietnamese army reached Phnom Penh in 1979 and expelled the Khmers Rouges, Cambodia's population had dropped to eight million and the nation's intellectual elite had been wiped out. All of Cambodia's teachers, bureaucrats, Buddhist monks, union organizers, businessmen, banking clerks, writers, and classical dancers were dead or in exile. Only sixty-five "intellectuals," he recalls, remained alive and inside the country.

A quarter-century later, the population has grown to fourteen million. Half are eighteen or younger, and eleven million live in farms or rural villages. With mathematical simplicity, two hundred thousand boys and girls come of age in the rural districts each year. Each must find a place.

Boys have some options. A young man can inherit the farm. His younger brothers can join the army, get work driving trucks, find construction jobs, and eke out livings as unlicensed taxi drivers.

Girls have fewer. Some stay home and marry. Some come to the capital, or to Siem Reap, to find work as a waitress or a maid in a tourist hotel. Easy to reach from Bangkok and Hong Kong, Cambodia is famous for the Angkor Wat archaeological park, which attracted two million tourists last year; dozens of hotels and hundreds of restaurants have sprouted up to serve the tourists. Other young women catch on in the noodle shops and bamboo stands selling fried fish and frogs along the upper reach of the Tonle Sap at Siem Reap, or in the karaoke bars and tourist restaurants by the Mekong in Phnom Penh.

The sex industry is also a common choice. Phnom Penh has a small army of prostitutes, estimated variously between thirty and a hundred thousand. Girls who join it, sometimes through criminal trafficking but often by choice, are said to earn about two dollars a day. A journalist describes the trail to the massage parlor:

> A 14-year-old girl is bored with living on the farm in the countryside. She has an older sister who left and went to Phnom Penh and hasn't been heard from since, but the girl believes that if she can get to Phnom Penh, she can find her sister and live with her and maybe get a job in a garment factory. So she sneaks away and gets on a bus and meets a woman who says she can help. She knows a restaurant that needs a dishwater, and she'll take her there. The girl thinks, great, what good fortune. But the restaurant turns out to be a brothel, and the woman sells the girl for $300 and walks away. The girl, being from a poor farm village and knowing virtually nothing of the world, believes this is a debt she has to pay back. It was just a woman on a bus, and the girl to her was like a wallet found on the street.[8]

Anecdotal accounts suggest that a prostitute can earn about as much in a year as a factory seamstress. But she can be robbed and beaten up at any time. A bribed policemen could easily take the side of a robber, and would almost invariably side with an abusive brothel owner. Despite an energetic national AIDS education program, one in five still leaves the work with HIV; and at best, a girl in the business will leave with some savings and a lifelong stigma. The garment jobs are prized for good reason.

Shadow World: The WTO and the Rules

At each juncture, this tangible world of seamstresses, factories, trucks, ports, ships, retail outlets, and shoppers has a shadow. This is the world of laws and international agreements, built up over sixty years, with the World Trade Organization at its center. The WTO oversees twenty agreements that bind 150 governments. The seven which apply to Srei's blouse join the Congress' quiet vote in 1996 as the reasons her factory and her job exist.

The oldest and most important WTO agreement is the General Agreement on Tariffs and Trade, or "GATT" for short. Dating to 1947 and revised eight times since, it requires America to limit its tariff on cotton pullover blouses to 16.5 percent. A second, the Agreement on Textiles and Clothing dates to 1994 and guarantees U.S. retailers the right to buy as many Cambodian shirts (or Chinese, Honduran, or Lesotho shirts) as they want. The Agreement on Safeguards lets the United States temporarily suspend either of the first two in an emergency.

The fourth, the Agreement on Customs Valuation, sets guidelines for the Customs Service officials who assess the shirts' value, making sure they do not overstate the shirts' cost to collect unwarranted tariff money or keep them off the market altogether. The Agreement on Rules of Origin, creates the common definition of what it means for a shirt to be "Cambodian" (or Chinese, Honduran, Lesotho, etc.) when Srei's factory uses dye from China, and American cotton knitted into fabric in Taiwan, to make the shirt.

The Agreement on Dispute Settlement, the sixth, lets Cambodia's government file a formal complaint and receive compensation if the U.S. were to apply a tariff of 17 percent or more to the shirt, or to limit the number of shirts the Gap can buy. The WTO's panels have already heard 360 cases, ranging from large ones like the dispute between the United States and Europe over airplane subsidies, to little ones like a Pakistani complaint over Egyptian match tariffs, a Korean suit against Japanese limits on edible seaweed, and a Costa Rican appeal—which the Costa Ricans won—against American limits on underwear trade. In the unlikely event that Cambodia's government were caught giving Srei's factory cash grants or low-interest loans to produce shirts at unnaturally low cost, the United States could protest a violation of the Agreement on Subsidies.

Of the remaining thirteen agreements, one limits farm subsidy programs in the U.S., Europe, Korea, and Japan, and another applies to services traded over the internet or through international banks, telecom companies, and law firms. The Agreement on Technical Barriers to Trade establishes procedures for creating technical standards, and the Trade-Related Aspects of Intellectual Property Agreement requires WTO members (with temporary exceptions for least-developed countries like Cambodia) to adopt copyright, trademark, and patent laws. The remaining eight run from telecommunications to inspections of farm products.

All the agreements apply to all 150 WTO members, though often in different ways. The GATT guarantees that United States will limit its tariff on cotton shirts to 16.5 percent. Cambodia, though, has a limit of 25 percent, and Europe's is 12 percent. The differences reflect long histories of negotiations and compromises among governments, which in their turn reflect the varying strengths and interests of lobbies in different countries. America's textile businesses have maintained a faith in tariffs for nearly two hundred years, and have used their Congressional friends to keep shirt tariffs high—the average American tariff is about 2.4 percent—long after many other tariffs vanished or dwindled into insignificance. Cambodia's higher tariff reflects a worry that free imports of shirts might wipe out its only industry.

The WTO "members," for their part, are almost all sovereign nations. (The exceptions are the European Union, which is an association of countries; Hong Kong and Macau, which are self-governing bits of China; and Taiwan whose status is a riddle.) Together, they come close to their self-declared "world" title, though there are still a few big gaps. Nervous, active little Cambodia and Honduras are members. So is gigantic America, and even larger China, with its three hundred thousand factories, its unquenchable appetite for tin and zinc and semiconductor chips and oil, and its roaring floods of exported television sets, cellular phones, computers, toys, and clothes. Oil-rich Kuwait, quirky Paraguay, and aristocratic Luxembourg accept the agreements as well. So do the little emerald atolls of Tonga in the South Pacific, whose 180,000 people and 280-pound king earn twenty million dollars a year selling coconuts, coral, and aquarium fish to wealthy Australians and Japanese.

In sum, the WTO members include nineteen of the world's twenty largest economies, from the United States and China down through Japan, Germany, and India, to France, Belgium, and Mexico. Russia is the sole exception, and only a temporary one. They unite seventeen of the twenty most populous nations—excepting again Russia, along with Ethiopia and Iran—and eighteen of the twenty largest exporters.

Together, they account for 97 percent of the world's $12 trillion in exports and almost 99 percent of its imports.

☙

THERE IS THE SKETCH PORTRAIT. The numbers illuminate a bewilderingly active and entangled world. The American who buys Valentine's Day flowers, wears a cotton blouse, sprinkles seed in a bird feeder, or turns on a computer is very close to the Andean farmers who raise our winter roses, the young Asian women who sew clothes for the world, the Ethiopians who grow the world's most valued birdseed, and the Chinese technicians who manage electronics factories. In each case, a shadowy network of rules, laws, and agreements developed over sixty years defines our treatment of the product and the country.

As many of America's modern liberals look at this world, and the agreements and laws that lie beneath it, they see exploitation, injustice, and folly—and are appalled.

An Indictment

TO MANY DETERMINED CRITICS, the WTO and its agreements are the product either of conspiracy, or of idiocy and naïveté on the part of self-important American diplomats perpetually outwitted by clever foreigners.

A garment-factory worker like Srei—or her counterparts in the Malaysian electronics business, the Central American textile mills, the Indian software industry, the tens of thousands of Chinese factories—is a victim cheated of the money she should earn. She can even be a sort of villain, not as an individual but as a type, whose job ought to be in the United States. Her employers are unambiguously rapacious and wicked. They sell us cheap shirts, exploit their workers and take the livelihood of unlucky Americans.

Bernie Sanders, the Independent-Socialist Senator from Vermont, makes the point emotionally and eloquently. With his shaggy white hair and blunt Brooklyn voice, he speaks of the more decent America, which the trading system has killed. Three decades ago, he says, factory jobs were plentiful, pay high and families secure. "The global economy didn't matter much to the average American," who did not compete with "desperate people in China who make thirty cents an hour."[9]

Within a generation a good life has collapsed:

> Thirty years ago there were decent paying jobs with good benefits available for [Americans without high school diplomas and college degrees] in manufacturing plants. Today the wages for those workers have declined precipitously, and they are now flipping hamburgers at McDonald's or working without health care at Wal-Mart.[10]

Because of the trading system, jobs are harder to find, pay less, and don't last. America's middle class is shrinking, and American factory industry close to collapse. Trade with China alone has cost 1.5 million jobs. The tens of millions of blouses arriving in the United States, and the twelve trillion dollars in annual world exports, are callous numerical abstractions. They barely disguise a "race to the bottom," pitting all the countries of the world against one another for jobs and investment, which has brought exploitation to poor countries and misery to America.

Ohio's newly elected Senator Sherrod Brown calls the system a triumph of business interest over the common good. His book, *Myths of Free Trade,* draws a parallel with the triumph of Gilded Age robber barons a century ago, allied with the money power of William McKinley's Republican Party. To Brown:

> The WTO represents another chapter in the essential American struggle—such as that inspired by [the Upton Sinclair novel] *The Jungle* over the division of power between democratically elected governments and private interests . . . Americans are beginning to see that the rules of international trade are fundamentally un-American and anti-democratic. NAFTA, the World Trade Organization, and almost every single trade agreement in front of the U.S. Congress shifts power dramatically from elected governments to private interest.[11]

Barney Frank, the brilliant Representative from the Boston suburbs, speaks in more nuanced terms of tragedy rather than plot. The global economy creates a brutal competition. As it continually drives down the price of goods, it forces even the best companies and most responsible managers to sacrifice values and ethics. They search the

globe for the lowest-cost workers—Srei in Cambodia, Meimei in Guangzhou, Grace in Lesotho, Flor in Honduras—simply to avoid bankruptcy
and failure. The result, even with the best intentions, is the sweatshop
and the incentive for child labor. And, of course, many businesses and
governments do not have the best intentions.

The AFL-CIO's melancholy and dignified President John Sweeney
falls somewhere in between. He points to an "unjust trading system
that increases corporate profits at the expense of workers' rights and
workers' dignity," and calls it the work of fools rather than outright
villains. It has emerged from "decisions and policies based on ideol-
ogy and—to be honest—crackpot ideas, rather than rational common
sense," and places the American worker in an impossible vise. "We have
the best workforce in the world," he says, "but our workers cannot compete against child labor, slave labor and sweatshop labor."[12]

And Jeff Faux, a labor intellectual and lately President of the Economic Policy Institute in Washington, finds the system's heart in the dis-
loyalty of American business executives. His book *The Global Class War*
asserts that after the Second World War, and as recently as the 1970s,
executives felt paternal responsibility for the national good. Since the
end of the Cold War, they have abandoned it for cheap labor. NAFTA told
them that the government believed they were right to do so; together
with the WTO, the newly created system "allowed the rich and powerful
to detach themselves from the bonds that had connected the economic
fate of Americans of all classes since World War II."

A different analysis, most ambitious of them all, comes from
the anti-globalization movement. This strand of thought, whose most
prominent advocate is Ralph Nader and whose most systematic work
is published by the International Forum on Globalization, suggests a
sort of world government behind the scenes, which designed the World
Bank, the IMF, and the General Agreement on Tariffs and Trade in the
1940s and reshaped it through the WTO after 1980. Its achievement,
"the most fundamental redesign of the planet's social, economic and
political arrangements since the Industrial Revolution," has created a
"power shift of stunning proportions." National governments and citizen movements have lost influence over life and development; in their
place, "at the expense of national sovereignty, community control, democracy, diversity and the natural world" stand banks, international

marketing chains, and global bureaucracies, who make democracy meaningless, force unwanted goods, and disruptive technologies upon people who don't need them, and drain life of its color and joy.[13]

Their explanations vary, sometimes widely. Their solutions cover still broader swaths of intellectual ground, and the anti-globalization movement's depart from anything recognizable as liberalism. But all the critiques share some basic points.

First, until the 1980s America was self-sufficient. (Or nearly so. The Americans of the golden age bought oil abroad because they had to, and coffee because they wanted to.) American factories competed only gently with a few wealthy foreign rivals, hired easily and kept workers for life. In this quiet world, strong trade unions could fight managers for higher wages, more generous health insurance plans, and reliable pensions. Activists concerned about public health and consumer safety could devise legal reforms to clean the air and water, or to protect children from harm, without fearing that businesses would move abroad. Rooted in values of equality and solidarity, the system created a good life.

Second, we've recently abandoned self-sufficiency. Faux points to the election of Ronald Reagan in 1980 as the turning point; Sanders suggests passage of the NAFTA in 1993; others cite the end of the Cold War. All agree that somewhere between 1980 and 1994, America quit the internal market and the good life, and embraced the global market and the Darwinian struggle for survival.

Third, the new approach is conservative doctrine. It reflects the values of the business class: investors should do as they please, profits come before people, and to get rich is glorious. Trade agreements, which let businesses move work abroad but continue to sell goods to the American public, are the incarnation of these values.

Fourth, the new approach degrades and impoverishes Americans and the developing world alike. Americans compete, as never before in our history, against Srei and millions of young low-wage factory workers exploited abroad. American industry has eroded away, as the opening world draws factories out of the United States to Mexico, China, and now India. The future promises only crisis and decline.

✺

SOLUTIONS RANGE FROM REFORMIST to radical. Ruy Teixeira and John Haplin, liberal political scientists from the Century Foundation and the Center for American Progress, fall into the moderate reformist camp. They suggest that:

> Progressives must insist that all efforts to expand global trade be conditioned upon genuine efforts to improve labor, environmental and political standards abroad and greater economic security, job preparedness, education and investment at home.[14]

Mr. Sweeney's response is similar: a "demand that all trade agreements contain basic guarantees of human rights and workers' rights and environmental protections."[15]

Senator Sanders is more ambitious than either. Where Teixeira and Haplin, and perhaps Sweeney, too, want a pause—albeit a long one, if trade policy is to wait for the social-democratic millennium in America *and* overseas—Sanders calls for reversing what is already done. Just as Barry Goldwater once pledged to repeal old laws rather than pass new ones, Sanders hopes to withdraw the United States from the WTO, cancel the NAFTA, and impose a high new tariff on everything made in China.

Dr. Faux's proposal is genuinely millennial. He suggests nothing less than revising the nature of the United States itself. His book proposes a political federation with Canada and Mexico, enclosed by a tariff wall to keep out the goods of other regions—a little oddly, he singles out Africa as a region that should be left to fend for itself—and hints at the name "Newland" for the nascent new sovereignty.

✺

THEIR STORIES HAVE EMOTIONAL FORCE. Exploited and miserable foreign workers swelter in dark tropical factories. A worried American father, poring over rent bills and food expenses, wonders if his paycheck will still be there in six months. A wealthy business-owner quietly initials a form and moves his factories away.

Moreover, this powerful emotional charge is not wholly wrong. Today's America is less egalitarian than the America of earlier years.

Businesses, pushed by competition, are pulling back from the roles they assumed decades ago as providers of health and pensions. The trade union movement, once a guarantor of security, has buckled and risks being pushed to the margin of economic life.

All these are legitimate complaints, and all require response. But the indictment as a whole is mistaken. Its view of the past is too rosy, its assessment of the present unreasonably bleak, and its guesses about the intellectual origin of the global economy wrong.

To sail three decades backward in time is to land in the middle of the 1970s and find American life not full of joy. Unemployment averaged 6 to 8 percent, the highest rate between the Depression and the present. The Arab oil embargo lay three years in the past and the Iranian shock two years in the future. Chrysler and U.S. Steel pleaded for relief from Japanese competition. America was neither self-sufficient nor industrially strong before 1980, and jobs were neither plentiful nor secure.

Since then, most change—though not all— has largely been for the better. We will return to this subject later with some more details, but the outlines are simple. Since the 1970s—even more so since the NAFTA—jobs have grown easier to find. American businesses employ more people, and fewer Americans are out of work. American factories produce more than they did in the past, and at the same time the country is cleaner and workers are healthier.

Nor did the opening of the American economy to trade break with any earlier liberal tradition. The strategy Brown and Sweeney ascribe to the 1980s, or to the passage of NAFTA, is much older than they realize. It dates to the 1930s and 1940s and has proceeded steadily ever since, advancing most rapidly during the great liberal presidencies. Rather than a novel and reckless attempt by conservative ideologues to create an integrated world in accord with academic free-market theories, it was a deliberate decision, based upon experience, to rebuild an earlier global economy that collapsed—and the decision was Franklin Roosevelt's.

☙

IN HIS GREAT SPEECHES on the postwar order, Roosevelt always speaks of the global economy and always portrays it as a guarantor of future prosperity and peace. His 1944 State of the Union address, the

fullest expression of his hope, explains that to reduce poverty would be
to create a world less prone to war and aggression, and that to encourage trade is to reduce poverty:

> All freedom-loving Nations shall join together in a just and durable
> system of peace . . . and a basic essential to peace is a decent stan-
> dard of living for all individual men and women and children in all
> Nations. Freedom from fear is eternally linked with freedom from
> want. There are people who burrow through our Nation like unsee-
> ing moles, and attempt to spread the suspicion that if other Nations
> are encouraged to raise their standards of living, our own American
> standard of living must of necessity be depressed. The fact is the
> very contrary. It has been shown time and again that if the standard
> of living of any country goes up, so does its purchasing power—and
> that such a rise that encourages a better standard of living in neigh-
> boring countries with whom it trades.

The trading system's origins are in the letter he wrote to Congress
a year later, to announce the opening of the first global trade negotiations. Calling the initiative—the first in the series of talks which, incre-
mentally, created all the WTO's agreements and rules—a chance to "lay
the economic basis for the secure and peaceful world we all desire,"
he closed the letter with a look far into the future toward the lives we
might live today:

> The point in history at which we stand is full of promise and danger.
> The world will either move toward unity and widely shared prosper-
> ity, or it will move apart . . . We have a chance, we citizens of the
> United States, to use our influence in favor of a more united and
> cooperating world. Whether we do so will determine, as far as it is in
> our power, the kind of lives our grandchildren will live.[16]

Roosevelt reached these conclusions conscious both of an old liberal intellectual inheritance now all but forgotten, and his own generation's searing encounter with the alternatives. His goals were the best
liberal aspirations—broadly shared prosperity, the rule of law, a stronger peace—and his project has largely succeeded.

II.

THE BACKGROUND

WHY DID ROOSEVELT, and his successor Truman, think in these terms?

Above all, because of their own experience in the Depression and the war. As middle-aged politicians, exiled from power during the first years of the Depression, they had seen countries close their borders to trade, watched the world economy come apart, and then seen the consequences unfold—first in economic contraction, mass unemployment, and misery, then in virulent nationalism and war. By reversing the closures they hoped to make a second Depression impossible.

They also inherited a century of American debate on trade, in particular the ideas of the 19th-century Democratic Party and the Progressives of the early century on economics, poverty, and the American tariff system—both in a way foreshadowing the positions their generation adopted on the global economy—and a much older tradition of liberal thought long predating the United States itself.

Hope, Gloom and Virtue

THE HOPES AND WORRIES of the 21th century are not new. "Global economies," even if they were not really global, always seem to have aroused the same emotions. At every point in history, trade sparks hopes for wealth and peace, creates fear of competition and financial drain, and raises the question of what a virtuous life might be.

Even the tiny economy of the 3rd millennium BC is no exception. This reached from Egypt through Mesopotamia, north to the Harappan towns of the Indus valley and the lapis mines of the Afghan plateau, south to the fisheries and pearl marts at Bahrain and Oman. The governments of these places—perhaps five towns, a few hundred villages and ten million people—attempted to regulate and civilize commerce just as modern ones do; and intellectuals worried about the consequences. Eight of Hammurabi's two hundred Babylonian statutes, published in 1800 BC on a polished pillar of black basalt regulate and suggest ways to arbitrate disputes over long-distance trade. Egyptian calligraphers, painting hieroglyphs onto the walls of their masters' tombs with reed brushes and ochre inks, admiringly recorded marine expeditions to Somalia and Greece. A Sumerian scribe, punching wedge-shaped letters into wet clay tablets, complains of inequity: *"How lowly is the poor man—his ripped garment will not be mended; what he has lost will not be sought."*

The classical civilizations, able to use ink and parchment, launched a more sophisticated debate. Their authors speculate about the links between wealth and virtue, commerce and war, imports and security. Their emotions presage ours, and some of their ideas remain instructive and valuable guides. We can use a few—a couple of Greeks, a Roman naturalist, a Chinese historian, a Biblical writer—to introduce the three parties who contend today for public favor and the liberal soul.

Party of Hope

The partisans of the party of hope look at trade and wealth with tolerant affection. They believe material desires are reasonable and peace among nations is possible, and that each can serve the other.

The expatriate Athenian soldier Xenophon, whose pamphlet *Ways and Means* is a unique economic-policy survival of the classical world, is a Greek example. Writing in 360 BC, he offered ideas to Athens' governing council on reviving an economy chronically depressed since the Peloponnesian war. Xenophon suggested infrastructure programs and new hostels at the Piraeus port, tax abatements and free drama-tickets for visiting ship-owners, and raids in Thrace to replenish the slave labor corps at the Laurion silver mine. He assured the council that his ideas would revive trade, create wealth, and expand power:

> Now, the greater the number of people attracted to Athens, clearly the greater the development of imports and exports. More goods will be sent out of the country, there will be more buying and selling, with a consequent influx of money in rents to individuals and customs dues for the state.

This was not, Xenophon explained, an end in itself. To revive trade, he argued, is to create wealth. To create wealth is to strengthen peace. And to strengthen peace is to guarantee a happy life:

> They are surely the happy states—in popular language, the most favored by fortune—which endure in peace the longest season. And

of all states Athens is best adapted by nature to flourish and grow strong in peace.

Who does not wish to live in a peaceful city? From the mariner and merchant upwards, all seek her—the wealthy dealers in corn and wine and oil, the owner of many cattle. Not only these, but the man who depends upon his wits, whose skill it is to do business and make gain out of money and its employment. And another crowd, artificers of all sorts, artists and artisans, professors of wisdom, philosophers and poets, with those who exhibit and popularize their works. And next a new train of pleasure-seekers, eager to feast on anything, sacred or secular, which may captivate and charm eye and ear. And once again, where are all those who seek to effect a rapid purchase or sale of a thousand commodities, if not at Athens?[17]

Three centuries later and five thousand miles east, the Han Dynasty historian Sima Qian expressed a similar idea with equal eloquence and more intellectual rigor. Founding genius of Chinese historical thought and unlucky servant of the "Martial" Emperor Han Wu,[18] Sima tied the global economy to prosperity, equity, and tolerance.

His monumental book *Shi ji,* or *Historical Records,* records the history of the early Chinese empire and the personalities who built it. It contains 130 separate and complementary essays, most of them the biographies of memorable people: kings and comedians, classical philosophers, assassins, an empress, famous merchants, and the ill-fated builder of the Great Wall.[19] The penultimate chapter is a review of economics and trade, mostly in the form of a catalogue of regional resources and agricultural specialties. (Forest products and spicy foods appear in the south, the western provinces are rich in mineral wealth, and so forth.) The introduction, just a few paragraphs long, is two thousand years ahead of its time:

There must be farmers to produce food, men to extract the wealth of mountains and marshes, artisans to process these things, and merchants to circulate them. There is no need to wait for government orders: each man will do his part as he gets what he desires. So cheap goods will go where they fetch more, while expensive goods will make men search for cheap ones. When all work willingly at their trades, just as water flows ceaselessly downhill day and night, things will appear unsought and people will produce them without being asked.

With a few words, Sima describes a diverse, self-regulating and happy economy. In a free society, the strengths and weaknesses of different regions will balance one another, just as the individual's delight in pleasure complements the merchant's hope for wealth. Together the two forces encourage artisans to specialize in different crafts, spark exchanges among the empire's different provinces, bring wealth everywhere, and make people happy.

♛

THE ANONYMOUS AUTHOR of the Bible's Book of Kings is not a theorist. He addresses no question of policy and makes no judgment on human nature. He is factual, tangible, and descriptive, making his views implicit in the stories he tells. Like the Greek soldier and the Chinese scholar, he associates commerce with peace and a secure, happy life.

Solomon, the writer tells us, lived in Jerusalem in a palace built of cedarwood and cut stone, directing commercial networks and alliances reaching across the Mediterranean and down the long arm of the Red Sea. His linen factories wove clothes for the aristocratic ladies of the Hittite kingdom to the north, and uniforms for the soldiers of the Egyptian pharaoh. The Hittite king and the Egyptian pharaoh—one of Solomon's many fathers-in-law—paid for their cloth with horses and chariots for Solomon's own armies; one horse cost sixty shekels and a chariot 150.[20]

Solomon dealt in spices, gems and incense with the Queen of Sheba, who ruled modern Yemen. He and his neighbor Hiram in Tyre pooled money and financed a merchant fleet. Every three years their fleet landed at Eilat, carrying "gold, and silver, ivory, and apes, and peacocks" from Ophir and Tartessus. The details of these stories may be fiction, but there is no reason to disbelieve the account of the commerce, which both later and earlier histories confirm.[21]

The Kings writer flavors his awe and celebration with some personal censure of Solomon. (He married too many women; they lured him into unsavory dabbling with foreign gods.) But the judgment is clear.

Solomon's ships sailed across the known world; his ports and capital were the markets for the most exotic foreign products; he recruited empires and misty faraway tribes as allies. Solomon's business networks meant not only opulence but security: the fleets sailed from Eilat; the caravans made the circuit of Egypt, Yemen, and the Hittite lands; Solomon "had peace on all sides round about him," and his people "dwelt in safety, every man under his fig tree and each man under his vine."

※

THE PARTY OF HOPE associates trade with peace, tolerance, and the good life. It also has a theoretical branch, which over two centuries has built a framework of intellectual support its critics have never been able to match. Its principal case is that economic "liberalization" is good mostly for the country which liberalizes: it becomes more efficient, living standards rise, it can grow more quickly without inflation and therefore support lower levels of unemployment.

Adam Smith, of course, is the founder of trade theory. His famous 18th-century example is the choice between wine and wool. Portugal—hilly, warm and dry—made wine more cheaply than Scotland. But Scotland, also hilly but cool and damp, was a perfect place to raise sheep, shear them for their wool, and stitch woolen fabrics into clothes. If Scotland chose to create a wine industry, it will have to block the Portuguese wine. The Scottish vintners may well grow rich, selling an acceptable wine for thirty times the cost of a foreign vintage. But the buyers of wine will spend far more on it than they should, and the British government may also need tax money to subsidize the vintners.

Therefore the buyers would have less money to spend on clothes, swords, boats and magazines. Makers of these things would lose customers and lay off workers. If Scotland simply stopped trying to grow grapes, bought the wine from Portugal, devoted more capital to sheepbreeding, and sold Portugal a bit of wool, all would be well.

Those who have not read Smith's book, *The Wealth of Nations,* often think of him as an austere friend of business, always lecturing the do-gooder and applauding the profiteer. This is sad because he was nothing of the sort. His book overflows with humanity and plain talk, colorful fact and weird anecdote, sympathy for the housewife and revulsion at the slavemaster, denunciations of treasure-hunting,[22] and the conviction—almost always based on powerful and entertaining evidence—that every rich man's pet project is a plot to rob the public.

Smith's attack on trade restrictions is characteristic. He give his readers a mocking list of the products forbidden by England's 18th-century mercantile laws: nobody could buy foreign-dug fuller's earth for tobacco pipes, or pipe-clay, or rawhides and tanned leather, or cattle horns. (The hope was to protect makers of drinking horns and combs.) No manufacturer could buy foreign-mined metal ores, with the exceptions of lead and tin. Nor could he buy brass, gun-metal, bell-metal, alum, coal, white wool cards, woolen cloth, coney hair and wool, hare's wool, or horses.[23]

He then makes two observations. The first is that a law of this type offends common sense:

> In every country it always is and must be the interest of the great body of the people to buy whatever they want from those who sell it cheapest. This proposition is so very manifest that it seems ridiculous to take any pains to prove it; nor could it ever have been called in question, had not the interested sophistry of merchants and manufactures confounded the common sense of mankind.[24]

The second is that they will financially damage the country that adopts them as a whole:

> To give the monopoly of the home market to the produce of domestic industry, in any particular art or manufacture, is in some measure to direct private people in what manner they ought to employ their capital and must in almost all cases be either useless or hurtful regulation. If the produce of domestic can be bought as cheap as that of foreign industry, the regulation is evidently useless. If it cannot, it must generally be hurtful.[25]

Smith then consoles the reader by observing that as bad as affairs may have got, all was once much worse. One example is a remarkable law passed during the reign of Elizabeth, banning exports of sheep at the urging of cloth-makers who hoped to keep the price of raw wool low:

The exporter of sheep, lambs, or rams was for the first offence to forfeit all his goods for ever, to suffer a year's imprisonment, and then to have his left hand cut off in the market town upon a market day, there to be nailed up; and for the second offence be adjudged a felon and to suffer death accordingly.[26]

His theories have been sharpened and revised over time, but never overthrown. Ricardo's doctrine of comparative advantage is more challenging than Smith's concept of 'absolute advantage,' but not impossibly so. Perhaps Portugal can also make cloth more efficiently than England. But its special excellence remains in vineyards—ninety Portuguese can do the work of a hundred English garment workers, but eighty Portuguese can equal a hundred English vintners—and if so, one can prove with arithmetic and graphs that England should continue to make clothes while Portugal concentrates on wine. Both countries will be better off.

Later writers refine this further, suggesting complementary roles for the state and public services. An example is the beautifully named Sir Lyon Playfair, chemist and MP for Edinburgh, who wrote an influential report for the British government in the 1850s arguing that the industrial development of Germany showed that competition among advanced countries had become mainly intellectual. The country with the best-educated workers would make the most sophisticated products and leave its rivals behind.

Generations of economists have made honorable careers in academia, or spotty ones in lobbying, poking holes in these ideas. Sometimes they find special cases in which theory requires temporary exception, or is outweighed by other considerations, or doesn't apply at all. An "infant" industry might benefit from temporary tariff protection, until it is large and strong enough to compete with established firms abroad. A temporary subsidy may help create an industry—aircraft manufacturing, railroads, satellite launches—in which the cost of building factories and lines can be so high that no private person could afford to start a business. An army may need weapons from domestic factories in an emergency; an unlimited world market for beluga caviar may spell doom for a fish which lives in Russia, where fishermen earn a thousand dollars a year and a single batch of roe can bring $100,000 in the Paris market.

Some exceptions apply easily to the real world. The WTO agreements recognize most, creating loopholes that help governments to control and manage wildlife trade, ban imports of environmentally harmful products, and exclude weapons and pornography. Others prove easier to imagine in principle than to execute in the real world. The American textile industry, for example, received 'infant' industry protection in 1816 and has it still. So does India's automobile industry, which is as old as Japan's but has yet to make a decent car. Acquiring a subsidy in the 1970s, the European Airbus consortium has never given it up. But in either case, justifiable or the result of self-interested lobbies, the exceptions do not overturn the basic theory.

Party of Gloom

The party of hope always meets a party of gloom, whose members have the conservative temperament. They remind us that all pleasures come with a price, worry about squandered savings, regret the erosion of old institutions and ways of life, and fear competition that might prove too powerful to meet.

Pliny, its founding member, was the first writer to total up an import bill and worry about the consequences. His stories of the frankincense business are only one example of a flood of luxuries—Greek ships unloading Indonesian pepper from the southern Spice Route, Iranian perfumes arriving on the Lebanon, Chinese silks coming west on the Silk Road—which he believed cost Rome a hundred million sesterces a year.

None of the Caesars had a sophisticated statistical service, so it is hard to see how Pliny got the figure. Perhaps he made it up. But modern writers estimate the imperial Roman GDP at around five billion sesterces. If they are right, and if Pliny was right about the import bill, and if his calculations included export revenues, first-century Rome ran a trade deficit equivalent to 2 percent of GDP.[27]

A modern counterpart to Pliny appeared in 17th-century Britain, as the East India Company's first shipments of Indian cotton arrived at London in 1670. Cheap, colorful and cool, the bales of printed "calico" (named for Calicut, the port of modern Kerala) found an enthusiastic shopping public. But they provoked riots among London garment-workers and a stream of appeals from textile baronets.

John Basset, Member for Barnstaple in 1680, saw ruin. Basset believed India's low wages would drive English mills into bankruptcy. "The people in India are such slaves," he says, that they are "willing to work for less than a penny a day, whereas ours here will not work under a shilling."[28] Unless Parliament halted the flood of Indian cotton, England would lose its export markets as calicoes pushed British silk and wool out of the continent; low-cost Bengali labor would then displace the well-paid Devonshire mechanic at home; and then British manufacturing would crumble.

Basset and his industry associates had an eloquent friend in Daniel Defoe. The author of *Robinson Crusoe* and *Moll Flanders* knew world markets well—in the 1690s he had exported socks to Spain and bought Virginia tobacco. Defoe thought Asian wages were a tenth of the British rate,[29] which is almost precisely the modern garment-wage disparity separating America and China. (In 2002, America's Bureau of Labor Standards reported that an American garment-worker earned about $9.50 an hour,[30] and the International Trade Commission found Chinese garment-workers making 90 cents an hour.[31]) The newly open world, Defoe insisted, meant that all had changed. A pamphlet he wrote for the Parliamentary session of 1700 told the Members that low-wage Asian competition was killing British industry:

> Above half of the woolen manufacture was entirely lost, half of the people scattered and ruined, and all this by the intercourse of the East India trade.

Parliament agreed and responded in 1701 with a law known as the Calico Act. Noting that "continuance of the trade to the East Indies . . . must inevitably be to the great detriment of this kingdom, by exhausting the treasure thereof, and melting down the coin, and taking away the labour of the people," it banned not only importing but wearing all "wrought silks and stuffs mixed with silk, of the manufacture of Persia, China or East India, and all calicoes [i.e. cotton] painted, dyed, printed or stained there."

The law failed. Manufacturing writers angrily found British ladies driven more by "their passion for their Fashion" than the balance of trade or the English factory interest. A second Calico Act accordingly passed in 1720, asserting that British manufacturing faced "utter ruin and destruction." It imposed a five-pound fine, the equivalent of four months' wages for a garment-worker, on anyone caught wearing Asian-made cotton clothes.[32]

Cottons flowed in nonetheless. Fines went higher. Calico's appeal to the London debutante remained strong. British manufacturers eventually solved the problem through technology, as they invented the water-loom, the spinning jenny, and the dark, satanic mills of the Industrial Revolution.

Party of Virtue

The last of the three, the party of virtue, is always small but also always, as with the Southern Agrarians in America's 1920s, influential. Its members are intellectuals, and spiritually-minded people—sometimes on the right fringe of politics, sometimes on the millennial left, at their best simply indifferent to politics—who consider wealth and trade sources of corruption. Often they offer valuable counsel to individuals; but for societies as a whole their advice is terribly flawed.

Pliny gives us a sample of its thinking. He called perfume "the most useless of all luxuries"—diamonds may be vanities but hold their value and can be passed to heirs; perfume just evaporates into the air—and denounced the Chinese silk trade as a threat to morals, asserting that "we travel to the end of the earth for this material simply so Roman women can parade around in see-through dresses."[33] The great classical example, though, is Plato.

Xenophon's merchants and party-goers lived in the Classical era's "globalizing" state. Athens was the most populous city in Greece and easily the richest. Its commercial ships—square-rigged, undecked vessels of up to four hundred tons, with banks of oars to maneuver in harbors—brought fish and wheat from the Ukraine, cheese and oil from Sicily, paper and cloth from Egypt, and incense from Persia to the Piraeus port and the Athenian agora. Silver Athenian coins, known as *drachmae,* were the Mediterranean's common currency; Athenian plays and jokes went into reruns in every Greek town after their debut in the metropolis.

Plato didn't much like any of it. He advised the rejection of wealth and common pleasures, and the embrace of virtue and the life of the mind. This argument, made with special force in *Phaedo,* inspires and consoles even today. Socrates, speaking to fifteen disciples in his prison cell a few hours before his death, explains his serenity to his grieving students with quiet compassion. He asks them why people are unhappy and why they fight, and answers by tracing misery back to the desire for wealth and sensual pleasure:

> The body fill us with loves, desires, fears and all sorts of fancies, and a great deal of nonsense, with the result that we literally never get an opportunity to think at all about anything. Wars and revolutions and battles are due simply to the body and its desires; all wars are under-taken for the acquisition of wealth; and the reason why we have to acquire wealth is the body, because we are slaves to its desires.[34]

We can easily free ourselves from these miseries, Socrates reminds the group. Logic and common sense show us that possessions are insignificant and death inevitable. Our own virtue and reason are all the soul can possess, and are all we need. To grasp this simple point is to win freedom from want and desire. Socrates has done so; he can face death without fear.

A man like Socrates earns admiration in every age. because he is a saint. He is serene in daily life and extremity alike, because he knows that wealth, family, and even life itself are not his to keep. He may enjoy them while he has them, but he can give them up with ease. The difficulties come when we transfer his personal renunciation to society.

Plato's later book *The Laws* attempts to describe such a society in detail, with prophetic and unattractive results. Its central character, known only as the Athenian Stranger, begins with the proposition that the earliest men and women lived happily, because their lives were so simple. Owning little more than the food and shelter they needed to survive, they had no reason to envy and compete with one another:

> The community which has neither poverty nor riches will always have the noblest principles; in it there is no insolence or injustice, nor, again, is there contention or envy. And therefore they were good,

and also because they were what is called simple-minded; and when they were told about good and evil, they in their simplicity believed what they heard to be very truth and practiced it.[35]

But moderns devote themselves to luxury, pleasure, and corruption. Therefore they have become shallow, easily angered with one another, covetous and violent, unwilling to take the time to cultivate self-reliance and appreciation of virtue and philosophy. No city has escaped corruption, and the only way to restore the happy past is for an enlightened few to escape. A new community must begin by leaving the modern cities for an empty valley far from the sea, surrounded by treeless rocky hills. In this deserted place, it can tend to its own needs—spending its days in clean honest work, growing its own food, making its own tools and clothes, and contemplating virtue in the evenings. That is all the people need for a happy life.

But Plato is too honest to end his narrative there. Though the people would have all they require, the Stranger concedes that corruption can easily return. Pleasure and luxury will tempt its young people constantly, until they are fully educated. Outsiders are the greatest source of this risk—"foreigners are always suggesting novelties"—and even in a state with good laws and virtuous people, "the mixture [with foreigners] causes the greatest possible injury." The citizens must therefore meet outsiders only rarely, and only under carefully controlled circumstances. A wise ruler will let nobody under forty go abroad for any reason, and permit even mature adults to leave only on public business—for an embassy, an athletic festival, or a religious pilgrimage.

Commerce is no safer than tourism. Any city needs a few imported goods to survive, which the city officials will monitor closely to keep luxuries off the market. (The Stranger suggests rigorous bans on incense and the purple dye made from the Lebanese murex snail; both are frivolities.) They will ban exports altogether. Selling goods abroad means a flow of coins and precious metals into the city. This means amassing of wealth, desire for more wealth, and the return of corruption—"a great export trade, and a great return of gold and silver have the most fatal results on a State whose aim is the attainment of just and noble sentiments."

As the Stranger talks, the city takes on authoritarian colors. A Nocturnal Council will keep the city's people away from strangers and arrest those attempting to travel without permission. Agents will accompany visiting strangers in the markets and keep them from mingling with the citizens. The Stranger hints at suppression of subversive literature, and creation of a Board to approve jokes:

> A comic poet, or maker of iambic or satirical lyric verse, shall not be permitted to ridicule any of the citizens, either by word or likeness, either in anger or without anger.[36]

By the end of the book, Plato has sketched a totalitarian horror, a classical counterpart to the modern North Korea—and one which is not wholly imaginary, but owes much to the great economically and culturally isolated state of Plato's age.

This was Athens' southern neighbor and eventual rival Sparta. Its constitution, known as the *rhaetrae* or "spoken laws," is one of the most effective sets of isolationist financial, commercial, and social systems ever designed. One rhaetra banned ownership of precious metal. Spartans found owning foreign coins, or gold and silver in bulk, would have it confiscated. Instead they used a cast-iron currency known as "obols" which Xenophon said were so heavy and bulky that their owners had to carry them around in wagons, and which no other classical state would accept.

Spartans took no part in trade of any sort. Like Plato's ideal community, they did import necessities—grain in lean years, metal for armor and weapons—but only through a small hereditary group of second-class citizens known as the *perioeki* or "border-dwellers," who could not vote and lived on the edges of the Spartan lands. If Sparta needed beef, an official ordered a *perioeki* family to make a few pots and go trade them for a cow.

Nor could they travel abroad. No Spartan citizen could leave the national territory except on military or diplomatic business. They even kept away from the Olympics. (Aristotle suggests that Cynisca, a Spartan princess and one of the only women ever to win an Olympic medal, entered her team only to humiliate Spartan boys and persuade them that athletic festivals were unmanly.) Nor did the Spartan state let Greeks from neighboring cities cross its borders, unless they were on accredited diplomatic missions or had exceptional value to the state.

The result, Xenophon says, was a state devoted to virtue and war. All Spartan men enrolled in the army, and spent their time drilling and preparing to fight. Living an egalitarian life, equal in law, possessions, and battle, Spartans cared nothing for material matters.

In other states, I suppose, all men make as much money as they can. One is a farmer, another a ship-owner, another a merchant, and others live by different handicrafts. But at Sparta, Lycurgus [the semi-legendary founder of the Spartan state] forbade freeborn citizens to have anything to do with business affairs. He insisted on their regarding as their own concern only those activities that make for civic freedom. Indeed, how should wealth be a serious object there, when he insisted on equal contributions to the food supply and on the same standard of living for all, and thus cut off the attraction of money for indulgence' sake? Why, there is not even any need of money to spend on cloaks: for their adornment is due not to the price of their clothes, but to the excellent condition of their bodies. Nor yet is there any reason for amassing money in order to spend it on one's messmates; for he made it more respectable to help one's fellows by toiling with the body than by spending money, pointing out that toil is an employment of the soul, spending an employment of wealth.

Plutarch agreed, calling Sparta a commercial and cultural desert. It had no financial links with its neighbors. It preserved national culture with jealous care and traded only in absolute necessities unavailable at home. Sparta "had no means of purchasing foreign goods and small wares, and merchants sent no shiploads into [its] ports. No rhetoric-master, itinerant fortune-teller, harlot-monger, gold or silversmith, engraver or jeweler set foot in a country which had no money."

The system survived through frank and continuous murder and terror. The ten thousand Spartan citizens lived on the labor of a gigantic population of hereditary serfs, nearly two hundred thousand of them, known as helots. These helots, descendants of communities conquered early in Spartan history, did not vote, own weapons, serve in the army, travel abroad, or travel within Sparta without permission. Each helot man had to wear a dog-skin hat as an identifying badge. The mission of the Spartan army was to not to attack the neighboring cities—until the Peloponnesian War, Sparta's reputation was that of a powerful but quiet and generally peaceful state—but to prevent a helot revolt.

Thucydides thought the entire *rhaetra* system was designed to preserve helotry. Spartan citizens learned war because they feared helot rebellion. They banned trade and travel to prevent impressionable Spartan boys from hearing foreign criticism. They kept other Greeks out of Sparta for the same reason, and to prevent them from spreading discontent among the helots. Sparta's economic isolation was simply one element, though among the most important, in this edifice of repression. Its restrictions on foreign trade, cultural exchange and financial flows were meant to keep citizens ignorant, soldiers and police focused solely on preserving the state, and slaves willing to accept their miserable lives.

This is the normal end of attempts to create isolated, virtuous states. All end with a small group—in Sparta's time, ultra-conservative aristocrats; in the modern era, more often secret police and military bureaucracies—living off a large population of suppressed people whose principal hope is to escape. Two communist experiments of the mid-century—Enver Hoxha's Albania and Kim Il-sung's North Korea—are examples, as is the Burmese socialist state founded by Gen. Ne Win in 1962. Before leaving the party of virtue (it will not reappear) we can look at one of its most interesting, and least-known incarnations: the isolated republic set up in Paraguay by Jose Gaspar Rodriguez de Francia in 1811 on the collapse of the Spanish empire in South America.

Francia had studied at the Jesuit seminary in Cordoba during the 1780s, and had become devoted to Jean-Jacques Rousseau's concepts of the simple life, virtue, and noble savagery. In the century's first decades, he was a striking dark-haired figure, always wearing a black suit and sometimes, in cool weather, offsetting it with a scarlet-lined cape. His abundant spare time went to contemplation of the careers of Napoleon and Maxime Robespierre, and experiments in astronomy.

He was one of those rare bookish people with a natural aptitude for politics—a born organizer, an intimidating negotiator and intuitive diplomat, a man utterly confident of his own intellectual superiority. He rose to the top of provincial politics within a year of the Spanish withdrawal—negotiating a treaty of independence with Argentina, building

43

up a local network of intelligence agents and military followers, then becoming acclaimed as President for Life. From this post he organized a program based upon Rousseau, designed to insulate Paraguay from the upheavals beyond its borders, erase the divisions between the local Guarani Indians and their erstwhile creole overlords, and abolish divisions between rich and poor.

Francia accordingly sealed the borders, dispatching military aides to the borders of Brazil and Argentina with orders to let nobody leave and admit only those foreigners he personally approved. Another decree closed the Asuncion port, except for shipments of yerba and furniture, again personally approved by Francia. A hundred riverboats lay abandoned in the mud, for decades, at the juncture of the Paraguay River and the Pilcomayo. New laws remade society, barring creoles from marrying one another, nationalizing church lands, abolishing the Inquisition, and closing the small Asuncion seminary.

Within six months Francia had created a new world. Nobody left it and few entered. Having smashed the church and the Inquisition, he replaced them with his own militias, prisons and intelligence services. The stunned creoles, outnumbered by Francia's regiments and watched by his agents, were powerless. Twice they conspired to overthrow him. Most of the prominent creoles died by firing squad, under an orange tree in the Asuncion town square, and several thousand more prisoners went to a rural prison camp three hundred miles north.

Francia's dictatorship lasted twenty-six years. During these years the state printed not a single newspaper or book. Nobody left and almost nobody got in. Europeans learned of events in the horrified book the Robertson brothers, two British merchants stranded on the Paraguay River in the first years of the republic, published after escaping down-river by night. Within a year of Francia's elevation to the Presidency, they wrote:

> The prisons were groaning with inmates; commerce was paralyzed; vessels were rotting on the river-banks, and produce going to decay in the warehouses; a system of espionage of the most searching kind prevailed; the higher classes were all depressed, the lower brought into notice; while the caprice of the Dictator was the sole rule of

government, and the insolence of his soldiers was systematically encouraged as the best means of striking terror into the hearts of the crouching and insulted citizens. Distrust and terror pervaded every habitation; the nearest relations and dearest friends looked afraid of each other; despondency or despair were more or less legibly written on every countenance.

Paraguay was quiet, law-abiding, and egalitarian. It was self-sufficient, selling its agricultural products when necessary to purchase necessities it could not produce at home. Its citizenry were equal by law and in condition, its government at uneasy peace with its turbulent neighbors, its people miserable.

Sima Qian, the Chinese historian, predicted this situation 1900 years before Francia created it. Any society attempting to live in frugal isolation, he thought, would end as a repressive dictatorship. Each time, its leaders would find their principles of frugality and virtuous poverty in conflict with human nature, and would have to impose their vision by coercive laws and punishments. Commenting on the Taoist Lao Tzu, who imagined an isolated society resembling Plato's, he observed that:

Lao Tzu has said that under the ideal form of government:

Though states exist side by side, so close they can hear the crowing of each other's roosters and the barking of each other's dogs, the people of each state will savor their own food, admire their own clothing, be content with their own customs and delight in their own occupations, and will grow old without ever wandering abroad.

Yet if one were to apply this type of government, striving to draw the present age back to the conditions of primitive times and close the eyes and ears of the people, I doubt one would have much success.

From ancient times to the present, eyes and ears have longed for the most beautiful forms and sounds, and bodies delighted in pleasure and luxury. So long have these habits permeated the lives of the people, that even if one were to go from door to door preaching the most subtle arguments of Lao Tzu, he could never succeed in changing them. The highest type of government accepts this as the nature of the people. The very worst compels them to act against their nature.[37]

If a habit is universal, Sima suggests, it is probably natural and unchangeable. No philosopher or ascetic can alter it. A powerful government might succeed by force, but this would bring only misery. So it has proven since, in Plato's day, Francia's and ours.

The American Background

AN UNBRIDGEABLE GAP OF TIME and culture separates us even from a man like Defoe—let alone Xenophon, the Kings writer, or Sima Qian. But their ideas are not strange at all. We see Defoe's anxious wool-industry friends in today's debate on the rise of Chinese competition, and Plato's utopians in the anti-globalization movement. We recognize Sima Qian's carefree pleasure-seekers in every crowd of Christmas shoppers; we see the descendants of Xenophon's Athens in the modern New York, London, or Hong Kong, and Sparta's children in Burma and North Korea.

Such things were part of the -century liberal inheritance. Most of the early liberals knew and treasured the Kings writer, many knew Smith and Ricardo, a few were familiar with Xenophon. Perhaps none knew of Sima Qian, but academic economics had long been an acceptable substitute. Roosevelt's generation accordingly built modern trade policy with a foundation partly of this classical inheritance, mixed with the debates, experiences, and experiments with alternatives piled up in the first 150 years of American history.

Hamilton and The Early Republic

Early America was in some ways as 'integrated' into the global economy as modern America. Statistics show this in a dry and impersonal way, just as they provide a pencil sketch of the modern world economy.

Alexander Hamilton's Treasury Department counted $20 million in exports and $23 million in imports for 1790. The size of the early republic's economy is not clear, but one historical-data service suggests that the American GDP of 1790 was roughly $190 million.[38] If it is roughly correct, trade was then the equivalent of 22.6 percent of GDP. The figure for 2005, at 26 percent, was only slightly higher.

A more tangible illustration comes from a famous product of the era. Now hanging in the entrance hall of the Smithsonian Museum of American History, it is the physical actual Star-Spangled Banner: the thirty-four foot flag which, flying over Fort McHenry in 1813, inspired Francis Scott Key to write the national anthem.

The Banner's stripes are pure wool, and the stars in its canton are cotton. The cotton is native to the United States, but the wool is a British import. The stripes are reddened with a dye called cochineal imported from Guatemala and southern Mexico, which also colored the famous wool coats of British Army officers. The most expensive red dye of the period, cochineal came from a bug, known as a "scale insect," native to Oaxaca, Chiapas and Guatemala. Maya women plucked them by the thousands from the stems of fleshy plants, dried and pounded them to paste. Reduced to a brilliant reddish powder, the cochineal went by ship to textile factories in Britain, Spain, and America's Atlantic coast.

The blue of the canton is indigo. Sixth color in the rainbow, indigo is a natural dye made from the boiled flowers of the indigo plant. As its name suggests, the plant is native to India. Arriving in Europe somewhere in the medieval era, the plant came to South Carolina during the 1740s. The Banner's blue dye is probably from a slave-worked Carolina plantation.

This was a typical product of the early republic. Americans, a crowd of three million people scattered through towns, ports, and farms along the Atlantic Coast, were a small part of a much larger world economy. They eased their lives through imports and earned money by exports. They imported twenty-five million pounds of sugar from the Caribbean islands and French Louisiana each year. They bought a million pounds of Chinese tea—as much per person as we buy today—along with two million pounds of nails, and fourteen million pounds of woolen and cotton clothing.[39] Dyes, textiles, vats for boiling indigo, gin and whiskey, metals and grains, clothing and silverware, tea and coffee flowed easily through the country's five great ports.

Meanwhile, South Carolina sent 150,000 barrels of rice to Europe each year, and the family of Elbridge Gerry—the Massachusetts Declaration signer and Vice President immortalized by invention of the "gerrymander"—grew wealthy by exporting salted codfish, caught off Newfoundland's Grand Bank, to Spain and Barbados. Virginia and Maryland sent Europe a hundred thousand tons of tobacco each year; New York and Pennsylvania exported 50 thousand tons of bar iron. This was the bread and fish that fed the people of London, Paris, and Madrid; the snuff and pipe-tobacco that enlivened the leisure time of their aristocrats; the metal Europe's factories worked into knives, gates, and cannons.

Trade naturally held a prominent place in the high diplomacy, domestic politics, and even ethical debates of the time. The Declaration of Independence placed "pretended legislation for cutting off our trade with all parts of the World" third on a list of nine abusive laws imposed by George III, and John Adams refused to conclude the peace agreement with Britain in 1783 without a guarantee that New England boats could continue to fish the Grand Bank. (Massachusetts' salted fish brought nearly $1 million a year, out of $20 million in exports, in the 1790s.) A few years later, the Constitution barred states from creating their own tariffs and import limits, and at the insistence of South Carolina's rice and indigo planters, barred any taxation of exports.

Most of the revolutionary generation's leading figures wrote on trade matters, and often in depth. Caustic Benjamin Franklin scoffed at pleas for tariffs in *Wail of a Protected Manufacturer*. Thomas Jefferson, after a term as governor of tobacco-exporting Virginia, argued for unconditional free-trade policies in Notes on the State of Virginia. As Secretary of State nine years later, he had a different perspective and reached a different conclusion in the *Report on the Privileges and Restrictions on the Commerce of the United States in Foreign Countries*.

This paper, sent to Congress in 1793, catalogues imports, exports, and foreign barriers to American goods much as the U.S. Trade Representative's *National Trade Estimate* does today. The Spanish and Portuguese courts, Jefferson says, forbid direct trade with Latin America. Britain banned salted fish, imposed a prohibitory tariff on whale oil, and barred American merchant shipping from ports in Canada and the Caribbean islands. Even Sweden blocked American rice. Jefferson remained eloquently convinced that trade ideally should have no restrictions—"instead of embarrassing commerce under piles of regulating laws, duties and prohibitions, could it be relieved from all its shackles in all parts of the world, could every country be employed in producing that which nature has best fitted it to produce, and each be free to exchange with others mutual surpluses for mutual wants, the greatest mass possible would then be produced of those things which contribute to human life and human happiness; the numbers of mankind would be increased, and their condition bettered."[40] But he suggested approaching this happy state one country at a time, through commercial treaties, and in the meantime treating others, Britain in particular, as shabbily as they treated Americans.

Social reformers found some types of trade ethically appalling. Quakers thought the sugar imports—slaves harvested it in the Caribbean, dying by the hundreds or thousands every year—a scandal. They suggested a national effort to substitute New England's maple sugar for the tainted cane sugar, and Thomas Jefferson's abolitionist friend, the Philadelphia Declaration signer Dr. Benjamin Rush, convinced Jefferson to plant maple trees at Monticello. The maple, regrettably, proved too expensive and seasonal to be a practical substitute for cane. On the other hand, Thomas Paine, the most "left" of the founders, came to a radically different conclusion, proposing in The Rights of Man that free trade might eliminate war:

> If commerce were permitted to act to the universal extent it is capable, it would extirpate the system of war, and produce a revolution in the uncivilised state of governments. The invention of commerce has arisen since those governments began, and is the greatest approach towards universal civilisation that has yet been made by any means not immediately flowing from moral principles. Commerce is no other than the traffic of two individuals, multiplied on a scale

of numbers; and by the same rule that nature intended for the intercourse of two, she intended that of all. For this purpose she has distributed the materials of manufactures and commerce, in various and distant parts of a nation and of the world; and as they cannot be procured by war so cheaply or so commodiously as by commerce, she has rendered the latter the means of extirpating the former.[41]

Alexander Hamilton, the first Treasury Secretary, is the most relevant of the Founders for modern debate. As Paine dreamed of universal civilization, he thought over the issue most alarming to today's liberals—competition between a rich country's highly paid factory workers and their low-income, low-cost rivals—and found an answer that remains convincing even now.

☙

HAMILTON'S 130-PAGE *Report on the Subject of Manufactures*, released in the winter of 1791, was the U.S. government's first paper on trade policy and "competitiveness." In it he looks decades ahead, and sees a gigantic and diversified American economy, in which factories coexist with farms and shipping firms; goods travel the continent's interior on broad, safe, nationally financed roads and canals; and American ships carry float cargo to Britain, Europe, the Caribbean, and Asia. Wealthy, able to equip itself with a powerful navy, this larger and richer United States would meet Spain, the Netherlands—even Britain and France—on equal terms.

These same foreign powers, though, stood between the early republic and its dazzling future. Already established as manufacturers, they worked tirelessly to prevent the emergence of rivals. They refused to share technological expertise. They blocked wool exports to foreign factories, they subsidized their own factories, they closed their markets to American corn, they enforced all the laws Defoe and his friends had devised in the 17th century and Smith had mocked in the 18th. These realities of life, Hamilton observed, made hopes of "full liberty of commerce" impossible to realize.

That conceded, the Report listed dozens of second-best ideas for counteracting the British and French mercantile policies. Higher tariffs, Hamilton suggested, should discourage imports of some finished goods, while lower rates on raw materials cut factory costs. He proposes a tax of two cents per pound on imported chocolate to encourage candy-refining; one of two cents per gallon on imported whisky and gin to launch distilleries; cotton clothes should get an additional tariff of 7.5 percent—a rate, incidentally, which is barely half the modern cotton-clothing tariffs—and glue an "excluding" duty of fifteen percent.[42] Simultaneously, Congress should scrap the three-cent per pound tariff on raw cotton, along with the two-cent per pound duty on the sulfur used to make gunpowder and the five percent ad valorem tariff on wood and a few dozen others. The combination—twenty-one tariff increases, a dozen or so cuts—would create a large manufacturing industry. Hamilton imagined wrought metals, book printing, cloth, coal, processed foods, candy, alcohol, and church bells.

Hamilton's critics preferred a rural economy based upon small farming families to urban industry. (Jefferson: "the mobs of great cities add just so much to the support of pure government as sores do to the strength of the human body.") They pointed to a structural problem none of Hamilton's policy gadgets could fix, one which made his visions idle dreams: American wages, far above the levels of Britain and France, were so high than American factories could never compete with foreign rivals.

Hamilton acknowledged this as an important objection. London, Paris, Antwerp, Glasgow, and Marseilles were all packed with immigrants from the countryside. The European factory-manager could pick and choose among them, forcing destitute and unskilled men and women to bid against each other for work. Their counterparts in a still largely empty America paid premiums to attract manual workers who could easily wander off to start a farm, join a shipping firm, or take up a skilled trade. As early as the nation's birth, we were competing against lower-cost rivals—and then, as is not true today, the rivals joined the advantage of expertises and control of the existing markets with their low costs. How, then, could Hamilton's imaginary factories ever succeed?

Here the Report shifts from period-piece to prophesy. Though Hamilton finds "much exaggeration" in reports of poverty wages in Europe, he accepts that "in the article of wages the comparison certainly turns against the United States," and that the high pay—the "dearness"— of American workers is a disadvantage. But he insisted that it is not an impossible disadvantage. Technology could solve the problem, since wage disparities fall when we make use of newly invented machines that reduce production costs overall:

> Let it be supposed that the difference of price in two countries of manual labor requisite to the fabrication of a given article is as ten, and that some mechanic power is introduced into both countries which, performing half the necessary labor, leaves only half to be done by hand, it is evident that the difference in cost of the fabrication of the article in question in the two countries, as far as it is connected with the price of labor, will be reduced from ten to five in consequence of the introduction of that power.[43]

Automation and inventiveness, then, can make workers more productive or replace them altogether. Labor costs will fall, wages will remain high, and American factories will succeed.

Hamilton bubbles with ideas on ways to get started. He advises Congress to pass a patent law to encourage inventors of new machines. He suggests cash prizes for American inventors and the best-run factories, and asks Congress to authorize money to send agents across the Atlantic to scour Europe for "implements and machines" that mechanize factories. (Not an easy or even safe assignment: Hamilton notes that most European states banned the export of these machines "under severe penalties," precisely to prevent rivals from learning how to make them.) Talented immigrants could help as well: Congress should pay the passage fees for accomplished "artists and manufacturers" willing to move to the United States. Technology, eventually, would make America a peer of Europe's industrial barons.

The 19th-Century Tariff Debate

The *Report*'s real-life legacy was small, though its ideas on technical advance remain relevant today. Jefferson, Madison, and their Republican friends agreed on the patent proposal, but they blocked all but a few of Hamilton's tariff increases, and authorized subsidies only for whaling and fishing. Then, whatever the future might have held, events overtook the Founders' debates. The 18th-century global economy shut down when the Napoleonic wars began in 1796, and stayed shut for twenty years. During the interlude, the Industrial Revolution reached Massachusetts and Rhode Island. By the 1810s, the factories and industrial working class Hamilton's report predicted had arrived.

Then the wars stopped and trade revived. Ships filled with imported clothes, harpoons, and furniture returned to the Boston and New York ports. Britain, its parliaments and governments interested in Smith's theories, began to buy southern cotton, indigo, and rice. New manufacturers considered peace a disaster. Planters to the south, suddenly able to buy cheaper clothes and farm equipment, had the opposite opinion. The division created a debate which lasted for a century.

The manufacturers may not have been wrong to believe they faced crisis. In the two years after Waterloo and the Battle of New Orleans, imports rose ten-fold, from $13 million in 1814 to $146 million in 1816. The resulting national deficit, probably close to nine percent of GDP in 1815, still exceeds even the Bush-era imbalance as the highest in American history. The Congressional debate over an import surge quickly became a more profound division, revealing conflicts between the economic interests of south and north, and still more basic divisions over the nature of national government.

The 19th-century tariff debate, intellectual as well as partisan, was a bright line dividing the populist Democrats from the conservative Whigs and their Republican successors for more than a hundred years. The split reflected differing views of trade and foreign competition, and also—because the tariff system was the main source of government revenue—a fundamental divergence over taxation and the role of government. The early Democrats led a coalition of farm lobbies, populists insistent on the rights of the common man, a few sympathizers with the poor, and southern opponents of strong federal government in dislike of high-tariffs. Whigs and the early Republicans who inherited their voters just before the Civil War joined manufacturers and northern supporters of activist government in support for high tariffs. The debate's resolution helped give birth to America's modern liberal politics during the Progressive era; and the renewed force of the Whig arguments is one of the main questions raised over liberalism today.

ONE WHIG ARGUMENT was about the role of government. No 19th-century argument over tariff rates could be about exports and competition alone. All were also debates over the size and power of national government. This is because 19th-century America, like all countries early in their history and economic development, found tariffs the easiest kind of tax to collect. Sophisticated tax bureaucracies, able to get accurate reports on incomes, inheritances, and land values and collect taxes on them, are difficult to create and even more difficult to run. But even a rudimentary government can operate the attentive, moderately honest customs service necessary to spot a ship arriving in port, surround it with revenue men and force the importers to pay. Tariffs are also politically convenient, as they are easy to portray as taxes on foreigners, though businesses which buy foreign goods invariably attach the tariff cost to the price of their chairs or shirts.

Throughout the 19th century, therefore, government revenue meant tariffs. The Whigs and early Republicans supported high tariffs in part because they had some good reasons to want money. They believed in strong, well-financed national government that could use public works to speed economic development. Sharing Hamilton's belief in "energetic administration," and his support for public spending on canals, roads, and other 'internal improvements,' they needed money and found a high tariff the easiest way to get it. Before the Civil War, tariffs raised eighty or ninety percent of the government's money. (In 1833, it provided $29 million of $34 million.) The Civil War's taxation of liquor and tobacco, and its creation of the Internal Revenue Service, changed the system but not decisively, and were accompanied by much higher tariff rates.

Whigs and early Republicans were also members of the party of worry. They argued—some from conviction, many for demagogic effect, most with campaign finances in mind—that America was too rich and American workers too well-paid to compete against low-income rivals. In contrast to Hamilton, they believed that American high wages were a permanent and irresolvable disadvantage.

Daniel Webster, the Massachusetts Whig Senator and perennial Presidential hopeful, was one of this gloomy theory's great advocates before the Civil War. A famously eloquent man with a gigantic head and "glowing" dark eyes, called "Godlike Daniel" by his friends, Webster's portraits show him in dark blue or black broadcloth, always made in New England mills, with a high white collar.

His voice was famous in an age when rhetoric was entertainment and popular art. We cannot recapture the voice, but the words of one of his speeches, delivered on a Pennsylvania hillside in 1832 during the Whigs' second campaign against Andrew Jackson, are a mesmerizing sample of party rhetoric. Before a crowd of Industrial Revolution workers and factory owners, Webster sketches a portrait of squalid Europe, celebrates the opulence of American life, and warns of a looming degradation of wages and working conditions. British workers starve at their looms and foundries, their cloth and ironwork selling for practically nothing. Absent a protective tariff, American wages are driven down or American factories close. Over and over Webster repeats a phrase, varied slightly each time: the "pauper labor" of Britain, the "cheap pauper labor" of Britain, the "unpaid and half-fed labor" of Europe. It is easy to imagine the fear and anger his audience must have felt.

Henry Clay, the Whigs' other leading figure, was Webster's Senatemate and frequent rival for the presidency. A tall and reedy man, he made the same argument (in "musical" tones rather than in Webster's deep and carrying voice) in his "American System" address of 1832. Recalling the import surge of 1815 and 1816, Clay argued that the end of the Napoleonic Wars had meant disaster for America's workers. Peace in Europe, in reviving British factories and shipping, had created "deep and general distress, general bankruptcy, and national ruin." Sixteen years later the English wolf waited just outside the gate. Pennsylvania's iron foundries and New England's textile mills were inches from ruin. In Louisiana, a "way of life" was at stake, as sugar plantations spread across the newly pacified British and Spanish West Indies and foolish politicians suggested cutting the sugar tariff.

Fear of pauper labor outlived the Whig party itself. Generations of colorful but forgotten conservative Republicans—William "Pig Iron" Kelley and Benjamin Harrison in the 1870s and 1880s, "Czar" Thomas B. Reed and Nelson Aldrich as the 19th century ended, William McKinley and the Taft family—picked up the phrase and the ideas, and kept repeating them until the 1930s. The argument was a simple logical chain. American factories cannot survive competition with low-cost labor; high tariffs provide the money for internal improvements; manufacturing, protected by a tariff wall, will create jobs and bring prosperity.

The theory always had organic links to political money. Webster spent his career on retainer from the Massachusetts wool lobby. William McKinley, a Congressional tax-and-tariff expert turned Republican President, fused politics with big business finance so adeptly that Karl Rove still gushes over it today.

McKinley was no match for Webster and Clay as an orator. His speeches are boring, peppered with undiscriminating statistics and irritating platitudes. They lacked the Whigs' clever sound-bites and striking bits of fact. But his financial backers were even better organized than Webster's textile men. Mark Hanna, McKinley's political wizard, collected hundreds of millions of dollars from bushels from the steel mills, wool spinners, and sugar refiners for the 1896 campaign that beat William Jennings Bryan. And the progressive journalist Ida Tarbell, a critic of the tariff, admitted that McKinley added a novelty: "an advantage which few of his colleagues enjoyed—that of believing with childlike faith that all he claimed for protection was true."

"Free trade gives to the foreign producer equal privileges with us," McKinley tells a Kansas crowd in 1892. "Upon what principle of fair play should he have them? It invites the product of his cheaper labor to this market to destroy the domestic product representing our higher and better-paid labor. It destroys our factories or reduces our labor to the level of his. It increases foreign production but diminishes home production . . . it destroys the dignity and independence of American labor, diminishes its pay and employment, decreases its ability to buy the products of the farm and the commodities of the merchant."

McKinley is certain that low European wages mean doom for American factories. "This country will not and can not prosper under any system that does not recognize the difference of conditions between Europe and America. Open competition between high-paid American labor and poorly paid European labor will either drive out of existence American industry or lower American wages." Triumphantly, and a little obviously, he adds that "either of these is unwise."[44]

❦

19TH-CENTURY DEMOCRATS PLACED LOW TAXES, the common man, state rights, and farming for export against Whig and Republican commitment to high tariffs, the wealthy and wise, a strong central government, and support for manufacturing.

Democrats could be as demagogic as their rivals. A mid-century party journal begins with a title so sedate as to drive readers away—*The Tariff: Its History and Influence*—and within four sentences devolves into a ranting tirade, terming the Whig tariff a "horrible tyranny," a "great evil," and an "heirloom of monarchy."[45]

Grover Cleveland, the only Democratic President between the Civil War and Woodrow Wilson, and perhaps deservedly forgotten, provides the best example of minimal-government Democratic thought and its link to trade and the tariff. A 280-pound Buffalo sheriff who married a 21-year-old girl while serving as President, he devoted the entire 1887 State of the Union Address to a call for tariff reduction.

The address begins by denouncing the tariff as regionally and industrially unjust. As it subsidized northern manufacturers by raising the price of machinery, it punished the southern farmers who bought the machinery. So far, true enough. It then observes that the tariff is also bad simply because it raises money, foiling the minimalist government that encourages hard work and thrift. Tariff money, says Cleveland, lures the nation into "schemes for public plunder," "unnecessary and extravagant appropriations," "reckless improvidence," and "the demoralization of all just conceptions of public duty." (He refers to ideas for canal-building, a larger navy, post offices, and pensions for Civil War veterans.) By cutting the tariff to the absolute minimum, Congress can avert "financial convulsion and widespread disaster."

19th-century Democrats also made a humanitarian argument against the tariff. In dual contrast to Cleveland's dislike of public services and fear of financial upheaval, this argument was appealing and true. However much money the government required, the tariff was the worst way to raise it because it took the money from the poor.

The tariff's highest rates, one finds in poring over old schedules, were always upon life necessities. Thomas Jefferson's old Treasury Secretary, Albert Gallatin, developed this point in his last arguments against Webster and Clay in the 1830s. Reviewing the Whig tariff, he found "all the coarser woolen articles of clothing, as well as salt, coal and sugar," facing vastly higher tariffs than luxuries and industrial supplies, and concludes that "the poor pay, in every instance considerably more than the rich."[46]

A later Democratic Treasury Secretary, Robert J. Walker, echoed him in 1846. Walker noted that the 100 percent tariff on cheap cottons was "five times higher on the cheap article consumed by the poor, than upon the fine article purchased by the more wealthy." Moving through cheap woolen goods, sugar, and similar staples, he charged the whole system with "discrimination against the poor and in favor of the rich." One example, anticipating Gandhi (though Walker was an exceptionally bellicose and sometimes slippery man) was his specific denunciation of the tariff on salt: "a necessary of life, [it] should be as free of tax as water or air."[47]

As the 19th century passed, the Democrats lost the tariff battle. Before the Civil War, the parties had been in rough balance. Tariff rates accordingly oscillated with the election cycles. (Democrats cut tariffs after their wins in the presidential election of1836, 1844, and 1856. Whigs and Republicans raised them after their victories in 1824, 1840, and 1860. After the Civil War, Democrats stopped winning elections. Between 1870 and 1930, with a brief but important exception for the Wilson administration, American tariffs were among the highest in the world.

Sometimes though, the Democrats lost with flair. Tarbell's book *The Tariff In Our Times* recalled New York's Democratic Congressman Samuel Cox as he ridicules pauper-labor appeals by forcing the House to vote on a mock amendment requiring all households in the country to seal their windows, "as also all openings, holes, chinks, clefts and fissures." The aim was to protect miners and "dealers in gas-coal" from the unfairly low-priced light of the sun, whose labor costs were zero. Another group of New Yorkers, she says, trained parrots to squawk "tariff is a tax" as an election-parade stunt.

A perfect Democratic response to Republican pauper-labor rhetoric came from Benton McMillin of Tennessee in 1897. He and his five colleagues on the House Ways and Means Committee were as outnumbered as their modern counterparts were during the Bush ascendancy. As William McKinley's lieutenants raised tariffs on flax, linen, burlap, cotton, salt, lumber, and books, McMillin protested with energetic jingoism:

> To say that the very intelligent and highly skilled laborers of this country cannot successfully compete with the ignorant and unskilled laborers of the Old World, is equivalent to saying that skill and intelligence are not of great advantage to the laborers who possess them. To our minds, it involves a contradiction in history as well as economic theory to hold that the factory labor of a civilized country needs protection against the factory labor of an uncivilized country. The fact that the unskilled laborers of a half-civilized country live more cheaply than the skilled laborers of a highly civilized country is more than counterbalanced by the greater productiveness of the skilled and intelligent laborers . . . The skill and intelligence of the American laborer are such that he is able to produce seven times as much as the less skillful and less intelligent laborer of Continental Europe and fifteen times as much as the ignorant and unskilled laborers of Asia. Surely it will be admitted that a productive capacity seven times as great as the one and fifteen times as great as the other should be all that the American laborer needs to protect himself against the competition of European drudges and Asiatic serfs.

Stripped of its scoffing at foreigners, McMillin's argument is sound. If Americans are more productive than Asians and Europeans, they will make more things and earn more money. If Asia's uneducated serfs and Europe's bone-headed drudges grow more productive, they will earn more money. The gap in wages will shrink. The same is true for Webster's half-starved Englishmen in the 1830s and Sanders' desperate Chinese—the International Labor Organization finds their wages are rising by ten percent a year—in the 21th century.

♛

NEITHER PARROTS nor mockery of foreigners won the debates for Democrats. But in a sense their losses were irrelevant. As Whigs and Republicans built walls around the United States, the tides of Victorian globalization flowed through them, around them, and over them with ease.

Victorian Globalization and Its Collapse

ROOSEVELT AND HIS COLLEAGUES were born into a world more "globalized" than that of the Founders, or of any other age until the present. They grew up in it as children, and as adults they saw it collapse.

In proportion to the economy, trade was smaller in the continental America of the Gilded Age than it had been in the 1790s. Cleveland's Customs Service recorded $858 million in exports and $789 million in imports in 1890, which came to 13 percent of GDP—less than the figures of the Founder's era, but not far below the 15 percent of 1990. Nevertheless, the Victorian version of the global economy is much closer to that of today than it was to the version of the 18th century, or most of the either.

Victorian Globalization

Protected by Britain's navy, a new global economy blossomed after the Napoleonic wars. More like that of today than that of the Founders' era, it featured much more than exchanges of goods: elaborate new communications technologies, multilateral agreements among governments, fears of cultural "homogenization." Commodities sped faster across oceans as steam replaced sail in the 1840s, and across continents as rails replaced hooves in the 1860s. Money and information slipped a mile beneath the sea through copper submarine cables—sealed in straw, iron, and the dried sap of the Malayan gutta-percha tree—laid down between 1850 and 1890.

The English language adopted words that now define America to the world. The *hamburger* arrived in the English language from northern Germany in 1905. Coca-Cola, invented in 1886 and bottled in 1894, combines the Quechua word for the *coca* plant with the Malinke word for the *cola* nut once used as a flavoring. Blue jeans arrived as well, from France: the term revives Marseilles dockside slang for denim-wearing Italian sailors from *Genes*, or Genoa, while *denim* is simply fabric "from Nimes." The *tycoon,* originally a high official of the Japanese empire, became an American baron in the 1860s.

Governments struggled to keep up. Their international agreements and conventions are remarkable even today. A seventeen-country convention, meeting in Paris in 1875, agreed upon the length of the meter, the weight of the gram, and the volume of the liter. Another, in 1886, concluded the first international intellectual-property agreement.

A third, in Washington, synchronized the clocks. This was the International Conference on the Meridian, called by President Chester Arthur in 1884. It joined representatives of Britain, France, Germany, Turkey, Haiti, the Kingdom of Hawaii, and the Empires of China, Brazil, and Japan to Washington in the hopes of synchronizing clocks. British and American delegates proposed that the day begin at 12:00 a.m. by the clock in the Greenwich Meteorological Observatory outside London. The French delegate proposed Paris, angrily rejecting British assertions that the City of Light was too plagued by air pollution. Had a French astronomer not, just two years before, discovered the planet Neptune? Britain and the United States ultimately won out on practical grounds, as British shipping carried seventy percent of the world's commerce and already used Greenwich time. (The Japanese delegate stayed quiet throughout. His country had adopted western hours in 1872, having previously used an ingenious sort of hand-made clock known as a "wadokei," which ran slow in the summer and fast in the winter.)

Trade barriers came down too, in almost every country but Republican-run America. Britain eliminated many of its industrial and agricultural tariffs in the 1840s. The other European powers were only a bit slower: forty commercial treaties concluded during the 1860s and 1870s—Austria with Belgium, Belgium with France, France with Italy, Italy with Germany, Germany with Britain—created a rickety, complicated, but workable set of legal guarantees that tariffs would be low and trade policies stable.

Most important among these was the Anglo-French Agreement. Concluded in 1860 by the British textile-magnate and founder of the *Economist* magazine, Richard Cobden, and the French diplomat Michel Chevalier, this scrapped all British tariffs but the one on wine, and abolished most of France's batteries of tariffs and prohibitions. Like Paine a century earlier, Cobden placed sadly excessive hope in his achievement:

> I see in the Free Trade principle that which shall act on the moral world as the principle of gravitation in the universe—drawing men together, thrusting aside the antagonism of race and creed and language, and uniting us in the bonds of eternal peace . . . I believe that the effect will be to change the face of the world, so as to introduce a system of government entirely distinct from that which now prevails. I believe that the desire and the motive for large and mighty empires—for gigantic armies and great navies—for those materials which are used for the destruction of life and the desolation of the rewards of labour—will die away; I believe that such things will cease to be necessary, or to be used, when man becomes one family and freely exchanges the fruits of his labour with his brother man. I believe that, if we could be allowed to reappear on this sublunary scene, we should see, at a far distant period, the governing system of this world revert to something like the municipal system; and I believe that the speculative philosopher of a thousand years hence will date the greatest revolution that ever happened in the world's history from the triumph of the principle which we have met here to advocate.[48]

Despite the best efforts of Gilded Age Republicans, by the 1870s goods flowed into American ports on a scale that the founding generation might have accepted, but would have made Clay and Webster gasp. Two million dollars in annual shipments of German-made blue, purple, green, yellow and red chemical dyes arrived in East Coast ports, driving Mexico's cochineal and Carolina's indigo off the national flags. Ninety thousand dollars worth of silk cocoons arrived each year. So did thousands of tons of zinc, half a million dollars worth of nutmeg, six million dollars' worth of barley, a million gallons of beer, two million square feet of plate glass, a million tons of steel, and six million pounds of glue.

From the ports of Boston, New York, Baltimore, Charleston, Galveston, and San Francisco a million dollars' worth of goods left for Costa Rica and four million more for Hong Kong. The Meiji Emperor's revolutionary Japan bought $5 million worth of American goods; so did chaotic Haiti. Britain bought everything from cotton to clothes to steel, and India bought American ice. Rudyard Kipling's crocodile story, *The Mugger of Mugger-Ghat*, recalls the enterprising Bostonian who developed an ingenious low-tech way to ship ice dug from Walden Pond by Irish immigrants (he lifted it off the decks in decks in huge plywood frames and packed it in straw) to Cuba, Bombay, Calcutta, and Singapore.[49]

Sixty years later, John Maynard Keynes looked back upon the era with awe. He called the period "an economic Utopia, an economic Eldorado." He thought it had been a time of material advance, social progress, and peace, something never before achieved and something never to be seen again:

Life offered, at a low cost and with the least trouble, conveniences, comforts, and amenities beyond the compass of the richest and most powerful monarchs of other ages. The inhabitant of London could order by telephone, sipping his morning tea in bed, the various products of the whole earth, in such quantity as he might see fit, and reasonably expect their early delivery upon his doorstep; he could at the same moment and by the same means adventure his wealth in the natural resources and new enterprises of any quarter of the world, and share, without exertion or even trouble, in their prospective fruits and advantages; or he could decide to couple the security of his fortunes with the good faith of the townspeople of any substantial municipality in any continent that fancy or information might recommend . . . Most important of all, he regarded this state of affairs as normal, certain, and permanent, except in the direction of further improvement, and any deviation from it as aberrant, scandalous, and avoidable.[50]

Wilson and the Progressives

For Americans, the later part of this era was the Progressive age. A bipartisan movement, Progressivism left laws and institutions so deeply rooted in public life that few notice them—the national forest system, the Food and Drug Administration, the Federal Reserve, the direct election of Senators—and created the urban reformist activism which remains the basis of American liberal politics today. Its Democratic wing has a less widely recognized legacy: under Woodrow Wilson it ended the 19th-century tariff debate, and in doing so made modern liberalism possible.

The tariff still provided half the government's revenue in 1912. As always, it reserved its highest rates for the necessities: clothes, soap, sugar, and the like. As Gallatin had in 1831, Wilson pointed out that taxing these goods meant taxing the poor. As Democrats and Progressives had since the 1880s, Wilson argued that high tariffs generally meant oppression of the consumer—a Republican Ways and Means Committee, fifteen years earlier, had laughed at his chief policy advisor, the young Louis Brandeis, for making this argument—along with support for the steel, wool, and sugar trusts, frustration of competition, and ultimately a stagnant economy.

Unlike the Cleveland type of Democrat, though, Wilson believed in strong national government able to provide the Whig type of public services. He wanted anti-trust powers and a central bank. He backed his rival Theodore Roosevelt's food safety laws and federally managed forests. By 1916 he wanted battleships and a powerful army able to fight a European War. He needed money, and his lasting achievement was to find it in the wealthy neighborhoods.

Forty-five days after his inauguration, Wilson called a joint session of Congress to deliver an address of 1,500 words. He devoted this speech—the first personal appearance by a President before Congress since John Adams' in 1798—to an attack upon the tariff system as a gift to the sugar, textile, and steel trusts. He followed this with a four-month campaign, quaintly using the press to shock the public with news that lobbyists for sugar refineries and wool mills were visiting Senators. By September he had his legislative triumph: sharply lower tariff rates, and a new income tax, written by Cordell Hull, later Franklin Roosevelt's Secretary of State and then Benton McMillin's successor as Tennessee Representative, to replace the lost money. A second bill three years later added the estate tax, which Theodore Roosevelt popularized and today's Republican party hopes to abolish. Aged, happy with a sinecure appointment as Ambassador to Peru, McMillin cheered in the *Saturday Evening Post*:

> Why lay tribute on what we eat and wear, and leave untaxed millions in the hands of those who can never personally consume it? . . . the concentrated wealth of the land should bear its share of our enormous expenses of government . . . it takes as many yard of cloth to clothe comfortably and as many pounds of sugar, coffee, salt, rice, meat and vegetables to feed bountifully a poor man as a rich one. Hence, when taxation is on consumption, as with tariff taxes, the burden is borne unequally—the poor paying more and the rich less than their fair share . . . Heretofore we have taxed want instead of wealth.[51]

By 1920, the income and estate taxes raised a billion dollars a year. Wilson used them to build a central government able to inspect meat, enforce factory safety laws, tend national forests and national parks, float a navy and equip the American Expeditionary Force in Europe. At the same time, he cut tariff rates from 40 percent to 12 percent, eliminated them altogether on sugar, eggs, and soap, and drastically cut them on clothes and bread.

This was the end of the tariff debate, and the birth of a liberal government able to combine kindness to the poor with national public works. With lower rates and the European war, tariff income plunged from a half to a twentieth of the government's revenue. Tariffs never again raised much money for the government, and the system lost much of its significance.

Conservative Reaction

Wilson's triumph as a tax reformer endured. It is still, even today, the reason an activist government can pay for public services without burdening the poor. But Wilson's tariff cuts died with his presidency and the League of Nations.

Republicans—and business lobbies along with them—had changed none of their opinions. They believed, as McKinley had, in an America isolated from the world economy, apart from international organizations, and indifferent to world politics. After the First World War a Republican Senate famously rejected the League of Nations Treaty. Warren Harding's victory in the 1920 Presidential election, pledging a "return to normalcy," underlined the decision. Harding's inaugural address rejects Wilson's concept of internationalism:

> America, our America, the America builded *[sic]* on the foundation laid by the inspired fathers, can be a party to no permanent military alliance. It can enter into no political commitments, nor assume any economic obligations which will subject our decisions to any other than our own authority.

Harding then proposes the same thing for trade, reprising the cheap-labor fears of a century of Whig and Republican politicians:

> It has been proved again and again that we cannot, while throwing our markets open to the world, maintain American standards of living and opportunity, and hold our industrial eminence in such unequal competition. There is a luring fallacy in the theory of banished barriers of trade, but preserved American standards require our higher production costs to be reflected in our tariffs on imports.[52]

Harding's awful Presidency lasted two years. We now remember it mainly for the Teapot Dome scandal (Albert Fall, the Secretary of the Interior, extorted $404,000 in bribes for oil-drilling rights in Wyoming) and Harding's romantic affair with a secretary, rather than for any positive accomplishment.

This judgment isn't unfair, judged even against Harding's own goals. By shifting taxation from want to wealth, Wilson's tax revolution unintentionally turned the Republicans into the party of small government and conservatism. Harding's hope, much like Cleveland's, was to accomplish as little as possible: "I must disavow any desire to enlarge the Executive's powers or add to the responsibilities of the office. They are already too large."

The one thing Harding did want, and did achieve, was a new tariff law. This aroused some misgivings—a new tariff penalty was not a friendly thing to do to our erstwhile Great War allies, with their wrecked economies. His first State of the Union speech did express perfunctory sympathy with the exhausted British and the miserable French, but quickly followed the sympathy with firm rejection of any interest in helping them, and then a grating series of platitudes on the rewards Europe could earn through thrift and hard work:

> With all my heart I wish restoration to the peoples blighted by the awful World War, but the process of restoration does not lie in our acceptance of like conditions. It were better to remain on firm ground, strive for ample employment and high standards of wage at home, and point the way to balanced budgets, rigid economies, and resolute, efficient work as the necessary remedies to cure disaster.[53]

Harding's 1922 tariff law, known as the Fordney-McCumber Act (for its Congressional authors Porter McCumber and Joe Fordney) made sure Europe would recover on its own. It restored most of the tariffs Wilson scrapped, the average tariff rate returning to 40 percent, and cut American trade in half, relative to the economy.

The debate puzzled a figure no less significant than Albert Einstein, who had arrived for a celebrity tour of the U.S. a month after Harding's inaugural. Amazed equally by the high quality of American-made furniture, cars, and household goods, and the "anxious care with which the United States keeps out foreign goods by means of prohibitive tariffs," he echoed Hamilton as he wondered about American economic ideas.

Einstein, who had worked for a short time as a patent examiner while writing the special relativity paper, looked to technology as the solution to competitive stress. He believed high wages made Americans clever. The cost of a worker, he suggested, made American businesses search constantly for technological devices and new procedures to cut costs. "The price of labor," he wrote on his return to Europe, "is the stimulus which evokes the marvelous development of technical devices and methods of work" he saw in New York, and "once the machine is sufficiently developed it is cheaper in the end than the cheapest labor." Einstein cited India and China as the gloomy contrast to inventive America. They were extinct volcanoes—giant, impoverished museum-nations in which "the low price of labor has stood in the way of the development of machinery." Their governments simply threw armies of unskilled workers at technical problems regardless of the human cost, and their histories had come to an end.[54] He thought the party of gloom foolish.

Hoover, Smoot-Hawley and Collapse

By the 1920s, though neither Einstein nor Harding knew it, the Victorian global economy was dying. Keynes had already written his elegiac lament; the earlier passage is from his book on the Versailles treaty, *The Economic Consequences of the Peace*, written a year after the war. Like the writer in the Book of Kings, who wrote of vanished palaces and long-sunken treasure ships, Keynes expressed awe at the past and sorrow for the present. To describe the new world emerging in place of the one lost in the War, he chose the words "starvation" and "lethargy," and the phrase "mad despair."

Russia had seceded from the world. In 1913, Nikolai II's empire bought a twentieth of world exports, Russia's peasants supplied the world with eleven million tons of wheat, and adventurous French and German businessmen ran factories in St. Petersburg and fisheries in Vladivostok. But the outbreak of war in 1914 sealed the empire off, the emperor abdicated in 1917. Within six months, the Bolsheviks had "picked up power" from the streets in which it lay.

Britain and France emerged from the war financially crippled. They owed immense debts to the United States, and their own demands for reparations payments pushed Germany into inflationary crisis. Calvin Coolidge and Herbert Hoover badgered them to abandon the reparations

payment, but insisted upon full payment of the war debts. The Fordney-McCumber law made matters worse, blocking their ability to earn
money by selling to American customers. By the time Hoover took office, Britain's exports to the United States had fallen by 20 percent, and
France's about the same. And Hoover's mistakes have pushed Harding's
out of history textbooks and memory.

Despite posterity's grim judgment, Mr. Hoover was not a villain. Cleveland's career has an aura of unimagination and stolid un-
generosity, and Harding's of bumbling folly. Hoover's has the mark
of tragedy.

He came to the White House successful in everything he tried.
In early life he was a mining engineer, then a mine safety expert for
the governments of Australia and China. (Hoover was also an unusually intellectual miner: in his spare time he translated, from medieval
Latin, a 670-page mining manual known as the *de re Metallica.*) During
World War I, as director of humanitarian relief for Belgium, he made
forty separate Atlantic crossings in the face of the German U-Boat pa-
trols. Much as Nixon remains a hero in China, Hoover remains for this
small country one of the most admired of American politicians. After
the war—tireless, capable, idealistic—he headed Wilson's much larger
famine relief program for the whole of Europe and Russia.

Under Harding and Coolidge, he was the most successful of America's Secretaries of Commerce. He oversaw creation of the national statistical services, launched public works and water projects, designed
safety standards for automobile brakes and elevators, and managed a
gigantic relief effort after the Mississippi River flood in the winter of
1927. His only failure was the great one.

The last American Presidential candidate to succeed with Webster's appeal to fears of pauper labor, Hoover campaigned in 1928 for
a second tariff law to replace Fordney-McCumber. It had not been effective enough to offset low wages abroad, he argued; time had passed,
competition had intensified, the country needed a new law. He cited in
particular the need for a new food-product tariff, hoping to prise rural
Democrats away from the exotic urban Catholic nominee, Al Smith. In
familiar language drawn from a century of Whig and Republican politicians, his platform says bluntly that American industries and workers

"cannot now successfully compete with foreign producers because of lower foreign wages and a lower cost of living abroad."

Four years later, by which time American life had changed noticeably for the worse, Hoover told the Republican Convention the same thing. The absence of a protective tariff would "place our farmers and our workers in competition with peasant and sweated-labor products from abroad." On the stump, he asked workers whether they "want to compete with laborers whose wages are only sufficient to buy from one eighth to one third of the amount of bread and butter which you can buy at the present rates of wages?"[55]

Hoover blended Webster-ish demagoguery with an engineer's precision and a Progressive's faith in expert government. Higher tariffs were one part of his plan. So was conversion of the tariff system into a sophisticated scientific instrument for managing trade. No longer essential to revenue, as streams of income and estate taxes flowed into the Treasury, tariffs could become a tool for industrial development. Hoover suggested that a non-partisan commission of experts should oversee it, continuously studying world markets, monitoring changes in the global economy and providing a dispassionate response. As wages in America's commercial rivals rose and fell, tariff rates would fall and rise in counterpoise.

Complementing this, Hoover proposed selective tariff exemptions to make the global economy serve American industry more efficiently. Tariffs on industrial raw materials for American factories would vanish, along with tariffs on tropical goods like coffee, tea, and bananas that American farms and mines could not produce. The whole system would come to resemble a hugely inflated and permanent version of the transitional plan Hamilton had devised 130 years earlier.

Hamilton's plan had died on contact with Madison's House of Representatives. Hoover's ideas met the opposite fate: Congress blew them up into something vastly larger, and then an accident made them larger still.

Willis Hawley, the Illinois Republican who led the Ways and Means Committee in 1929, alerted Washington's business community to hearings on a new tariff law, scheduled to begin after New Year's Day. More than 1,100 businesses, trade associations, lobbyists and trade unionists applied to testify. The result was the still-famous Smoot-Hawley Act of 1930.

Hawley's Committee held forty-three days of hearings in January and February of 1929. Its staff compiled eight fat bound volumes of testimony, which extend across 9,744 pages. Each day twenty-five businessmen, farmers, lawyers, and lobbyists appeared before the Committee, representing thousands of businesses and industries: steel mills, cigar factories, gold-fish pond managers, wheat-growers, necktie makers, reindeer herders, and telescope-makers, the diversity of their occupations matched only by the monotony of their ideas.

One of the early witnesses—an Indianan named E.C. Shireman—arrived before the Committee on a thirty-degree January day to testify on behalf of the American Goldfish Producers Association. This Association was a group of forty to fifty pond entrepreneurs, who hatched a million dollars worth of glittering little fish each year for America's aquariums and ornamental gardens. Shireman told the Committee his industry's future was bleak. Low Japanese wages were driving America's native goldfish farmers from a market which ought to be theirs:

> In this country [America] the work is practically all performed by hired labor. In Japan the labor is produced by the man, his wife and his family. Their labor costs are very low, and they depend almost entirely on natural food, that is, the minute crustaceans that breed in the water. We feed an average of 50 tons [of commercially bought fish-food] per week. These two items, labor and food, make it almost impossible to compete with the Japanese.[a56]

Thomas Cheney of the Silk Association of America showed up the next day to make the same complaint about the same country. Japanese silk-factory wages were an eighth of America's, and since the mid-1920s "a great lot of Japanese goods have been brought in, at prices which are almost impossible of comprehension." A trade unionist, Mr. Flynn of the Neckwear Workers of America, sat at the same table and echoed him, brandishing a statistical table which itemized the almost equally low wages of silk-workers in Italy, France, Germany, and England.

The arguments united farm and factory as effectively as they joined factory owner and union chief. S.A. Knapp, of the Domestic Rice Growers and Millers, warned of competition with the miserable peasants of Southeast Asia:

This rice that competes with us comes from Burma, Siam, and French Indo-China. It is impossible to get any costs of production at those points, but under the travel methods, they simply put in a crop that under any conditions will give them enough to eat, and what is balanced is dumped.[57]

Chester Gray of the eight-year-old American Farm Bureau Federation said the same thing about eggs. He pointed to China as the principal threat:

The prevailing wage rates in China for farm labor average from ten to twenty times less than the rates prevailing in the United States. With the improvement of political conditions in China and the improved facilities for the shipment of eggs from the interior of China to the seaboard, and the development of better transportation facilities from the Orient to the U.S., particularly refrigerator service, greatly increased competition from China may be expected to the injury of the domestic poultry industry.[58]

The American Iron and Steel Institute, as potent in those days as any lobby on earth, told the Committee that European steelworker wages are between half and a third of America's. Its President argued that "iron and steel are products vital to the welfare and safety of the Nation as a matter of national defense, and for these reasons is [sic] entitled to such protection as will ensure its future development and well-being."[59]

Dr. Roberts of the Scientific Apparatus Makers Association made the same appeal. Audaciously claiming that labor costs made up 85 percent of the price of microscopes, telescopes and laboratory scales, he concludes "it is therefore increasingly necessary that the tariff be adjusted to accordance with the rates of labor paid in this country as compared to foreign countries," if the nation hoped to retain the industrial might to defend itself in war. Roberts alludes darkly to the lessons of history. "Had the scientific industry been properly supported and protected in our country," he reminds the committee, "we would not have found ourselves with a serious lack of skilled instrument workers and scientific apparatus makers such as we had in 1914 and subsequent years."[60]

On it went through captains of industry, union leaders, farmers, and forgotten niche-businesses. The chairman of the Deep Sea Otter-Trawl Fisheries Association appeared to argue against duty-free treatment of manila-made nets from the Philippines. The Manufacturers of Surgical Instruments tried emotional blackmail. ("It is up to you gentlemen to say if you want surgical instrument-making to stay" in the United States.) Mr. Ogren of Sanduk Watch Corporation noted that Swiss watchmakers earn 29 cents an hour, barely a third of the 86-cent American wage. The Lomen Reindeer Corporation said that with a tariff of nine rather than four cents per pound, Alaskan reindeer could supply the nation with meat. The Cotton Manufacturers Association, the Wool Manufacturers Association, forty-five separate dairy industry associations and the Cigar-Makers International Union all made their appearance, and all delivered the same message. The only praiseworthy exception was the Book Publishers Association, whose Chairman proudly told the Committee that "the book publishing industry is unique among the great American industries in that, so far as is known, it has never appealed to Congress for tariff protection.

The audience for this parade of scoundrels was always sympathetic, often enthusiastic. By May of 1929 the Committee's work was done. Hawley published a Committee Report to prepare for House debate. It opened by pointing out that foreign workers in Britain, France, Germany, China and Japan earn, on average, barely forty percent of American wages. It asserted that new competition, at least as difficult to meet, is appearing "from Italy and Czechoslovakia" and insisted America needed a tariff of at least forty percent to make up the difference. Hawley understood that foreigners will dislike the new tariff law:

> We appreciate the importance of our relations to foreign countries, and that, under the comity [sic] of nations, our nationals have the privilege of trade in their territories as their nationals have of trade in ours; but we believed that our first duty was to our own people and the maintenance of their prosperity.[61]

Hawley's law, "an Act to provide revenue, to regulate commerce with foreign countries, to encourage the industries of the United States, to protect American labor, and for other purposes," joins Prohibition as one of the two Jazz Age policies we still vaguely remember today.

Hoover signed it a little glumly, complaining that Congress had given him far more than he had hoped for.

☗

THE SMOOT-HAWLEY ACT did not cause the Depression, which began with the stock market crash in the autumn of 1929. (Or, alternatively, with a fall in the industrial production indexes the previous spring.) Some recent attempts at revisionism even suggest that the law's break with the past was overstated, and the new tariffs were not vastly higher than those of the 1922 law. Alfred Eckes, in his 1996 history of American trade policy, goes beyond this to argue that the law had little actual effect at all. Senator Sherrod Brown's book, *Myths of Free Trade,* enthusiastically accepts the argument.[62]

In such readings, the law had little effect on the economy—perhaps it even did a bit of good. It looms so large in memory only because Franklin Roosevelt's campaign press operation used it to demonize Hoover and blame him for the Depression.

This assertion is silly. Roosevelt had no special reason to single out the Smoot-Hawley tariff as responsible for the Depression, other than that as a Democrat he inherited the party's low-tariff doctrine. Hoover would have been easy to blame on any grounds. Elected in 1928, he inherited an economy of $103 billion that employed 32 million men and women. Leaving in 1933, he left an economy of $56 billion with 24 million workers. There is every reason to think Roosevelt, in blaming the Smoot-Hawley Act for the country's misery, believed what he was saying.

The argument that the law's tariff increases have been exaggerated needs some more explanation, because in a way it is true. Contemporary statistics place the average Smoot-Hawley tariff rate somewhere between 42 percent and 59 percent. This reflects an arithmetical calculation—the division of the tariff revenue by the total value of imports. (In 1932, the law raised $260 million, on imports valued at $459 million. The division of the first figure by the second yields a 57 percent average tariff rate.) The same calculation measures the Fordney-McCumber tariff at 39 percent in 1928. The increase, though not trivial, is smaller than the surge most history books imply. How could it, then, cause an international disaster?

One minor reason is that the Smoot-Hawley wall had many loopholes, reducing its aggregate impact and therefore its average rate. It eliminated some tariffs, in accord with Hoover's plan, to ensure duty-free flows of industrial inputs. These included petroleum, the ores of iron, copper, and tin, the chicle used to make chewing gum, and the cocoa used to make chocolate. It also eliminated tariffs on tropical products unsuited for production in the United States, like coffee, bananas, and tea. Hawley, whose Illinois district had some processed-food factories, personally exempted fifteen spices—cinnamon, ginger, cardamoms, nutmeg, black pepper, mace—as long as they were un-ground. His associates added 325 more duty-free products, though most were curiosities: ant eggs, turtles, Gobelin tapestries, whalebone, skeletons, cod-liver oil, bars of platinum, dried blood, books "and pamphlets" in languages other than English, Indian water-buffalo hides, parchment and vellum, fossils, and potassium cyanide. All of this brought the average down a bit.

But the Smoot-Hawley law raised many more tariffs than it cut. Its wall rose higher than ever before on farm products and manufactured goods, and added turrets and buttresses against the cheapest and simplest goods. It charged, for example, $1.81 for a kilo of butter and imposed, on top of a 50 percent tariff, a fee of $3 per dozen on straw hats. Still more important, half the Smoot-Hawley tariff increases were much larger than they seem on paper. Many of the tariffs were not the percentage-based *ad valorem* percentage tariffs used today, but flat fees known as "specific duties."

The tariff on eggs is an example, and one which helps to explain the law's impact. Advice from Mr. Gray's lobby led the Committee to raise the egg tariff from eight to ten cents per dozen. In print this is a smaller increase than Harding's. (Wilson had abolished a five-cent per dozen tariff on eggs in 1913, and Harding revived it and raised it to eight cents in 1922.) The law's authors may have expected their work to be effective but limited.

But the Act passed in the first year of a powerful, intense and prolonged deflation. Prices of goods began falling after the stock market crash, fell faster as bank failures continued, and continued to fall until 1932. Unemployed shoppers stopped buying goods. Businesses stopped buying the things they needed to make goods. The prices of metals, wheat, fabrics—almost everything—dropped. As they fell, the law evolved from a sharp one-time tariff increase into something far more powerful, for as prices fell, the "specific duty" fixed tariff rose in percentage terms.

The egg war between the United States and Canada, inadvertently launched by Mr. Gray's fears of peace and agricultural development in China, is simply one of many consequent disasters. Eggs cost thirty cents per dozen in 1929. The move from eight to ten cents meant that the Smoot-Hawley Act authors intended to raise tariff rates from the equivalent of 27 percent to 33 percent. But egg prices dropped to twenty-four cents per dozen by 1930, eighteen cents in 1931 and less than fourteen cents by 1933. Each month, therefore, the ten-cent tariff grew higher. By 1933 it was the equivalent of 72 percent, and Americans stopped buying foreign eggs.[63] The Chinese egg threat never materialized, and Canadian egg exports to the United States fell by half. Canada then retaliated by raising its own egg tariff, from three to ten cents per dozen. American egg sales to Canada then also collapsed, falling from over two million eggs in 1929 to 160,000.

Specific duties applied to more than half of the 3,000 goods listed in the tariff schedule Hawley's Committee published in 1930. The tariff on gloves was $6 per dozen, and that on perfume is forty cents per pound, plus a 75 percent *ad valorem* tariff for good measure. The tariff on onions is 2½ cents per pound; anvils get 1½ cents per pound, and paint 8¼ cents per ounce. Other specific duties show up on shoes, wool, cotton clothes, hats, copper pots, pistols, silverware, playing cards, water, soap, brooms, perfume, dental floss, toothbrushes, paint, buttons, clay, fountain and ballpoint pens, cork, film for movie cameras, blue and black dyes, onions, oranges, railway ties, and gypsum. This list is far from inclusive.

The egg fiasco occurred in hundreds of industries. Deflation converted the Smoot-Hawley Act from a sharp one-time tariff hike on onions, perfumes, gloves, paint, and the like into a gigantic rolling four-year increase. Rather than trimming imports, it hacked them off at the base. American imports fell from $4.4 billion in 1929 to $1.1 billion in 1933. Only two events in American history—Jefferson's 1808 embargo and the British blockade imposed during the War of 1812—have ever produced a comparable collapse of trade. Not even the Civil War or World War II achieved anything close.

By 1930 American decisions had international consequences. Jefferson's embargo was a disaster for New England, but a mild annoyance to Napoleon and Castlereagh. The 19th-century obsessions of "Pig Iron" Kelley and William McKinley were diplomatic irritants for British Ambassadors and disappointments to idealists of the Cobden type, but little threat to the global economy. After the First World War the utopias and El Dorados had gone. The major European economies had never recovered, and the United States was no longer the trivial economy of Jefferson's age nor even the second-tier power of the 1870s. After the war it had replaced Britain as the center of finance and as the world's export market. America's collapsing trade, credit, and financial assets traveled around the world like a propagating wave.

☙

DOZENS OF COUNTRIES MATCHED Canada's egg retaliation. Britain created an 'imperial preference' tariff of 10 percent in 1931. Australia and Canada joined and built it higher in 1932 through an arrangement known as the Ottawa Agreements. France created its own array of tariffs and quotas. Cuba, Denmark, Egypt, Germany, India, Iran, Italy, Mexico, New Zealand, Portugal, Siam, Spain, Sweden, and Switzerland all added their own.[64] By the 1932 election campaign, Hoover was undercounting when he complained about "twelve new tariff walls" built up all over the world. When tariffs were exhausted, countries began devaluing their money.

The resulting trade collapse was only one of several simultaneous calamities. The stock market crash provoked bank failures and bankruptcies. Mass unemployment meant falling consumption and price deflation. The effect of the trade catastrophe was more to close the exits than to launch anything new.

A nation struck by financial crisis normally escapes by exporting. During the financial crisis of the 1990s, for example, the twenty WTO agreements kept markets open. Thailand, Indonesia, Korea, Russia, and Brazil sold enough rice, clothes, steel, computer chips, oil, and soybeans to recover after a traumatic year or two. In the 1930s all of these escape routes were closed. The tariff war of 1930-1932 and the collapse of trade accelerated these crises, intensified them, and made solutions harder to find. Tariff hikes and currency devaluations closed the usual paths to escape and held them closed. Once economies fell, they stayed down.

Within four years, according to tables kept by gloomy economists at the League of Nations in Geneva, worldwide trade had fallen from $68 to $24 billion. Britain's trade was down from $3.5 to $1.3 billion, Germany's from $3.4 to $1.3 billion. Smaller countries suffered just as much. South Africa's exports of gold and fruit fell from 84 to 35 million pounds. Vietnam's rice exports fell from 2.7 to one billion francs, and China's exports from $420 million to $120 million. Bulgaria's exports fell by 60 percent, and Poland's by more than 75 percent.[65]

Latin America suffered most, though (understandably in light of events elsewhere) its fate got little attention. Traveling south from Rio by train in 1933, Cordell Hull saw "huge columns of smoke rising into the sky" from piles of burning coffee on the wharfs at Santos, incinerated by growers unable to sell the stuff at any price. Chile's trade, mainly metals and nitrates, dropped 90 percent. [66] With no money to spend, the Chileans who bought ten thousand American cars in 1929 bought only forty-two three years later. Argentina's sales of wheat, wool and beef fell from $920 million to $330 million dollars. Hoover took this as vindication, telling an Iowa crowd in 1932 that without the new law, "corn and wheat could be sold in New York from the Argentine at prices below yours at this moment."[67]

Prolonged economic disasters never remain confined to jobs and profits. They spread to psychology and politics. Jobless men and women become depressed, turn more frequently to crime and suicide, grow interested in conspiracy theories that purport to explain their misery, discard long-established institutions, and look for revolutionary cures. South American governments toppled like wooden men on a shaking chess-board.

Ibanez, the President of Chile, escaped over the Andes in the summer of 1931. Nine military officers followed him into office and out in the next eighteen months. Peru's Leguia, attempting to flee by boat, was caught by a warship off Callao. Like Argentina's Yrigoyen, he ended in jail. A civil war known as *la matanza,* "the massacre," erupted among destitute coffee-growers in El Salvador. Ecuador went through fourteen

Presidents in seven years, one of whom attempted to win German aid through an ordinance expelling the country's Jewish residents.

Bolivia and Paraguay went to war in 1932 over an expanse of jungly land known as the Chaco. Both governments wrongly thought it contained oil. Bolivian soldiers in particular, brought up on the high arid Altiplano, caught malaria and died by platoons. By 1935, sixty thousand Bolivian conscripts and forty thousand Paraguayans were dead. Bolivia had a population of a bit more than two million at the time, Paraguay less than one million.

The upheavals of Depression Europe are well-known and often repeated. The smaller important stories of South America and Southeast Asia, and the more fateful decisions of the Japanese government, reveal the era just as clearly.

The Thai peasants whose "rice-dumping" scared Mr. Knapp in 1929 were bankrupt by 1931. The Smoot-Hawley law had doubled America's rice tariff, and world rice prices had fallen by half. Siam's rice exports evaporated by the end of 1930, its own rice prices were down two-thirds by 1931, and the value of peasant farm-lots fell faster still. Unable to pay land-rent or service their loans, hundreds of thousands of farmers lost their land. The banks which lent them money collapsed along with the farms.

In Bangkok, the disaster left well-meaning King Prajadhipok anxious, confused, and ultimately overwhelmed. He explained to an audience of military officers, themselves receiving daily appeals from families and rural dependents, that:

> Even experts contradict one another until they become hoarse. Each offers a different suggestion. I myself know nothing at all about finances, and all I can do is listen to the opinion of others and choose the best. I have never experienced such a hardship; if I have made a mistake I deserve to be forgiven by the officials and people.[68]

The unlucky king was overthrown the next year. His abdication brought a modestly bloody revolt by dispossessed nobles in 1932, then rule by a succession of generals. The first of them, Plaek Pibulsongkram, is the most appealing of Depression-era strongmen. He ruled through a quirky series of new laws. One, perhaps inspired by his older contemporary Ataturk, required all men to wear hats. Bus-drivers could be arrested for accepting fares from men without hats, and Interior Ministry officers pasted up posters around Bangkok: "Wearing a hat will enable Thailand to achieve great-power status."[69] Another decree changed the Thai word for "thank you," and a third changed the kingdom's name from "Siam" to "Thailand" on grounds of national authenticity.[70] But Pibul's jails never filled up, and a few years later, he kept Thailand, more or less, out of the war.

Two thousand miles away, half of Japan's farmers earned money by cultivating silkworms. They sold the raw silk to Tokyo factories which employed the low-wage workers so alarming to the Silk Association's Thomas Cheney. The American markets for silk ties, dresses, and underwear shut down in 1930, victim of one of the more modest Smoot-Hawley tariff increases and the general lack of interest in buying silk. The price of raw silk fell by 75 percent, and without the extra earnings, a crop failure in 1932 induced a food crisis verging on famine. A contemporary traveler saw farmers "reduced to eating millet, roots, bracken, barnyard grass, rice husks mixed with chestnuts and acorns, the stems of water lilies and bark stripped from trees." A modern historian, Richard Storrey, explains the sinister as well as tragic consequence:

> The core of the army came from the peasantry, and many of the officers belonged to medium and small land-owning families. No decent company or platoon commander could be unmoved at the distress afflicting the families of so many of his men; for in extreme privation there was only one sure way for a farmer to obtain cash—namely to sell a daughter to the city brokers who toured the land on behalf of tea-houses, cafes and brothels. Such conditions increased the exasperation of those officers who believed that parliamentary politics were ruining Japan, and that only by some drastic program could the nation be saved.[71]

Finance Minister Korekiyo Takahashi improvised a "Keynesian" solution: public works, government loans, mass printing of money. In retrospect his burst of activity looks successful. Japan pulled out of the Depression before any other industrial country. It was not successful enough, as Army officers had already improvised their own solution;

known as the as the "Imperial Way" or "Showa Restoration," this was an attack upon China to secure export markets and raw materials for Japan's factories, employment for its farmers, and glory for themselves. Takahashi struggled on for four years, raising money and lobbying against the China war, until he was assassinated in 1936.

Europe's evolution requires little comment. In 1928, one million Germans were unemployed. Three million were out of work by 1930, and more than six million by 1932. Chancellor Bruning, remembering the hyperinflation of the early 1920s, made the opposite mistakes. He cut spending, raised taxes, balanced the national budget and further depressed the German economy. The Nazi party had received 2.6 percent of the 1928 vote, but became the largest bloc in parliament in the election of 1933. Bruning, a lucky man, escaped in 1934 and lived out a long life as a political science professor at Harvard.

Liberal Internationalism and the Trading System

ROOSEVELT OFFERED A JUDGMENT on these events four years later. Visiting Argentina for the "Inter-American Conference on the Maintenance of Peace"—it was a forum for arbitration of the Chaco war as well as worries over Europe—he spoke at length on the collapse of trade and its political effect:

> The welfare and prosperity of each of our Nations depend in large part on the benefits derived from commerce among ourselves and with other Nations, for our present civilization rests on the basis of an international exchange of commodities. Every Nation of the world has felt the evil effects of recent efforts to erect trade barriers of every known kind. Every individual citizen has suffered from them. It is no accident that the Nations which have carried this process farthest are those which proclaim most loudly that they require war as an instrument of their policy. It is no accident that attempts to be self-sufficient have led to falling standards for their people and to ever-increasing loss of the democratic ideals in a mad race to pile armament on armament. It is no accident that, because of these suicidal policies and the suffering attending them, many of their people

have come to believe with despair that the price of war seems less than the price of peace.[72]

But if his diagnosis was correct, the disease had no easy remedy. Roosevelt and Hull were convinced that the collapse of trade was prolonging the Depression, and that the Depression was spreading a virulent and aggressive nationalism through Europe, Asia, and even the Americas. Neither knew quite what to do.

At home, it was easier to denounce the Smoot-Hawley Act than to repeal it. Dying American businesses wanted no new competitors. Exporters injured by new tariff walls in Europe and Asia wanted their own markets back before solving problems for foreigners. Roosevelt judged Wilson's tariff-cutting achievement of 1913, completed in a world of prosperity and open markets, impossible in the new world of Depression and tariff walls.

Abroad, things were no easier. The Good Neighbor Address, in May of 1933, suggested a free trade zone in the western hemisphere. With South American Presidents sneaking away over mountain ranges, imprisoned on desert islands, or studying Mussolini, little emerged beyond some good feeling.

Larger diplomatic efforts fared no better. The "World Economic and Monetary Conference," held in London a month after the Good Neighbor talk, attracted sixty-six of the world's seventy-five sovereign nations. Ramsay MacDonald and Neville Chamberlain attended, as did Soviet Foreign Minister Maxim Litvinov, the ill-fated Dollfuss of Austria and the unlucky Benes of Czechoslovakia. Hjalmar Schacht of Germany, the Nazi party banker, came as well. T.V. Soong, brother-in-law of both Sun Yat-sen and Chiang Kai-shek and by then Chinese Central Bank Governor, arrived on a boat, while the Japanese delegate came overland by train.

The principal diplomatic effort to solve the Depression, the Conference achieved nothing at all. Delegates from Britain, France, and the Netherlands hoped to readjust exchange rates. The American delegation wanted a "tariff truce" as a prelude to trade negotiations. Some Europeans wanted international loans, others a coordinated international spending effort. MacDonald raised Britain's old grievance over First World War debt. All the ideas look reasonable eighty years later. At the time, the participants were unable to agree upon any of them. The conference dragged on for a month, then disbanded in July. Its failure became a lesson in the difficulties of *ad hoc* solution to deep, tangled, and evolving crises.

Roosevelt developed a modestly successful trade program a year later, based upon the law passed in 1934, conceived by Hull and authorized by Congress as the "Reciprocal Trade Agreements Act," and reasonably dated as the beginnings of the modern global economy. Hull described it as a way to "descend in an elevator, rather than jumping off the roof" by attempting to write a new tariff law.

The program envisioned agreements with individual countries, one at a time. The United States and each partner would agree to cut tariffs or eliminate them altogether. The U.S. would then apply the tariff cuts to other countries. Cuba came first in the fall of 1934. Brazil, Belgium, Haiti, Sweden, Colombia, Canada, Honduras, and the Netherlands followed the next year. By 1939, Hull proudly counted twenty-two agreements. Switzerland had come along in 1936, joined by Nicaragua, Guatemala, France, Finland, and Costa Rica, then El Salvador in 1937. The series wound up with Czechoslovakia in 1938. then Ecuador, Turkey later in that year, and Canada and Great Britain in 1939.

None of it made much difference. As everyone knows, the political events set in motion by the Depression did not stop peacefully.

⚜

THE ALLIES RETURNED TO THE MATTER after the war. Their invention of the trading system was one part of a burst of foreign-policy activism as remarkable and lasting as the Progressive era's domestic-policy creativity.

The Allies drew two political lessons from their experience. Abuse of human rights within the fascist countries foreshadowed aggression and genocide. Pacific, well-intentioned democracies had failed first to understand these aggressors, and then to unite against them when their aims became plain. In future, peaceful nations must be willing to unite against potential new aggressors and stand against human rights abuse abroad. Here are the foundations of the UN and its Security Council, and later the NATO alliance, the Universal Declaration of Human Rights and the ILO's Philadelphia Declaration.

They also drew economic lessons. The stock market crash of 1929, the bank failures of 1931 and 1932, as well as the ill-fated World Economic and Monetary Conference, all showed that an economic crisis could spread beyond the borders of one major economy to others, and that attempts to arrest such a crisis through *ad hoc* meetings and agreements would often fail. The experience of the Smoot-Hawley law showed that trade barriers could spread as well, making recovery from crises more difficult or even impossible. Prolonged suffering, finally, could produce waves of anger, nationalism, and ultimately aggression. Hull explains the lesson in his memoir:

> Economic warfare results in a lowering of living standards through-out the world. It foments internal strife. It offers constant temptation to use force, or threat of force, to obtain what could have been got through normal process of trade. A people driven to desperation by unemployment, want and misery is a constant threat of disorder and chaos, both internal and external. It falls an easy prey to dictators and desperadoes.[73]

Aging New Dealers hoped the converse might also be true. Reopening the world economy might develop common interests among nations. Governments with economic interest in their neighbors' security and prosperity would hesitate to threaten or damage those neighbors. Sometime in the future a world subject to disagreement like that of the Victorian age might be rebuilt. This time, international organizations and great powers would guard it. In such a world, the chance of war would be diminished:

> In so far as we make it easier for ourselves and everyone else to live, we diminish the pressure on any country to seek economic betterment through war . . . The principles underlying the trade agreements program are therefore an indispensable cornerstone for the edifice of peace[74]

Here are the origins of economic internationalism. The World Bank and the International Monetary Fund date to 1944; and two weeks before his death, Roosevelt proposed to Congress an enlarged "multilateral" version of the Reciprocal Trade Agreements program of the 1930s. Simultaneous negotiations among many governments would bring down the tariffs of the 1930s. Growth would return as markets opened. Standards of living would rise as governments abolished border taxes on food, cars, appliances, and clothes. As years passed, the nations that had failed to develop in isolation would prosper as parts of a single larger world economy like the one that developed after the Napoleonic Wars and vanished after the First World War.

Meanwhile, countries which sold one another food and manufactured goods would see more value in their neighbors' security and prosperity than in attempts to seize land and resources. Joining the UN's collective security commitment and the financial support provided by the IMF and World Bank, the trading system would be another barrier to war. Roosevelt's letter to Congress concluded with the hope that a reintegrated world economy would become "the economic foundation for the peaceful world we all desire."

This hope is the basis of the rules and agreements that, sixty years later, allow (among many other things) blouses to flow easily from Cambodia to Europe and the United States. At their peak of influence and power, 20th-century liberals welded Roosevelt's vision of postwar internationalist foreign policy—collective security, human rights, international law, an integrated economy—to the foundation of Wilson's Progressive-era tax revolution. The United States and the Allies, then the Latin American republics and the new countries of Asia, Africa emerging from colonial rule, most recently the new democracies and reforming communist states, took it up and have stuck to it ever since. The WTO's twenty agreements are its consequence.

※

TRUMAN PICKED UP ROOSEVELT'S initiative after his death. For a few months the idea must have been inspiring: a bold and utterly new approach to a question as old as the nation, driven by a vision of economics and foreign policy on a global scale, aimed at the great hopes of equity, prosperity, and a stable peace. It had little precedent in world history—the closest parallels are the 19th-century conventions on copyright, weights, measures, and time—and none in the American past.[75]

But ever since then, the days of Roosevelt's trade policy have looked confusing, dull, and somewhat mercenary. A visionary idea taken as a whole, the rebuilding of the global economy proceeded bit by bit—through painstaking negotiations over eggs, fruit and railway ties, helicopters, rice, shirts, books, chocolate, glue, and other utterly mundane things—each explained, to make matters worse, in dull and impenetrable technical jargon. The public learned of the results in terminology so detailed as to be boring, or so opaque as to be meaningless.

In 1947, Truman's State Department nonetheless concluded the first international trade agreement, the General Agreement on Tariffs and Trade (GATT). Twenty-three countries participated, ranging from World War II Allies like the U.S, China, Britain, France, and the Netherlands to Brazil, Uruguay and Cuba. South Africa and its even less respectable neighbor "Rhodesia," India, Pakistan, Sri Lanka, and Burma, which had emerged from the British Empire the previous summer, joined too.

This was far less than Truman had hoped to achieve. He had wanted to create an "International Trade Organization" comparable to the modern WTO, and a 1947 agreement known as the Havana Charter sketched out the whole thing, complete with an Executive Board, suggestions of negotiations on labor rights and investment policies, technical assistance programs, and more. A Republican Senate refused to approve it.[76]

The agreement nonetheless cut tariffs on about $10 billion worth of trade. The agreement—the first "GATT," whose descendant now limits tariffs on shirts made in Cambodia—covered forty-seven products. Eggs were among them, with the American tariff rates dropping to nine cents per dozen. Others included acids, aluminum, arms, auto parts, barbed wire, cash registers, cattle, chinaware, chocolate, cigarettes, cocoa, coffee, costumes, dresses, fish, fruit, glass, glassware, glue, hats, iron, jewelry, knives, liquor, meters, oils, paper, pipes, printing machines, quilts, railway ties, refrigerators, robes, seeds, silk, soap, speedometers, spices, sports equipment, steel, sugar, tobacco, tools, tractors, and zinc.

Each of Roosevelt's successors worked away at the task. Over the next forty-five years, administrations had concluded seven more "rounds" of negotiations, culminating in the creation of the World Trade Organization in 1995, followed by four international agreements through the WTO. To describe each of them would be pointless and dull, but a brief outline can provide a sense of the system's scope and its progress.

Between 1949 and 1961, The GATT made four agreements known as the Annecy, Torquay, Geneva II, and Dillon Rounds.[77] Each added another bleary list of products to Truman's original forty-seven. The Torquay Round, for example, included beer, liquor, dried fruit, licorice, nuts, rubber clothes, hats, handkerchiefs, paper-cutting and folding machines, drilling machines, wicker, bamboo, cane, timber, bricks, motorcycle parts, carriages and wagons, harmonicas, dental drills, horses, bovine cattle, sheep, wine, gas meters, church organs, musical instruments, dyes, glue, cigarette paper, bells, amplifiers, cigarette lighters, street rollers, lawn mowers, carpet sweepers, curtain stretchers, synthetic wax, light bulbs, clothing ribbons, electric washing machines, raw tobacco, and religious pictures larger than nine by fourteen centimeters, along with post cards, gelatin, box-making machines, and animal skins.

John F. Kennedy expanded the agenda in 1961, four years after the Treaty of Rome launched the creation of the European Union. With the war almost two decades past, fears of industrial competition had revived. (Eckes quotes a ball-bearing industry executive who could just as easily be speaking today: "the great danger of a policy of uncontrolled imports can no longer be disregarded or minimized. The evidence is all around us, in chronic unemployment and underemployment, in factories going abroad and going south."[78]) Kennedy argued that the experience of two postwar decades proved that a Europe without internal trade barriers was more peaceful, and the hopes Roosevelt's generation had placed in trade policy were proving largely correct: that the future of American industry lay in exporting, and that the creation of such a large new commercial partner and rival meant America needed to become more ambitious to avoid discrimination against its own goods.

For this purpose, and to ease Congressional fears of State Department squishiness on foreigners, Kennedy created a professional trade negotiating agency. Known as the Office of the U.S. Trade Representative, it is a minnow among the Cabinet's dolphins and whales. Its two hundred employees—a small fraction of the State Department's five thousand or the Commerce Department's thirty thousand—are the government's official trade negotiators. Their job (briefly mine, as an employee of the agency in the late 1990s) is to consult with Congress on national trade strategy; evaluate the demands of businesses, farmers, unions, and Members of Congress in particular agreements; and decide which to accept and which to reject as unreasonable, impossible, or contrary to larger goals. The agency's recent chiefs have been figures without the political prominence to head the State or Treasury Departments, but intelligent and forceful enough to trust with complex and politically sensitive work.

As Kennedy reshaped the bureaucracy, he also changed the standard method of negotiations—a dull decision on the surface, but one with large and permanent consequences. Under Truman and Eisenhower, trade negotiators asked one another for tariff cuts on goods especially interesting to exporting businesses. An American administration might ask the European Economic Community (as it was called from 1960 to 1985) to cut tariffs on poultry and cars. Europeans would agree to cut car tariffs, reject the chicken demand, and ask in exchange for lower American tariffs on paintings and wine.

Kennedy suggested scrapping this method, and instead agreeing to cut all tariffs except for those a government specifically asked to exempt. Kennedy bluntly told the National Association of Manufacturers that the sheltered businesses should accept the challenge or die:

> Industries which would benefit the most from increased trade are our most efficient—even though in many cases they pay our highest wages, their goods can compete with the goods of any other nation. Those who would benefit the least, and are unwilling to adjust to competition, are standing in the way . . . of greater growth and a higher standard of living. They are endangering the profits and jobs of others . . . and in the long run their own economic well-being because they will suffer from competition in the U.S. inevitably, if not from abroad—for, in order to avoid exertion, they accept paralysis.[79]

The resulting agreement, completed in 1969 and named the Kennedy Round, took longer than its predecessors but accomplished more. It cut most tariffs in half, though familiar pressures excluded most farm products, shoes, and clothes. It also went back past the tariff innovations of the Smoot-Hawley law to address the "non-tariff barriers" Harding's administration created in 1921 and 1922. These were the anti-dumping law and a device used by the chemical industry known as the "American selling price."[80]

The agenda continued to evolve and grow more elaborate in the 1970s and 1980s. By then tariffs had fallen to ten percent or so, and businesses and economists, therefore government agencies—grew interested in a larger range of topics. Non-tariff issues accordingly overshadowed tariff negotiations. This, we will see later, had a rather sad real-life consequence.

The seventh agreement, known as the Tokyo Round for its launch in Japan, began during the Ford Administration in 1974 and ended five years later under Carter. It created a new agreement, known as the Agreement on Technical Barriers to Trade, covering the technical standards that make, for example, electrical cords and light-bulbs compatible with sockets and lamps. Another new agreement abolished "import licenses," and a third new agreement limited industrial subsidies. Its focus on non-tariff issues made it still more arcane and confusing to the public than its predecessors had been.

The WTO itself is a product of the eighth round, and to this date the last. Known as the "Uruguay Round" for its 1986 launch at the tip of South America, this agreement eventually stretched out to nearly ten thousand pages, and covered much more than all the earlier ones. It abolished quota limits on clothing and textiles, which is why Srei's factory can sell the Gap all the clothes it wishes to buy. It took the first steps toward classifying services trade—a fiendishly complicated subject brought rapidly to prominence by the Internet—and created a controversial worldwide agreement on copyright, patent, and trademark laws. It also began limiting agricultural tariffs, quotas, and subsidies, which earlier talks had set aside as topics too emotional to touch. For Congress and the administration, its 30 percent cut in tariffs was close to an afterthought.

The Uruguay Round also created a new and busy system to settle disputes among the WTO members. If a government believes one of its trade partners to be breaking promises, this system enables it to get a judgment from panels, whose members are trade-law experts recruited from countries neutral in the dispute. By mid-2007, over its first twelve years, the WTO had handled 360 of these complaints, ranging from big ones about airplane subsidies and biotechnology to small ones over leather, seaweed, matches, and milk.

In practical terms, were the United States to impose a new egg tariff today, Canada could file a protest with the WTO (Egg tariffs are now 2.8 cents per dozen—still higher than Wilson's duty-free egg law of 1913). A panel of judges, none permitted to come from Canada or the United States, would assemble to hear Canada's grievance. Unless the American lawyers could show that an emergency had made the tariff hike necessary, the panel would ask the United States to drop the tariff. If the U.S. refused, it would give Canada a right to impose an equivalent tariff on American products.

The Uruguay Round, though last in the series of rounds, was not the last major agreement. In 1997 and 1998 it completed four more agreements on single issues and industries. One abolished American, Asian, and European tariffs on computers, semiconductor chips, and telecom equipment. Two others covered financial services and telecommunications. The last guaranteed duty-free treatment for electronic transmissions, like e-mails.

Meanwhile, new countries were joining the system as its agreements grew. The Axis powers of the 1940s, now democracies and allies, maneuvered themselves back into the liberal community not only by joining NATO and the Pacific alliance, but by membership in the GATT system: Italy joined in 1950; Germany and Austria in 1951, during the Geneva II Round; Japan in 1955.

Since then, decolonization and the end of the Cold War have brought in most of the remaining countries. By 1986, when the Uruguay Round began, the system had ninety members. In early 2007 it has 150: thirty-seven African nations, all the East Asian states except Laos and North Korea, and every nation of Latin America and the Caribbean, with the sole exception of the Bahamas. The most recent group of members are the old adversaries of the cold war, first a string of small new democracies—Bulgaria, Armenia, the Baltic states, Mongolia, Georgia, Albania—then China in 2001, Vietnam in 2006, and perhaps soon Russia.

As time passed, hundreds of smaller arrangements sprang up around the central WTO system. One is extremely large, deep, and sophisticated. (Or, to its detractors, madly intrusive and over-negotiated.)

This is the European Union, whose rules—typed up in Bulgarian, Dutch, English, Estonian, Finnish, Gaelic, French, German, Greek, Italian, Latvian, Portuguese, Slovak, Slovene, Spanish, and ten additional languages—extend far beyond trade and investment to most aspects of economic law and governance. An EU member must now accept an internationally negotiated antitrust law, farm and fishery subsidies, government budgets, labor movement, safety rules for indoor tanning lamps, a common currency, and over a hundred pages of regulations on wine bottling and labeling.

Less ambitious, the North American Free Trade Agreement (NAFTA) still covers two-fifths of American trade. Latin America, parts of Africa, and Southeast Asia have their own Free Trade Agreements (FTAs). The younger Bush has been especially enthusiastic about this approach. When he took office America had free trade agreements with Canada, Mexico, Israel, and Jordan. By the end of 2006, his administration had raised the count of FTA partners to sixteen, and another ten were in line.

Economists often dislike FTAs as complicating factors in a system that should be simple. They are also decisions to pick winners; as such, they always create unintended losers. A special benefit for one country, or ten, by definition means not only more complicated tariffs, but brutally complicated import rules. How does one define whether a shirt whose cotton, fabric, yarn, dye and buttons are all from different countries is really 'from' Jordan or El Salvador? No answer can be anything other than arbitrary. And if done well enough to work, the decision to make Jordan and El Salvador winners by reducing tariffs for them alone inevitably makes someone else a loser. Nonetheless they have been popular, at least as the WTO system has grown and its agreements slowed.

The richer countries also have sets of programs known as "preferences," which exempt some favored poor countries from tariffs not yet negotiated away to nothing. The United States has five. The earliest, known as the Generalized System of Preferences, dates to 1974 and extends to products from 150 countries. Most are fairly complex manufactured goods—pianos, felt-tipped pens, TV sets, elemental titanium—with tariffs varying from 1 or 2 to 6 or 7 percent, while food and simpler products like clothes are excluded. The beneficiaries, accordingly, are

mainly middle-income countries with sophisticated manufacturing industries, like Brazil, Thailand, India, and the Philippines. The four programs created more recently are more "generous" in that they include
more products, but are also limited to particular regions: the Caribbean
islands and Central America, Haiti, four Andean republics, and sub-Sa-
haran Africa. Europe's analogous program, known as "Everything But
Arms," applies to all the world's least-developed countries.

Re-Enter China

THE AGREEMENT WHICH BROUGHT China into the WTO, concluded by Clinton's second U.S. Trade Representative Charlene Barshefsky in 1999 and implemented in 2001, was the last genuinely big change in the global trading system. Centerpiece of Clinton's second term, it mirrored the earliest GATT negotiations in its combination of high ideals and visionary goals with grubby detail work; and also, though with more success so far, Roosevelt's efforts of the 1930s to use trade to head off political conflict. The agreement and its aftermath offer a convenient lens through which to see today's system as a whole—and then to calculate the price of success.

⚜

FOR TWO CENTURIES China has been the shape-shifter among the powers. Like the little god Proteus in Homeric legend—first a seal, then a fish, a tree, a gush of water, a serpent, at last a man—China takes a new form each decade. Its present incarnation, as the world's smoking and roaring industrial park, is only the most recent of many.

The Europeans of the Enlightenment thought the Qing Dynasty's 18th-century empire a serene and impenetrable mystery. Voltaire and Rousseau believed it wisely governed by an aristocracy of the intellect.

Adam Smith was less certain. Had they known of the debate, the Chinese courtiers would have sided with the French rather than the Scottish Enlightenment. They believed the outside world had little of value to offer the Empire, and foreigners nothing to teach the Chinese.

In 1795, the last great Qing Emperor, known by the reign-name Qianlong, received a British envoy named Macartney with some surprise and much displeasure. Macartney requested the right to open an embassy in Beijing and begin coastal trade outside the single authorized port at Canton. The Emperor calmly replied:

> Our Celestial Empire possesses all things in prolific abundance and lacks no product within its borders. There is therefore no need to import the manufactures of outside barbarians in exchange for our own produce. But as the tea, silk, and porcelain which the Celestial Empire produces are absolute necessities to European nations and to yourselves, we have permitted, as a signal mark of favor, that foreign *hongs* should be established at Canton, so that your wants might be supplied.

Qianlong had ruled the empire longer than anyone in two thousand years. Not only an administrator but a poet and art collector, he had good reason for his condescension. Qianlong's government, according to economic historian Angus Maddison, controlled a third of the world's wealth and a quarter of its people,[81] loosely united in a peaceful empire stretching from Siberia to Burma. But neither he nor his classically educated court understood the person he had met or the stormy forces he represented; and they did not bother to try.

Within a few decades China had began to collapse. Though Europe was not much better-educated than old China, European technology and political organization had surpassed the empire. By the 1830s, piratical drug-dealing foreigners raided its coasts at will. Internal order broke down entirely a decade later, as an eccentric scholar in Guangdong, thinking himself the younger brother of Jesus Christ, recruited an army and launched a rebellion capable of capturing Nanjing and sending an army to the Tiananmen Gate. A series of late-19th century reforms, hoping to preserve the essentials of the Confucian political system while adopting western technology, sequentially failed; and by the century, China was shedding and assuming identities almost annually.

In the 1920s it was an anarchic jungle patrolled by feuding generals; the writer Lu Xun famously called it "a dish of loose sand." Then it was a budding democracy. Then a martyr and embattled friend in the Second World War; then a communist state. By the 1960s China was no longer a state at all, but a fanatical revolutionary movement.

China between 1950 and 1973 was less open to foreigners than the Qing empire had ever been. In 1950, as the United States entered the Korean War and imposed a trade embargo upon China, the Mao government evicted foreign factory-owners from the marts of Shanghai and foreign trucks from the beaten-earth highways of Sichuan. Within a decade it had "nationalized" the entire Chinese economy, taking each of the country's millions of warehouses, factories, shops, and ports from its owner, and embarked upon the oddly named "campaigns"—the Anti-Rightist Campaign, the Great Leap Forward, the Cultural Revolution, Smash the Four Olds, "Criticize Confucius and Lin Biao"—which eventually left the country demoralized and bankrupt.

This most significant attempt by any big country to leave the global economy did not wholly succeed, but came close. In the 1960s and 1970s Congress held no hearings on "outsourcing" of manufacturing orders to China or on theft of copyrighted music and movies. Trade unions made no complaints about the suppression of worker rights, and textile mill owners no appeals for limits on imported sweaters.

The experiments and campaigns left China poorer than ever before. Maddison calculates that by 1973—still with a fifth of the world's people—China made up barely 4 percent of the world economy. Its rulers, at least, had become aware of the fact, and hoped for cash, technology, and allies against their new enemies in Russia.

NIXON'S VISIT TO BEIJING IN 1973 reopened trade with China after a quarter-century break. Six years later, Congress approved, with minimal debate, President Carter's Commercial Agreement, through a grant of Most Favored Nation status. This meant China received in a night, though on a probationary basis, the cumulative results of eight

GATT rounds. The decision remains the largest trade "concession" America has ever made to China.

A year later the National Security Council's China specialist, Michel Oksenberg, proudly noted that trade had doubled to $4 billion. Fifteen years later, though the Chinese identity had changed again—from Cold War ally to conservative police state—after the end of the Cold War and the suppression of the democracy demonstrations at Tiananmen Square in 1989. But trade had continued to grow as Maoist-era controls on contacts with Hong Kong, Korea, Japan, and the west relaxed. By the early months of the Clinton administration, trade with China was close to $40 billion, and *BusinessWeek* was running the first of many cover stories (a black cityscape, lit up in crimson and yellow) on the awakening giant.

In Clinton's second term, China's hope to join the WTO was also the center of American trade policy, and as close as trade policy has come since the 1940s to the center of foreign affairs. The end of the Cold War had destroyed Nixon's security foundation for American relations with China, and the Tiananmen killings had wrecked the Chinese government's reputation. After that, crises came almost annually: over human rights, over Chinese diplomacy, over Taiwan, and more. The decade's principal foreign-policy question quickly became the possibility of any stable and mutually beneficial relationship between the world's two largest economies.

China's WTO membership was the principal goal the Chinese shared with the United States. China's government had come to rely—for its own stability and for national economic development—on exports as a creator of urban jobs, foreign investment as a quick way to acquire technology, and trade as a source of wealth. The forceful Premier of the later 1990s, Zhu Rongji, believed WTO membership would help to secure all these things. For their part, American foreign policy thinkers— joined by prominent Chinese dissidents—expected that WTO membership would force concepts of law, limited government, and transparency upon the Politburo. American businesses thought in more practical terms, as their old dream of a billion Chinese consumers roared back to life.

Barshefsky, who held the U.S. Trade Representative job between 1996 and 2000,[82] planned and led the negotiation with China. She and her China staff—jovial General Counsel Bob Novick; pugnacious, white-haired Bob Cassidy with his boxing-thickened ear; his deputy, erstwhile Zaire Peace Corps volunteer Christina Lund; and arrays of lawyers and specialists drawn from within the USTR or borrowed from the Agriculture, Treasury, and Commerce Departments—negotiated with the Chinese, and took the public's demands as they arrived.

All modern trade negotiations have two sides: one with a foreign government, another with squadrons of Americans trying to influence the outcome. The requests come either directly from interest groups, or through their Congressional friends. Almost everyone had something to say about China. Hollywood studios wanted to show a few dozen first-run movies a year in Chinese theaters. The Farm Bureau, more open-minded than its egg-phobic ancestor, wanted China to cut tariffs on meat and vegetables, reduce limits on imports of grains, end a ban on wheat imports from the Pacific Northwest, and agree never to subsidize farm exports. The AFL-CIO hoped for a ten-year retention of quotas on Chinese-made clothes, special anti-dumping rules that would enable businesses to impose protective tariffs on Chinese steel more easily, and labor rights provisions no other WTO member had ever accepted. The American Textile Manufacturers Institute asked for extended rights to impose quotas on Chinese clothes; auto firms sought to cut a high car tariff and end import quotas; semiconductor companies like Intel and Advanced Micro-Devices asked for abolition of Chinese chip tariffs and quotas.

Each recruited supporters from Congress as insurance for their demands. Letters filtered in from rural Senators requesting tariff cuts on beef and a clear path for ships carrying Pacific wheat. Other letters came from Silicon Valley representatives' technology centers asking for better copyright protection, and from steel-mill towns hoping for assurance that the American anti-dumping law would not be touched.

The USTR staff's goal is always to meet as many of the demands as it thinks are within reason. The China agreement, like the earlier GATT Rounds, needed approval from Congress in the end, through a legislative grant of Permanent Normal Trade Relations. The more Congressional requests negotiators can grant, the more Members of Congress can feel pride in accomplishment and show a specific benefit to a constituent. Thus their support, and therefore ratification, becomes more likely.

The USTR's inclination, therefore, is to accept as many of the requests as they could, and to reject as few as possible on the grounds of impracticality or bad faith.

Barshefsky herself brought her own remarkable combination of skills: an earned reputation as a relentless negotiator, a sense of the commitments most important to Congress, and a personal conviction that common interests make negotiations succeed more often than threats and pressure. (And a lively interest in Chinese history. In the off-hours she read scholarly books on Chinese history: Jonathan Spence's biography of Mao, a history of the first Opium War, and so forth. One afternoon she ordered the entire China staff to the National Gallery of Art to tour a Chinese-archaeology exhibit.)

The conclusion of this agreement in November 1999—after three years of more or less continuous talks, and despite powerful political jolts from a negotiating breakdown that April and the accidental bombing of the Chinese Embassy in Belgrade during the Kosovo war a month later—looked wildly one-sided. GATT Rounds all require a balance of mutual concessions. This one did not. China wanted to get into the WTO, and would have to give. Its government promised thousands of things, and the United States only three. Barshefsky pointed this out firmly at a Congressional hearing in May of 2000. A slice of her testimony reads:

> To enter the World Trade Organization, China has made comprehensive, one-way trade concessions addressing each of our major concerns. These concessions open China's markets to American exports of industrial goods, services, and agriculture to a degree unprecedented in the modern era, strengthen our guarantees of fair trade ,and give us far greater ability to enforce China's trade commitments.
>
> By contrast, as is clear in the legislation before the Committee, we change no market access policies—not a single tariff line. We amend none of our trade laws. We change none of our laws controlling the export of sensitive technology. To win the benefits of China's concessions, we agree only to maintain the market access policies we already apply to China, and have for over twenty years, by making China's current Normal Trade Relations status permanent.

To be more specific, the agreement committed China to six thousand tariff cuts and 2,500 amendments to national and provincial law. They were exceptionally complex, and as always generally dull, but can be summarized in the image of a large onion:

The topmost shell is a series of tariff cuts, about 160 pages long. China agreed to cut tariffs on bedroom furniture from 15 percent to zero, on air-conditioner compressors from 25 to 10 percent, on floor fans 15 to 10 percent, on blank CDs from 25 to zero, on frozen lobster 30 to 15, on satellite earth stations from 15 to zero, on ornamental aquarium fish 40 to 17.5, and so on through airplane parts, haunches of pork and legs of frog, royal jelly, unshelled shrimp and headless rabbits, hygrometers and rifles, butter, telescopes, mushroom spawn, pistachios, magnetic resonance imagers, bamboo shoots, roasted coffee, dried apricots, and more.

The second shell abolishes quotas and licenses. Before 2001, China imposed limit—often secret limits—on the number of cars, semiconductor chips, chemicals, and many other products a foreigner could sell to a Chinese customer. A Chinese buyer would have to ask the government's permission to buy the product and file a form explaining the reason. A clerk would judge whether the rationale was good enough, and—even if it was—then reject the request if the annual quota had been filled. The agreement abolished all these quotas and forms for cars, motorcycles, refrigerators, television sets and VCRs, washing machines, cameras, microscopes, cyanide, rubber, yarn, VCRs, and construction cranes—as well as urea, wristwatches, textile carding machines, gasoline, fax machines, and asphalt pourers; not to mention burglar alarms, snowmobiles, dentists' chairs, and vermouth.

The next layers address older policies, some dating to the first years after the 1949 revolution. One was a state monopoly over of transport and travel companies, much eroded since 1980 but still a legal principle of the Communist Party. Another was the right of government agencies to publish regulations, or decide not to publish them, as they chose. Another was a government monopoly on communications. A sixty-page set of services trade agreement reshapes all of them, allowing foreigners to run trucking and warehousing businesses, buy and own Internet service companies and offer long-distance phone services, and sell insurance policies first in three cities, then ten, then all towns. Foreign law firms could offer advice, first to foreigners only and then to Chinese. Foreigners could once again buy and build luxury hotels, reach agreements with Chinese sports federations to hold matches in Chinese stadiums, and show movies. Banks could set up branches, first in Shanghai and Beijing and Shenzhen, then later around the country.

Next, close to the core of the agreement, comes a layer of 'rules.' China's government is to drop contracts demanding technology transfers as conditions for investment, let foreign businesses with factories or offices in China import and export the supplies and equipment they need, move their goods and personnel around China in their own trucks and cars, and pass and enforce copyright and patent laws.

Last is enforcement through the WTO's dispute panels. A WTO member dissatisfied with China's performance on any of the thousands of commitments can, in essence, take China to court and get satisfaction. With her government's backing, a Thai vendor of amphibians could do it for the tariff cut on frogs' legs. An American movie studio can do it for factories printing video discs without permission. China's government had agreed to nothing of the sort since the collapse of the League of Nations.

By contrast, the American negotiators agreed to three changes, each already promised to all other WTO members. One guaranteed that the United States would drop quota limits on China's exports of clothes, linens and other textiles in 2005, but would retain an option to reimpose them until 2009. The second was an arcane change in anti-dumping law policy, long since for other WTO members, which committed the United States to treat China as a "market economy" by 2015. Most significant, and the only change Congress would have to approve by vote, was a permanent grant of Normal Trade Relations. This, a technical matter of tariff law,[83] changed no actual tariff rate but instead made the existing rates permanent. Larry Summers, the Treasury secretary, joked that the agreement was one-sided enough to be not only trade policy but good mercantilism.

⚜

IN A WAY, the WTO agreement was a mirror of Carter's Bilateral Trade Agreement in 1979. That awarded China the cumulative result of seven GATT agreements; this did the opposite, with China accepting the cumulative result of those seven agreements plus the five that had followed. The agreement's commercial merit struck most observers as obvious.

When the Members trooped to the floor to May of 2000, most argued about human rights and great power diplomacy—appropriately, as its supporters generally believed stable and productive relations with China were possible, and its opponents generally did not.

The agreement's conservative opponents made a bleak but internally consistent argument. They were convinced that a Cold War with China, or even a real war, was inevitable. With collision looming a few years in the future, they believed trade would merely helps a future enemy arm itself for the struggle. Duncan Hunter of California, then the Chairman of the Armed Services Committee, was a colorful example:

> American dollars are arming Communist China today. . . . The [Sovremenny] class missile destroyers, straight from the Russians, designed for one purpose, to kill American aircraft carriers, were purchased with American trade dollars. The SU-27 fighter aircraft, high performance aircraft, capable of effective warfare against America's top line fighters, were purchased with American trade dollars. On top of that, kilo class submarines, AWACS aircraft, air-to-air refueling capability, sophisticated communications equipment, all purchased with American trade dollars . . . . [T]he tragedy of the 21st century, could happen if this country through a massive infusion of cash produces, by our own hand, another military superpower, and if the cemeteries of this country one day hold the bodies of Americans in uniform killed with weapons purchased by American trade dollars.

Liberal opponents made a moral appeal, on the grounds that PNTR would reward China for repression. Richard Gephardt, then Democratic leader, insisted that "the issue today is not trade"—the one-sided nature of the agreement struck even him as so clear—but rather America's willingness to stand against repressive government in China. Nancy Pelosi, soon to succeed Gephardt and now Speaker of the House, spoke in even stronger terms:

What credibility do we have as a country that is the leader of the free world to speak about freedom? . . . What credibility do we have as the leader of the free world to speak out against human rights abuses anywhere in the world if we will put deals ahead of ideals in China? What does it profit a country if it gains the whole world and suffers the loss of its soul?

Max Baucus, Senator from Montana and one of the administration's prominent supporters, made the opposite case:

Do we bring China into the orbit of the global trading community with its rule of law? Or do we choose to isolate and contain China, creating a 21st century version of a cold war in Asia? China is not our enemy. China is not our friend. The issue for us is how to engage China, and this means engagement with no illusions—engagement with a purpose. How do we steer China's energies into productive, peaceful, and stable relationships within the region and globally? For just as we isolate China at our peril, we engage them to our advantage.

Others had questions. Steny Hoyer of Maryland, a twenty-year participant in Europe's Helsinki Act human rights dialogue and now Democratic House Majority Leader, asked about the opinions of Chinese dissidents. Senator Biden, the Foreign Relations Committee's chief Democrat, asked about Chinese missile sales to Pakistan. Others wondered about the fate of Tibet, the illicit copying of software, or the outlook for exports of lemons, movies, financial services, and beef.

Anticipating each of the arguments, the Clinton administration took great pains to rebut them. Each Cabinet member was directed to give a major speech, preferably outside Washington, to support the effort. To back them up, the White House assembled a 'war room,' modeled on Clinton's presidential campaign staffing and recruiting experts from the Commerce, Treasury, and Agriculture Departments, the U.S. Trade Representative office, and its own National Economic Council. They worked eighteen hours a day, preparing model answers to questions, drafting "fact sheets" crammed with statistics and quotations from supporters of the agreement—Asia scholars, Chinese dissidents, business executives, retired members of the Clinton, Bush, Reagan, and Carter Cabinets—to place in three-inch-thick briefing books for Congressional offices, state governors, newspaper columnists and experts of all sorts. A typical page would begin with a question and a few "talking points" along the following lines:

Q. *Won't PNTR reward China for holding political prisoners?*

A. • The agreement is generally one that will help our human rights diplomacy by encouraging the rule of law and transparency within China, subjecting Chinese government decisions to international oversight, and opening China more fully to foreign Influence.

   • This is why many dissidents like Ren Wanding and Xu Wanli, who have spent years in Chinese prisons, or Hong Kong democrats like Martin Lee, support the agreement and PNTR.

   • To reject it is to make an ineffective statement that in practice keeps China closed and slows development of the rule of law.

To illustrate and bring home the talking points, the briefing books would then present backup material: transcripts of dissident interviews, reviews of the implications of telecommunications trade liberalization for information flows, and so on. Similar pages went to nonproliferation, Taiwan policy—what did the government of Taiwan think about PNTR? Taiwan hoped it would pass, but would say nothing in public—and the like.

The administration campaigned for four months, from February to May of 2000—Barshefsky visited seventy members of Congress—and then closed by observing that China had made thousands of concessions and the United States essentially none. If Congress approved these concessions by granting PNTR, China would grow more dependent on an open and stable world economy, and gain a larger stake in peace and calm. It might become a more open society. Somewhere in the distance, one might see China as a full participant in the liberal world order. To reject the agreement, by contrast, would be to teach the Chinese leaders that America could agree to settle no contentious issue—even when the concessions were almost solely China's. They would conclude that America had decided it could not live with a communist party government. They would likely be right to do so. America and China would then slip towards a confrontation which neither wanted and the world could not afford.

When Congress voted to approve PNTR, all seemed settled. The Chinese Premier had used the talks to cement his own vision of economic reform. The American businesses and farmers, on the whole, won the tariff cuts, quota eliminations, and trading rights they sought. The Clinton administration left office believing the American relationship with China was on a stronger foundation, and that predictions from left and right of a new Cold War were likely to be proven wrong.

Happy Ending?

SO WE COME TO THE PRESENT, and perhaps a period of stasis. Geographically, the system is almost complete. Russia is the only great power still outside the WTO, and will probably join in 2007 or 2008. A deepening of the system looks unlikely, as the cycle of international agreements, votes, and talks came to a halt with the breakdown of the WTO's "Doha Round" in the summer of 2007. An unraveling looks equally unlikely. No WTO member is threatening to leave the system; nor has anyone assembled a group intent on undoing the existing agreements. The pause may be healthy or regrettable—but either way, it is a convenient point to stop and assess.

⚜

SIXTY YEARS AFTER they began the work, most of the goals Roosevelt and his successors set have been met.

A strong institution exists where none did during the Victorian or the Depression eras. The WTO's twenty agreements bind all the world's great powers but Russia, and the second-tier powers of every region but the Middle East. They regulate the vast majority of trade in manufactures and natural resources, and—to some extent—most of agricultural and services trade. When governments disagree, they settle their problems through dispute panels rather than threats and tariff wars. Trade policies operate by laws, agreements, and international consensus.

The world economy has been reopened. The trade barriers set up in the early 1930s are mostly gone. In Europe, North America and wealthy Asia, tariffs have fallen by 90 percent and quotas vanished. More of these relics survive in the big developing countries such as Brazil, India, South Africa, China, and Pakistan, but there, too, they have dwindled into exceptions to the general rule. Sometime in the late 1990s, the era of Victorian globalization was finally matched and eclipsed, as trade surpassed the 17 percent share of global GDP it held in the 1890s.

Thus the world Keynes mourned—the economic "Utopia" and "El Dorado" of his youth—has quietly been restored in a more stable form. The unity Roosevelt hoped to create in the 1940s has emerged, and the grandchildren he imagined in his letter can judge the results.

No human creation can ever be perfect, and the trading system is no exception. The WTO is surely a flawed institution. In 2003 the European Union's Trade Commissioner, Pascal Lamy, said its procedures were "medieval," shortly before accepting a job as its boss. Four years earlier, the Clinton administration was echoing the unhappiness of American consumer groups and environmentalists with dispute-panel procedures.

Its agreements are uneven. They have done more to open trade in new industries than in traditional businesses, and more to integrate Europe, Asia, and the Americas than Africa, the Pacific islands, and the Muslim world. The New Dealers' generation did not foresee the environmental crises of the 21st century—the vanishing fishing stocks, the clouds of carbon dioxide and methane changing the world's climate—and neither the WTO, nor the UN, the World Bank, nor any liberal internationalist institution does much to help.

But just as no human creation is perfect, no reform can satisfy every critic. Some activists and politicians in rich countries want the WTO to guarantee labor standards, but most poor-country governments hate the idea. A few financial thinkers want it to assist in managing currency flows, while most others want it to stay out. Some like its agreement on intellectual property as a stimulant to art and invention, while others detest it as likely to raise prices. Some believe the WTO panels biased against the United States, others think them structurally tilted against poor countries.

But judged against the genuinely important questions it was meant to solve—mass unemployment, wars among the great powers, the risks of financial panics and global depressions—the record is good. Though one never knows how much credit to assign to the global growth that trade policy has helped to spur, how much to technological change, and how much to domestic policies, some combination of these things has changed the world drastically and for the better.

In the rich world, material life is easier than ever. Fresh raspberries appear in midwinter on breakfast tables, flown in daily from Chile. Red long-stemmed roses appear on snowy February Valentine's Days, grown in ranks of greenhouses in the hills outside Bogota. A quarter of the shrimp in American seafood markets comes from warm briny ponds by the Andaman Sea, lazily aerated by little plastic propellers, and gigantic color television sets light the apartments of the urban poor. To be a bit less anecdotal, the Bureau of Labor Standards finds that American families spend far less of their money on necessities—a typical family spent twenty-seven cents of every dollar earned on food and clothes in the early 1970s, and seventeen cents today[84]—and accordingly much more on college, health care, books, movies, and other good things.

Life is also better in the poor world, though too few recognize it. With obvious and painful exceptions—starving North Korea, AIDS-afflicted southern Africa, the violent Middle East—incomes are rising, life expectancy growing, and conflicts fading throughout the developing world. A Bangladeshi girl, in 1980 could expect 48 years of life; her daughter, born this year, has 63. The World Health Organization finds infant mortality down by two thirds, from fifteen doomed babies to five in every hundred, between 1955 and 2000.[85] Small and technical decisions in big rich countries change lives for the better in poor and desperate places. Contrary to Congressman Frank's fear, child labor is fading: the International Labor Organization, which counted 174 million children working in hazardous conditions in the late 1990s, now finds only 111 million and suggests that Latin America may soon join the rich world as largely free from child labor altogether.[86]

The catastrophe of the 1930s remains unique. The global economy has the rules and institutions it lacked when crisis erupted eighty years ago. In their two great tests since the war—the oil shock of the 1970s and the Asian financial crisis of 1997-1999—the rules and institutions of liberal internationalism held up, ensuring that temporary economic crisis did not become disaster.

Even war itself seems to be receding. Two years ago, the governments of Sweden, Canada and Britain commissioned a study of the warring world, done by academics at the University of British Columbia. The results which show a "radical decline" in warfare almost everywhere, stunned the researchers themselves. The 1990s and the early 21st century feature fewer and less bloody wars than any decade since the 1820s. The peace in Europe has been unbroken for sixty years—longer than any comparable period of calm since at least 1000 AD, when records get shaky—and shows no signs of strain. The calm in East Asia and Latin America, though newer and shakier, is holding, too. With surprise and pleasure, the survey concludes that "the 1990s was the least violent decade since the end of World War II," and that "the probability of any country being embroiled in an armed conflict was lower than at any time since the early 1950s."

The authors, wisely refusing to insist upon a single explanation, suggest a mix of causes. Ideological conflict has waned since the Cold War, decolonization has removed a cause of grievance, UN peacekeeping missions have become surprisingly effective. The global economy, they believe, deserves credit as well:

> The most effective path to prosperity in modern economies is through increasing productivity and international trade, not through seizing land and raw materials. In addition, the existence of an open global trading regime means it is nearly always cheaper to buy resources from overseas than to use force to acquire them.[87]

Roosevelt, his aides, and their party of hope believed a more integrated world would be wealthier and more peaceful. Evidently they were right. But their modern heirs are none too happy.

PART II

I.

BACKLASH: CRITIQUES OF THE SYSTEM

Loss of Faith

HARRY JOHNSON, A CANADIAN trade economist of the 1960s and 1970s, observed that the scientists who study physics and chemistry learn a new fact only once. Once they establish it and make the appropriate adjustment to their theories, they remember it forever. Not so with social science. Each generation comes fresh, its collective mind a clean slate, to matters the preceding generation knew from experience.

So it has happened in trade. Old worries emerge and strike us as utterly new. Arguments stale in the 1920s return and seem fresh. It is just that different factions adopt the worries, and different actors make the arguments.

⟁

ON THE FLAT AND LONELY PLACE from which Presidents survey the world, liberal trade policy has remained constant. Each Democratic President since Roosevelt has come to see trade as a guarantor of growth and peace, and each has completed at least one multilateral trade agreement. The unusually energetic Clinton managed four.[88]

Among interest groups on the lower slopes, some of trade policy's early enemies have given up or changed sides. The high-tariff business lobbies that financed Webster and McKinley survive only in shreds and patches. The manufacturing industries who opposed Roosevelt in the 1930s received Kennedy with cautious approval in 1961 and now mostly lobby for tariff cuts and trade agreements.

America's public is sophisticated and ambivalent. As shoppers, Americans enthusiastically buy the world's shirts, cars, and cheese. If public opinion polls are reliable guides, they also wonder and worry. Like the Quakers of the early republic, they have ethical concerns, sincerely held—is the young woman who sewed my shirt fairly paid? Is her factory safe?—and like the mechanics listening to Webster on the hillside in 1832, they fear competition with poorer rivals.

National debates on trade bills reflect this ambivalence well. So do opinion polls. A recent survey, done by the Pew Center in December 2006, finds a distinction between the national and personal meaning of trade liberalization. Asked whether "free trade agreements like NAFTA and the WTO" are "a good thing or a bad thing for the country;" a fairly strong plurality replied that the agreements help the nation. Asked whether the agreements helped or hurt their personal financial situations, the same respondents split evenly, thirty-five to thirty-six.

The divergence may shed light on political debate over trade agreements. Expecting Presidents to serve a broad national interest even in the face of local resistance, the public rewards the President who concludes a major trade agreement. The same public could expect Members of Congress to oppose a trade agreement which may be good national policy but is personally worrisome. Hispanics, African-Americans, "blue-state" residents and young people seem to like the agreements most. (Though African-Americans are sharply split: more likely than the general population to consider trade agreements good for the country, but also more likely to view the agreements as threatening to personal finances). The elderly, rural Americans, poor people, and "red-state" residents are least happy.

⚜

THE TRULY SURPRISING SHIFT is among the liberals whose ancestors built the system, and the Democrats who are their voice in politics. And where Roosevelt's generation saw trade as a guarantor of peace and growth, many—perhaps most—modern liberals see it as a source of threat to workers at home, exploitation abroad, and loss of industry.

A trail of votes on trade negotiating authority records the migration. In 1962, Kennedy brought the AFL-CIO's famous President George Meany to the White House for the press conference which launched his Trade Act. Seven House Democrats in eight supported them. Twelve years later only half would vote to launch the Tokyo Round, and by 1997 Bill Clinton counted only forty-two supporters. Five years later, fewer than thirty—often facing puzzled looks from friends and glares from caucus whips—supported George W. Bush's bid for authority to start the Doha Round.

Table 1: **A Generation of Trade Votes**

Year	Democrats For	Democrats Against
1962	218	35
1974	112	121
1991	91	170
1997	42	156
2002	27	190

The votes reflect disillusion, seeping in for forty years like water saturating a bed of limestone. As time passed, personal experience of mass unemployment and great-power wars faded and then vanished, along with first-hand acquaintance with the alternatives. As early as the 1970s, liberals were wondering whether the price of Roosevelt's vision had been too high. Three decades later many—perhaps most—have forgotten his ideas entirely. They often think trade policy is a conservative plot.

Trade unions lost their faith during the late 1960s and early 1970s, first as clothes began to flow in from Japan and its less wealthy neighbors Korea and Taiwan; then, more powerfully, as Japanese heavy industry pressed upon American steel, electronics, and cars. In 1958, unions enrolled two American workers in five. Twenty years later the figure was one in four, and the Garment Workers' Vice President warned in the intellectual journal *Foreign Policy* that falling tariffs had enabled businesses to begin moving abroad to avoid collective bargaining. The succeeding three decades brought a sort of fugue: worried unions appealed to liberal politicians for relief from Asian competition; politicians echoed them with charges of unfair trade.

The phenomenon is, like all changes in the economy, a complicated thing. The opening to trade arrived as part of a much larger set of changes, from computerization and the Internet to environmental regulation, workplace-safety laws, and the expansion of the labor force through feminism, mass immigration, and civil rights. And trade cannot be the sole reason for the weakening of unions—union "density," meaning the share of trade unions in employment, has fallen as fast in areas such as construction and retail, where there is no trade competition, as in manufacturing. The best explanation for the decline in unionism is probably the waning appeal of traditional union services—bargaining for a pool of long-term employees in a particular firm for seniority-based promotion, raises, and benefits—to a different generation of workers.

But trade has had its price, at least in accelerating change in the economy as a whole, and it has not eased with the passage of time. I.M. Destler, the University of Maryland's encyclopedic authority on trade politics after the 1970s, notes that between 1960 and 1980, Japan's share of the world economy rose from 3 to 10 percent and that "any large country rising so rapidly was bound to cause problems for the world trading system."[89] The Japanese boom brought cheap televisions and beautifully designed cars to the American family, and alarm—followed by anger and then despair—to businesses and unions.

By the 1990s, having stumbled, American industry recovered by adopting Japanese techniques. But even as Japan's boom ended, Mexico and then China—whose share of the world economy, to borrow Destler's illustrative stat, has risen from 5 to 15 percent since 1985—replaced Japan as the source of alarm. This has reawakened a version of the Whigs' argument against trade with low-income nations, but this time in the liberal church rather than its old conservative home.

☗

THE CENTRAL POLITICAL FIGURE in this evolution is Richard Gephardt—St. Louis Congressman, Presidential candidate in 1988 and 2004, Democratic House leader in the grim years after 1994. A big earnest man with pale blonde hair, early in his career he was an iconoclast among the older leaders—Foley, Mitchell, Rostenkowski, even O'Neill—who had come into politics before the global-economy visions of Roosevelt and Kennedy began to take on sepia tints around the edges.

Unlike his disciples, Gephardt could date the origin of trade policy accurately, though he evidently found its ideological origins either uncomfortable or irrelevant. (In 1997, speaking to a Washington think-tank, he asserted that the Clinton administration's trade policy embodied a "laissez faire post World War II model.") His concerns in the 1980s were Korea and Japan; in speeches and floor debates, he would challenge older party leaders to see that trade with Japan differed essentially from trade with Europe. Borrowing from "revisionist" writers Clyde Prestowitz and James Fallows, he termed Japan a closed, mercantilist economy, using strategic plans and administrative guidance to develop heavy industry and high technology through exports. The price for its postwar recovery, still more for its industrial boom in the 1970s and 1980s, was the demise of the unionized heavy manufacturing industries of the United States—automobiles, steel, consumer electronics—and perhaps soon semiconductor fabrication and airplanes.

Like McKinley in Tarbell's century-old book, Gephardt's arguments drew strength from his sincerity. He spoke with a tangible sense of outrage and loss, and powerful nostalgic affection for the great days of the steel and auto unions. His announcement for President in 1988 is a sample:

> We can't afford more trade negotiations in which American workers and American farmers are always the losers. . . . We can no longer accept a situation in which they [South Korea] can invade our market with Hyundais sold cheap because we are paying dearly for the tanks that defend their borders. I know this position will not be popular with everyone. But people sitting in cushy offices, in secure jobs, have no right to tell workers on assembly line that their hopes and livelihood have to be sacrificed on the altar of a false and rigid free trade ideology.[90]

Gephardt's protest was strong enough to win on the miniature playing field of the Iowa caucuses in 1988, but not elsewhere. Fear of Japan then faded in the early 1990s as Japan's boom died and America's began; but Gephardt then found a new cause for worry in the low wages of the developing world.

By 1993, opposing the free trade agreement with Mexico, he was speaking in words McKinley or Hoover would have recognized—"our wages and our standard of living will seek their own level and, drawn down by the lower wages in Mexico, our standard of living will continue to stagnate or decline"—and giving pauper-labor arguments an idealistic twist by arguing for use of trade sanctions to force better factory conditions and environmental regulation in poor countries. Jesse Jackson said much the same thing, finding disadvantage for wealthy America in the low wages of poor Mexico, just as Webster found them in Europe: "we can compete with Mexican workers, but we cannot compete with 50 cent an hour wages."

More often the argument skates around wages, and rests instead on the assertion that low labor and environmental standards—lack of independent unions, corrupt or weak pollution monitors—are competitive advantages for poor countries. The rarely expressed converse is gnawing worry that, with good motives but tragic results, we have crippled ourselves. The achievements of liberal domestic policy, in this view—rigorous clean air and water laws, minimum wages, workplace safety laws, and trade union rights—are a competitive disadvantage for the United States, inducing businesses to stream off to locations more tolerant of pollution and less willing to enforce labor law.

The formula has a powerful appeal, to workers anxious that businesses might flee or succumb to lower-priced imports and to activists for social reform abroad. Environmental and consumer groups often find it attractive as well, fearing companies might use the threat of departure to force repeal of American environmental and factory-safety laws, or that WTO panels—thought ignorant about social and environmental affairs but fanatical about safeguarding trade flows—might strike down the environmental laws themselves.

☙

MR. GEPHARDT, though now in retirement, is close to winning the argument. If the table of votes or the most recent debates are evidence, his case against the global economy has become something close to conventional wisdom. Having sketched the trading system and explained its origins, we can now come back to the indictment. The bill includes five particulars:

1. Trade liberalization is hollowing out American industry and costing jobs.
2. Trade liberalization causes exploitation of workers in foreign countries.
3. Trade institutions intrude upon national sovereignty.
4. Trade liberalization is environmentally destructive.
5. Trade policy is unfair to the poor.

Some of these are wrong. Others contain grains of truth, or much truth. We can even add one more: trade policy does too little to secure peace. As we take them up one by one, we can use them to develop an agenda for the next liberal president.

Trade & Labor: The New Whig Argument

THE FIRST CHARGE IS the new version of the Whig argument. The revival of China and India, once shorthand for starvation and upheaval but now the world's fastest-growing big economies, has come at American expense. As Chinese factories push out their ceaseless streams of goods, their American rivals—weighed down by environment and labor law—cannot compete. China is the largest and most visible competitor, but not the only one: America suffers in the aggregate from competition with low-cost countries, in which workers have no unions and governments care little about air and water quality. Jobs and industry accordingly drain away, as is inevitable when the rich compete with the unscrupulous poor. The appropriate response is the use of threats and trade sanctions to force poorer countries to adopt higher standards of labor and environmental law.

To respond by saying that trade has no cost is facile. The price of success has indeed been high. It was high as the revival of Europe and Japan changed the world, remains high as the revival of China and India changes it again, and will stay high if and when Africa and the Muslim world join them. But the charge is basically wrong. Trade with developing countries is not, in fact, eroding American industry. The combination of open markets with clean air and water and modern labor law has not weakened the rich world—for thirty years the United States has consistently grown cleaner, healthier, richer, and busier—and what we need are good national policies and healthy civil society institutions to ease adjustment to change.

The best response to a charge is to take it up directly, with facts. Quickly look back thirty years, to the era often cited as the rosy time before the global economy burst upon us. The United States then conducted no trade with China and barely any with India. Trade was a considerably smaller factor in the national economy than it is today, while American labor and environmental laws were weaker.

The United States has self-evidently higher environmental standards now than it did in 1975. The reformist laws of the 1970s—the Clean Air Act, the Occupational Health and Safety Act, the Clean Water Act, the Endangered Species Act, and so on—have worked. Streams are cleaner and air healthier. In the early 1970s, factories and cars pumped 197 million tons of carbon monoxide, and 12 million tons of soot and ash into the American air, along with 31 million tons of sulfur dioxide and 220,000 tons of lead. The surfaces of rivers occasionally caught on fire. The national bird was almost extinct. Thirty years later carbon monoxide and sulfur dioxide emissions have dropped by half, the particulate matter count is down to two million tons, and lead has almost completely vanished from the air. Figures on "fishable" and "swimmable" rivers and lakes are equally good. Alaska's bald eagles are more like pests crowding around docks and dumps than mournful symbols of the vanishing past.

The factory safety laws of the 1970s have worked, too. The AFL-CIO's records report that fourteen thousand of America's eighty million workers died at their jobs each year. As American GDP has grown—in real terms, tripling—and private-sector employment has nearly doubled, workplace deaths and injuries are rarer not only relative to the number of workers but in total. To choose the worst of them, workplace deaths are 5,500 or so each year.

The consequence of all this for jobs and unemployment rates seems either nonexistent, or else good. Businesses now employ almost twice as many men and women as they did in the 1970s, and unemployment has steadily fallen.

Table 2: **Jobs, Imports And GDP Since 1975**[91]

1975	1985	1995	2005
U.S. GDP			
$1.7 trillion	$4.2 trillion	$7.4 trillion	$12.5 trillion
Imports			
$120 billion	$410 billion	$890 billion	$1990 billion
Imports/GDP Ratio			
7.1%	9.7%	12.0%	16.0%
Private-Sector Jobs			
62.3 million	81.0 million	97.9 million	111.7 million
Unemployment Rate			
8.5%	7.2%	5.6%	5.1%

Nor have businesses fled, at least in the mass, to poor countries with weaker labor and environmental laws. American businesses do spend more on factories and offices abroad than they did twenty or thirty years ago. But they spend most of their money in Europe, just as they did in 1985 (little Ireland receives as much American manufacturing investment as big Mexico) and favor rich countries more emphatically they did in Kennedy's day. Meanwhile, foreign business investment in the United States—Chinese refrigerator-maker Hai'er in South Carolina, Toyota and Honda plants in Tennessee, Australian-run shopping malls in suburban Maryland—has grown about as fast as American investment abroad[92]

Table 3: **Businesses Not Fleeing**[93]

1960	1985	2005
Total U.S. Foreign Direct Investment (FDI) stock		
$33.7 billion	$230 billion	$2070 billion
Rich world		
57%	83%	82%
Europe, Canada, and Japan		
$18.1	$162	$1370
Other wealthy economies*		
$1.0	$29	$330
Developing Countries		
$14.6	$39	$370
Total FDI Stock in United States		
$6.9billion	$185 billion	$1640 billion

* Australia, Bermuda, Hong Kong, Israel, New Zealand, Singapore,
  South Korea, Taiwan

There is, then, no reason to believe that high labor and environmental standards are a disadvantage. Americans do not need to accept dirty air and water, or mismanaged and dangerous factories, to compete with foreigners or hold onto industry. Nor does the American public want anything of the sort. Ten years ago, the "revolutionary" Congress of Gingrich and Delay attempted to convert the Clean Water Act into a "voluntary" program and scrap most wetlands protection. Public outrage forced them to abandon the plan by within months. It has never revived, and has no prospect of reviving.

If nostalgia for the 1970s is misplaced, should we look to the North American Free Trade Agreement as an inflection point? No. Since the NAFTA, just as since the 1970s, unemployment has dropped while employment and factory production have grown. The unemployment rate, averaging 7.1% in the twelve years before the agreement, has averaged 5.2% in the thirteen years since. A still more important figure, the total number of unemployed Americans has fallen by 1.8 million. And the better figures show up not only for the country as a whole, but also for young people and African-Americans.

Table 4: **Unemployment Falling Since Nafta**[94]

1982–1993	1993	1994–2006	2006
(Average)		(Average)	
National Unemployment Rate			
7.1%	6.9%	5.2%	4.6%
Workers Unemployed (in millions)			
8.4	8.9	6.6	7.1
African-American Unemployment Rate			
14.2%	13.0%	9.7%	9.2%
African-Americans Unemployed (in millions)			
1.8	1.9	1.6	1.6
Youth Unemployment Rate			
13.5%	13.5%	11.2%	10.5%
Total Youth Unemployed (in millions)			
3.1	2.8	2.8	2.3

Neither has American industry eroded since the NAFTA. In 1993, before Congress voted on free trade with Mexico, American factories accounted for about 21 percent of the world's "value-added" production. A decade later, the figure had risen to 23 percent. Using constant dollars, which adjust for the low and sometimes falling inflation in manufacturing and the high and rising inflation of health and real estate, factories account for more of America's production in 2006 than they did in 1992.

Table 5: **Stable Manufacturing In The U.S. Economy**[95]

1993	1995	2000	2005
U.S. GDP			
$7.533	$8.032	$9.817	$11.134
Manufacturing Value Added			
$0.974	$1.096	$1.426	$1.537
Manufacturing as % of GDP			
12.9%	13.6%	14.5%	13.6%

[Source: Bureau of Economic Analysis]

Trade does, of course, cost jobs in some industries. But the actual number seems quite low. Each year—as businesses compete with one another for customers, technological change creates new industries and turns others into relics, and recessions come and go—American businesses lay off fifteen to nineteen million workers. Gary Hufbauer's survey for the Institute for International Economics, the most comprehensive study of the literature, estimates the annual jobs lost to trade competition at about 200,000 a year, with a somewhat smaller loss to overseas investments. Even the highest estimate—by Kate Bronfenbrenner of Cornell—raises the combined total to about 900,000, which is below 5 percent of layoffs. 95 percent of America's job losers are wait staff gas station attendants, construction workers, secretaries, maids, and the like, whose troubles come from recessions, bad management, computers, and robots or superior nearby competitors.

What, then, of China? If there has been no loss of industry since the 1970s, and no drain of jobs since the NAFTA, is the rise of China—the world's most populous country, the new industrial colossus, a nation whose government bars the formation of independent unions—not different and unique? Is it mistaken to believe the Chinese government has found a way to manipulate trade, and develop at the expense of others? Here the answers require more than a few facts and numbers.

Return to China

TEN YEARS AGO, the shape-shifter among the powers was a baleful conservative police state. Now it is a gigantic factory floor.

When Nixon visited China in 1973, China sold the world some artistic curiosities and a lot of junk—a few silks, some carefully chosen antiques, cheap plastic shoes, tea sealed into rough tin cans with peeling labels. Thirty years later it is the pounding heart of world industry. Twenty thousand factories sprout along its coasts each year, and a towering pillar of smoke rises off every Chinese city. China sends thirty million television sets to American electronics outlets each year: Six million Chinese-made new wooden beds grace American bedrooms each year, double the three million arriving in 2003. Two million Chinese-made telescopes serve America's amateur astronomers, and school bands buy a million Chinese-made trumpets and trombones.

Altogether the bounty cost Americans 300 billion dollars last year—the equivalent of a third of the world's printed bills and coined cash, and enough money to make a chain of dollar bills reaching from the Earth to the planet Venus. Americans buy it all happily in stores, then go home to worry as they read stories of hot grim factories and exploited Chinese workers, and shuttered plants in the American midwest.

Few of the debaters of 2000 imagined such a thing. The administration, its supporters in Congress, and its critics alike all assumed the economics were simple. China made concessions; America did not. It was an agreement with one side—and therefore an export boom for America, unless China ignored its promises.

This assumption rested not only on the general nature of the agreement, but upon more formal analyses, most ambitious among them a study by the descendant of Hoover's Tariff Commission. Renamed the International Trade Commission in the 1960s, it remains alive today—hidden on a quiet Washington street a few blocks south of the Museum of the American Indian—and employs 250 economists, whose main jobs are to update the tariff schedule and to evaluate business complaints about low-cost imports and foreign subsidies. Upon government request, they also forecast the effects of trade agreements, by feeding changes in tariff rates and quota policies into computerized models and using the results to predict the real-world changes the agreements may bring.

In the spring of 1999 the ITC assigned a tenth of its staff for one such study of an early draft of the China agreement. By fall it published a 270-page book, suggesting that "accounting for both static and growth effects," America could expect $2.7 billion in extra exports after five years. The trade imbalance with China would widen slightly, as China became a more attractive place to make things; the smaller trade deficit with the world at large would decline a bit.[96]

The export boom arrived on schedule. In fact the ITC's forecasts look modest. By 2006, American exports to China had risen from $13 to $50 billion. China first passed the Netherlands and Brazil as an export market, then Germany and Britain, and is now level with Japan. Citrus groves in California and Arizona which sent fifteen tons of lemons to China in 1999, sold a 15,000 tons a year by 2003. Semiconductor firms sent $700 million worth of chips to China in 1999, and $5 billion in 2006. Even the textile mills, as they predicted disaster and (successfully) demanded limits on Chinese-made shirts, tripled their sales of fabric and yarn to Chinese mills. Willy Lin, a Hong Kong textile prince, told me that at least by 2004, American textile businesses refused to accept the small and specialized orders Chinese businesses prefer to make, and that he could remember no American textile business ever sending an export mission to Hong Kong. Nonetheless, $80 million in fabrics and yarns turned to $260 million in five years.

The money has brought no joy. As the flow of exports to China broadened from a stream into a river, the flows of imports came to resemble the tidal bore. American businesses imagined a billion consumers in 1999. Within five years they were wide-eyed, fearing an invincible competitor—a giant grabbing and gobbling up the world's steel, copper, cement, fish-meal, and petroleum—an economy rising in the sky like a planet, with a gravitational pull reshaping the entire world. Battered by recession and unexpected competition, American factories shed three million of their seventeen million workers. Businesses began campaigning for a new strategy. A member of the "U.S.-China Economic and Security Commission," a group set up by China's Congressional critics, caught the mood with a colorful expression of the general fear: China is ripping out the foundation of America's industrial economy.

Why? The explanation favored by worried manufacturing-industry economists points to manipulation of the exchange rate. An undervalued currency lets a country sell its goods cheaply and forces up the cost of imported products, and therefore tends to create a trade surplus. China has fixed its currency, known as the yuan, at an unreasonably low level, in order to rig the world market for its exporters.

China has certainly developed a surplus since 2005, with the world as well as the U.S. As of 2007, the yuan probably should trade at higher rates. But China's imports have grown nearly as fast as its exports. America's export boom to China, as powerful as it has been, looks feeble against those of the developing countries; and of Asia especially, where China is surpassing the United States as the market of choice.

Peru's fishing boats and copper mines sent $215 million worth of fishmeal and ore to China in 1999, and $1.9 billion in 2004. Turkey's iron, cloth, and steel exports rose five-fold in four years. South Africa's sales of gold, gems and fruit rose six-fold, from $240 million to $1.4 billion. Within Asia, trade patterns nearly 150 years old have vanished within the space of five years.

From the 1870s to the millennial year 2000, all Asian countries relied on the west for markets. Since the Second World War in particular, Southeast Asia, Korea and Japan used the opening American market, and the fondness of American shoppers for cheap clothes and gadgets, to become industrial powers. Between 2001 and 2005, like a field of sunflowers along the Pacific rim, they turned their faces toward China.

China replaced America as South Korea's main export market in 2003, and as Southeast Asia's in 2005. By the end of 2006, even mighty Japan, the world's second economy, is turning away. Setting aside the war era, Japanese businesses have relied on America as their principal market ever since 1873, when Meiji-era customs officers used their wooden abacuses to record 4.3 million yen worth of exports to China and 4.2 million to Ulysses Grant's America.[97] By 2006, China had come almost even with the United States again. Japan, remember, did not abolish the samurai orders until 1876. Within sixty months, a pattern that has endured since warriors wearing kimono and swords walked Tokyo streets has vanished. An overvalued yuan cannot account for this alone.

♔

THE LABOR MOVEMENT offers a different explanation—an especially important one, which is offered with special conviction for China but applies to the developing world as a whole. This rests upon exploitation.

Senator Sanders revives the Whig fears of pauper labor unchanged: 30 cent jobs in China mean lost jobs here. We have clean water and high wages. They have pollution and low wages. Therefore, they can make cheaper products than ours; therefore, trade with China is eviscerating American jobs and industry.

The AFL-CIO's analysis is more subtle. Its economists and intellectuals argue that China succeeds because its government refuses to respect the rights of workers. Instead, officials and business managers collaborate to suppress unions and ignore minimum wages. Therefore Chinese factories become less costly and more efficient. Producing goods at lower prices, they are driving more scrupulous producers into bankruptcy. Decent factories, clean air, trade unions, and reasonably-paid workers make a country's industry weak; exploitation, low wages, and pollution make it strong. In effect, the federation has concluded that the bad guys win.

The most detailed version of the case appears in a 102-page petition filed with the U.S. Trade Representative office in 2004. This demands a 77 percent tariff on all Chinese goods to compensate for advantages gained by suppressing labor rights. Mark Barenberg, the Columbia law professor who drafted it, opens with an appeal to emotion:

> Each year, millions of Chinese citizens travel from impoverished inland villages to take their first industrial jobs in China's export factories. Young and mostly female . . . They enter the factory system, and often step into a nightmare. . . . Attempts to organize unions or to strike are met with summary detention, long-term imprisonment, and torture. Enmeshed in bonded labor, they frequently cannot even leave their factory jobs, no matter how abusive.[98]

The trade-petition genre is not often a literary one. Barenberg tries to be the exception. His first three paragraphs alone include the words, "stripped," "nightmare," "meager," "sickness, disfiguration, and death," "submerged caste" (a leitmotif repeated five times in different sections of the petition), "cramped," "militaristic," "abuse," "misery," "ruthlessly," "long-term imprisonment and torture," "enmeshed," "bonded," "abusive," "impotence," "desperate," "shocking," and "suicides."

Logical argument comes next. China's advantage, he says, is not efficient infrastructure, literacy, savings, or work ethic. Instead it is a mesh of three national policies designed to lower wages and draw in unscrupulous foreign investors:

1. The requirement for a work-permit, known as a *hukou,* which allows a rural Chinese to emigrate legally to cities to work, assigns her to a job, and holds her there. Unable to change jobs, she has no bargaining power and must accept the wages and maltreatment she gets.

2. Suppression of independent trade unions. Chinese workers cannot bargain collectively on their own. Instead they are enrolled in, and constantly sold out by, the All-China Federation of Trade Unions, which is an arm of the Communist Party closely allied to managers and police.

3. Cheating. Some companies pay less than the wage they promise. Many keep account books with false data entries, hiding profits while exaggerating wage and benefit costs. Still others conspire with local officials to avoid paying minimum wages or force overtime shifts upon the workers. The government refuses to enforce the laws.

Chinese factories thus make low-cost, high quality shoes, trumpets, and telescopes by suppressing unions and refusing to pay workers wages fairly earned. The petition suggests that Chinese wages frequently run at 15 to 30 cents an hour, or 13 percent of the cost of manufacturing in China. A 'fair' wage would make labor 23 percent of production cost, or even half, and inflate the price of Chinese-made shoes, toys, and telescopes somewhere between 12 and 77 percent.[99] In effect, labor suppression cuts the cost of Chinese goods by almost half and guts foreign businesses: "China's labor repression displaces approximately 727,000 manufacturing jobs in the United States alone, and perhaps many more."

On this basis it requests a 77 percent tariff on Chinese-made products, to remain in place until China signed an enforceable agreement to abolish the hukou system, guarantee freedom to emigrate from villages to cities, establish a right to form independent trade unions, and create an internationally monitored system to enforce salaries, minimum wages, and factory safety laws.

The petition's facts are open to some question. The claim that Chinese export workers earn wages "as low as 15 to 30 cents per hour" is slippery. The International Trade Commission's investigation of the question in 2003 found Chinese garment workers—in most countries the lowest-paid factory workers—earning on average 70 to 90 cents per hour. The figure is roughly the same wage Filipino and Thai workers earned, well above the 35-cent rates common in Indonesia, India, Kenya, and Pakistan, and even further above Srei's entry-level $45 per month.[100]

Nor is it obvious that the *hukou* system keeps wages low. Even if it were strictly enforced, its effects would be complicated. (And it isn't strictly enforced: in Shanghai alone, three million of the city's twenty million people are rural emigrants without *hukou*, filling jobs as waitresses, construction workers, street-sweepers, and factory hands.) By limiting the flow of farmers to cities, and so reducing the supply of workers for factories, *hukou* laws could more easily raise factory wages than keep them down by reducing supply. Statistics kept by the International Labor Organization, the reports by Japanese businesses operating factories in China, Chinese Central Bank report showing average annual wages rising by 14.1 percent in 2005—a simple glance at the pink-haired daughters of the Shanghai middle class—all show the Chinese earning money and getting rich.[101]

The petition's remedy, meanwhile, would be painful to Americans, but far more to the Chinese workers it intends to help. A 77 percent tariff on Chinese products, if trade patterns remained the same, would be a tax of about $240 billion a year and not on wealth but on shoes, clothes, toys and television sets. Easily it would be the most regressive major tax since the tariff Wilson cut in 1913. More likely, though, unless it were applied worldwide at an even higher cost to the American public, the tariff would only spread imports from China to other countries. American textile mills have been running a test-case since the autumn of 2005. The China WTO agreement of 1999 allowed the U.S. government to reimpose quotas on Chinese clothes until 2009. Shedding two thousand jobs every month, industry lobbyists demanded and got an agreement imposing this quota in November 2005. Retailers simply bought more clothes from neighboring Asian countries; textile mills continued to shed two thousand jobs a month in 2006, and continue to do so in 2007, though the limit remains in place.The petition's implicit premise is that a tariff system like this ought to apply worldwide, as a remedy for all low-income competition.

The vehicle would be a general agreement that all imports should pass a labor-rights test, based upon the eight "core" Conventions of the International Labor Organization, with goods from countries whose factories do not meet the standards facing a tariff to offset their "advantage." If applied rigorously, this test would be rather difficult for any country to pass; it would almost certainly, for example, disqualify America from agricultural trade with itself, as the Senate has ratified only two of the eight core conventions, and American farm laws are out of compliance with the convention on child labor. Thirty-one states have agricultural minimum working ages below sixteen outside school time—Oregon's minimum working age for berry-pickers is nine, and Hawaii's is ten for the coffee business—and eight fail even during school months.[102]

The petition's basic weakness, though, is its misperception of the realities of life for workers—not only in China but in all poor countries. A job in a Chinese shoe factory might seem awful to an American, or even an urban Chinese. Chinese migrant workers who get them feel differently. Barenburg's petition carefully rejects all evidence from businesses and surveys of Chinese factories, on the grounds that managers hide the facts. But if one hopes to help workers in Chinese factories, this is a grave mistake.

Pietra Rivoli, a young Georgetown University professor, has looked and asked. Her book on the garment business, *Travels of a T-Shirt in the Global Economy*, tells the story of a young woman, chosen from an extensive series of interviews with Chinese factory workers.

This is He Yuanzhi, a worker at the Shanghai Brightness #3 factory. Interviewed in 2003, she had been at her job for eight years after moving from an inland province, making T-shirts for western retail chains. These chains worry about petitions like the AFL-CIO's and bad publicity from student activists, and push factory owners to raise standards. Yuanzhi accordingly works a fifty-hour week earns $150 a month—roughly five times a farm family's income—and saves a hundred dollars a month. Looking ahead a few years, she imagined herself taking a better job with a western company for higher pay, or going back to Hunan and opening a small business with the savings.[103] *Hukou* or not, new jobs are fairly easy to find; Yuanzhi and her friends use their phones to alert one another to openings in higher-paying factories. Her world looks hard, but not cruel.

Hong Kong sociologist Ching Kwan Lee has also looked and asked. Her book *Gender and the South China Miracle*, written in the late 1990s, reports on the lives of young women working in a Shenzhen electronics factory. 22-year-old Chi-ying had moved from Hubei to Shenzhen, just across the Guangdong Province border from Hong Kong, to assemble CD-players systems. The factory often sounds like a nasty one—eleven-hour days, bathroom permits, the constant smell of solder; at one point the workers cause a sensation by complaining to the provincial Labor

Bureau about bad food and obnoxious rules—but Chi-ying thought her experience one of independence and self-reliance rather than exploitation. In two months she could earn more than her father made in a year (the father earned 700 yuan a year, and Chi-ying earned 300 a month), keeping half for herself and sending the other half home. She was able to buy a gold ring and visit the cinema on days off; she felt, Lee reports, "modern, free, and young."[104] Another young woman, Liang Ying, thought factory life simple in comparison to the rubber-tapping she had done at home—"every morning from 4 AM to 7 AM you have to cut through the bark of 400 rubber trees in total darkness"—and had easily evaded the *hukou*, leaving factory jobs for better ones elsewhere no fewer than eight times.[105]

These descriptions of Chinese factory life are not bits of boosterism. The *hukou* system, though ineffective in holding migrant workers to particular jobs in particular factories, does mean they earn less than people born in the cities. Apartments cost more for migrants, and offer fewer services. Factories can cheat on wages. But the workers Lee and Rivoli meet are not stripped, miserable, or suicidal. More often they are hopeful, excited, and proud of earning a high status in their village and family. They are resourceful people, energetic and a bit clannish (production line leaders, Lee finds, promote workers from their own villages or counties, while funneling outsiders into the soldering jobs) but almost always pleased to have their jobs. Rivoli reaches ambivalent conclusions:

> The suffocating labor practices in textile and apparel production, the curfews and locked dormitories, the timed bathroom visits and the production quotas, the forced church attendance and the high fences—all of the factors throughout industrial history designed to control young women—were at the same time part of the women's economic liberation and autonomy. [106]

We sympathize with people like Yuanzhi and Chi-ying. Their jobs seem to pay little, and their work is very hard. They seem close to us as we wear the clothes they make on our bodies and watch the television sets they screw together. Sympathy is natural—but carelessly translated into policy, it can harm as easily as it can help.

China's young factory workers are financial supports for whole extended rural families. Their jobs can be passages for rural women to new and exciting lives. To impose tariffs and trade bans, even with the best intent, is to strip them of those jobs. Barring revolutionary change in Chinese governance, a 77 percent tariff would keep Chinese shirts, TV sets, and shoes out of American malls. The Shanghai plant would close, and Yuanzhi would lose her job and get back on the bus to Hunan. Chi-ying and her friends would see their cell-phone messages, earrings, and weekly movies evaporate. A humanitarian crisis would erupt across coastal China as countless young people like them suddenly lost jobs. Then, as it ebbed, millions of young women would troop back to villages, arranged marriages, and pre-dawn appointments with rubber trees. They would not thank Professor Barenberg for his sympathy, and one wonders whether he would inquire into their fate.

And how should a conscientious Chinese official respond? The petition says China boosts exports and creates jobs by suppressing labor unions and keeping wages low. If this is correct, China would lose jobs by allowing free labor unions and enforcing minimum wages. The Chi-yings and Liang Yings would stay home and their families would stay poor. If labor rights mean fewer jobs, a decent Chinese Minister of Labor contemplating the 170 million rural Chinese, hoping to find jobs in the cities, might easily conclude that labor rights improve life for a few workers but worsen it for many. If so, labor standards would on balance be a bad thing. And the minister's dilemma, though on a very large scale, would be the same one that confronts the government of almost every poor country.

Cambodia and the Refutation of Pauper Labor Theory

Developing-country governments—Brazil and South Africa, China and India, the Philippines and Jamaica—have furiously resisted links between trade and labor standards for twenty years. This is in part because they have heard American activists constantly telling them for a decade—not intentionally, but in effect—that low labor standards attract investment and high standards drive it away. But if the liberal goal is not a neo-Whig conviction that low wages and labor standards are advantages, there is another option. One government has chosen to link the issues. We can examine its experience, by turning for a moment away from Guangdong and Shanghai, and back to Srei and her factory in Phnom Penh.

※

A YOUNG CAMBODIAN GIRL has few choices. If the alternatives to a garment job are a chancy job as a maid in a tourist hotel, or a more likely choice between picking rags in garbage dumps or taking work in Phnom Penh's karaoke bars and massage parlors, even Barenberg's satanic mills might not be the worst option. Jobs in the tough, well-run factories described in Rivoli's *Travels of a T-Shirt* would be prized—and Cambodia's three hundred thousand garment jobs are far better. They are, in fact, some of the best factory jobs in the developing world. Srei's factory survives, in part and for the moment, precisely because Cambodia has chosen a humane strategy.

Like the Cambodian garment industry itself, this choice is the unanticipated result of an American decision. Two years after Congress renewed trade with Cambodia in 1996, Washington's brazen textile lobbyists began to complain that Cambodia was "disrupting" the American garment business. The quota system gave them a right to demand a limit on Cambodian shirts and blouses, which they asserted forcefully.

The Clinton State Department and U.S. Trade Representative Office, partially staffed by Vietnam War protesters, felt some pangs of guilt. Their novel response was an agreement, signed in 1999, which gave Cambodia's factories a quota more generous than most other countries received. Cambodia's clothing exports could grow by 14 percent each year, rather than by 5 or 6 percent. The additional "market access" came with two conditions: one, Cambodia's government would invite the International Labor Organization to Phnom Penh to write a labor code consistent with the ILO's core conventions, and with a reasonable interpretation of its ideas on minimum wages, sexual harassment law, and factory safety; two, Cambodia would allow experts from the International Labor Organization to monitor factories around Phnom Penh and make sure the code went into force.

The agreement succeeded beyond anyone's hopes. Within a year, Cambodia's Parliament had passed a new labor law. Twenty monitors, hired and trained by the ILO, were making the circuit of the factories, with unannounced visits to mentor each plant and ensure that it was living by the law. Cham Prasidh, the Commerce Minister, personally vowed to block exports from any factory that refused to live up to the code.

The program is unique but effective. The ILO monitors declared the factories free of child labor. They found the laws guaranteeing minimum wages and barring sexual harassment were generally enforced. They noted that unions formed when workers wanted them. Labor costs rose a bit, but the factory owners found to their surprise that the labor code was a blessing for them. For, while American shoppers may not care much about foreign garment factories, they care enough to watch the news, and a story about an ugly factory is certain to damage sales and drive down the price of stock. Srei's shirts come with the equivalent of an ILO seal of approval, so the retailers who buy them know they will avoid such an event.

Seven years later the quota system is gone. Cambodia no longer gets any tangible reward for its labor program. But Cham Prasidh has kept it going anyway. The ILO's visits continue. Its monitors report minimum wages paid, child labor banned, and sexual harassment laws enforced. Most of Cambodia's 300,000 factory women are union members, enrolled in fifteen national labor federations. This may mean somewhat higher wages—as I visited factories in the summer of 2006, the Garment Manufacturers Association of Cambodia was negotiating with the union federations to raise the minimum wage from $45 to $52 per month. But it has not stopped or even slowed clothing sales. In fact the labor code has been one of the main reasons for Cambodia's success.

The Commerce Ministry does not keep the program going because its officials are fools or unworldly activists. They believe Cambodia can succeed only if it offers something China doesn't. Srei, Nuon, and Rith have their jobs and wear their silver bangles in part because their factories' practices are good, and buyers in the American retail industry need not worry about criticism. (Or at least fair and informed criticism.) Liberal-minded urban Cambodians may find the whole thing strange. Why the intense American concern about relatively well-paid garment workers? Why the comparative unconcern with genuinely exploited prostitutes, and the absence of any interest at all in destitute farmers? But for the factory girls and the country, it works.

Copying the experience elsewhere might be difficult. The ILO has the money and people to monitor Cambodia's three hundred factories. It could easily buckle if asked to monitor the four thousand factories of Bangladesh, let alone China's three hundred thousand. But neither is it unthinkable. If a reward were available—if activists struggled to recognize poor countries which set high standards, rather than punishing those which fall short, and encouraged companies to buy their goods—China might well find a way to do it. And it is hard to see why this would make competition easier.

If Yuanzhi, Chi-ying, Liang Ying, and their twenty million colleagues earn more money and enjoy rather than tolerate their jobs, they will probably make better shoes, TV sets, auto parts, and shirts. China would gain the reputation it now lacks for ethics and high standards, on top of the reputation it has justly earned for efficiency, low cost, and high quality. It would become not weaker, but altogether more formidable.

The China Challenge and the Relevance of Hamilton

Currency values can explain a bit about imbalances, but not China's sudden ability to make high-quality products. Labor exploitation fails as well. To insist that China succeeds because its workers are miserable is to lose confidence in a bedrock liberal principle: a happy and well-treated worker will do her job, or his job, better than an angry and mistreated worker.

The best explanation for China's success is simpler. China once made mistakes—horrific mistakes—and now gets more things right. Chinese children read and learn; Chinese parents work and save. Chinese universities graduate two hundred thousand engineers and scientists annually, who move on to factories and laboratories. China's government spends money to build good roads and ports. China's government has accepted part of the liberal order it once rejected. Through the WTO agreement, by virtue of its one-way concessions, China has opened up to the world. Thus it can capitalize not only upon its own strengths—savings, work ethic, low costs—but upon its neighbors' wealth and technological sophistication.

Between 1950 and 1975, Mao created a strange, upside-down

society. Businesses produced goods so as to lose money, and university professors traveled to remote rural districts to learn from illiterate peasants. But the people did learn to read; and a large pool of low-cost, literate workers built up behind the policy dams isolating them from the world.

The rest of Asia evolved alongside, very differently. Japan grew rich and strong: first a textile-mill haven, then a designer of cars, more recently a financial giant and an inventor. The smaller Asian countries followed; a stock Japanese phrase of the period described the region as a flock of "geese flying in formation." South Korea tracked Japan's industrial footsteps. Singapore and Hong Kong, once the commercial *entrepots* of the British empire, retained their status as hubs of shipping and developed into financial centers as well. Each had its mountain of cash, its army of bankers and engineers, its corps of educated urban workers. Malaysia, Thailand, Indonesia, and the Philippines sought to keep pace as best they could.

Thus two Asias evolved in isolation from each other. On one side of the divide, China: rural and poor, populous, and better-educated than ever before. On the other, Japan and the "tigers." The two Asias fit each other perfectly. Ching Kwan Lee explains the natural links between Guangdong Province and Hong Kong:

> A principal asset of the province [was] a vast network of overseas Chinese businessmen, many of whom had family and ancestral roots in the villages of Guangdong. The ebb and flow of state ideologies and the gulf separating economic systems had not weakened the tenacity of these ties of blood. . . . The divergent paths of development in Hong Kong and Guangdong laid the groundwork for a gigantic joint venture once China's door was opened and the two partners discovered their complementarities.[107]

When Hong Kong returned to Chinese rule in 1997, its businesses had been blurring the border for fifteen years. Chinese diplomacy created the same complementarities elsewhere on the coast: China and South Korea made peace in 1992, and flights of South Korean businessmen followed the Korean ambassador to northern China; Taiwan's government, either charmed by pleas from its manufacturers or concluding it could not stop them, scrapped laws banning mainland investment. Meanwhile, China's domestic-policy ministries invented tax dodges and subsidies to bring in foreign factories and spent $50 billion between 1998 and 2002 to build five of the world's most efficient complexes of roads, air cargo terminals, container ports, and telecom networks around Hong Kong, Xiamen, Shanghai, Dalian, and Tianjin.

WTO membership accelerated the merger and reduced the costs of Chinese industry, precisely by making it easier for foreigners to export to China. As semiconductor tariffs fell from 10 percent to nothing, and the permission slips and secret quotas for chips vanished, American chip factories doubled their sales to China; and Chinese factories paid less for the chips that run television sets, personal computers, and refrigerators. Likewise with foreign truckers offering low-cost transport and international telephone companies charging less for phone calls and Internet connections, the paths from factories to ports smoothed out.

China quickly became a more attractive place to make things, and the flow of investment into China grew to a flood, nearly doubling from $40 billion in 1999 to $72 billion by 2005. Each year, China now receives about $50 to $60 billion worth of foreign direct investment (FDI). Each year the figure is the largest sum in the world, or second to the United States.

American and European businesses are part of it, of course, but the vast majority is Asian. Hong Kong and Taiwan account for about half of the foreign investment in China. Another $15 billion arrives from Japan, South Korea, and Southeast Asia. The Asian money, according to a 2003 report by the Chinese Commerce Ministry, builds 15,000 to 20,000 "manufacturing facilities" on the Chinese mainland each year, each blending the mainland's still fairly low costs with the technology and financial strengths of China's neighbors. To put it in perspective, while the Ministry's definitions are probably not quite identical to ours, the United States has about 360,000 operating factories. The world's manufacturing industry has thus changed rather drastically since 2000. It is no surprise that American businesses and workers are worried.

In this light the Chinese challenge is less mysterious. There is no need to explain it through low currency rates—though these can certainly affect the balance of payments—or through exploitation. China has become so strong so quickly because (with much urging and prodding from the United States) it has opened to the world and let the complementarities work.

Ten years ago, Asia was a string of accomplished, unconnected high-tech economies. Now it is more like a single national economy; an informal "Asian Union" driven by businesses rather than formal agreements. China provides educated labor to run the plants and the infrastructure. Capital and technology arrive from Japan and the ex-tigers. Southeast Asia, Russia, the Middle East, Africa, and South America offer oil, metals, rubber, and wood. Asia has accomplished in a few years the integration that took Europe forty, and China has become its productive center.

Trade policy as worked more or less according to theory. As economists suggest, liberalization is proving most valuable to the country that does it. As China opens to the world, it is able to use its own strengths more effectively, and take advantage of the strengths of others. As governments make fewer mistakes, literacy rises, infrastructure improves, and economies grow more open. Poverty begins to fade and confidence grows.

In a way, the agreement is working as Clinton hoped it might in 2000—or as Roosevelt might have hoped the GATT would work in 1945. Chinese hotels and businesses buy our oranges, semiconductor chips, and airplanes. Chinese workers make shoes, TV sets, and personal computers, and soon will make semiconductor chips and cars. As the prices fall, America's poor get a few more trips to the movie theater and can buy fresh vegetables instead of canned corn. The two superpowers develop common interests, and the chance of coexistence grows stronger.

But the success has had an unexpected price. As China's darkly glamorous industrial belts turn on the power, lights go on in the South African mines, Japanese auto-parts production lines and Taiwanese machine-tool shops that keep Chinese industry running, and in American art galleries, medical laboratories, and lemon groves. But factories elsewhere can go dark, though their workers are not lazy, their managers are not fools, and their products are good.

It is the price of trade with China, and the price of Roosevelt's vision generally. We now remember the birth of European unity and the rise of Japanese industrial power as comfortable and gentlemanly forms of competition among the rich. In reality, the revival of Europe and the Japanese boom required a massive and painful adjustment lasting twenty years. By the early 1990s, the United States had emerged from the challenge with lower unemployment, faster growth and more rapid technological advance—but also with more anxiety, faster cycles of industrial rise and fall, and an economy less egalitarian than it had been since the 1920s.

The revival of China may be even more stressful. It is always, of course, worse for a great civilization to fail than to succeed—without the collapse of the Chinese empire there could have been no Pacific war in the 1930s and 1940s; without the Chinese revolution, the Korean War would have been unlikely and the Vietnam War unthinkable—but this is not much consolation for workers who must navigate the transition.

Even the China challenge may not be the most painful one. Just as trade liberalization and container traffic allow China to take a central place in manufacturing, the Internet is enabling India to capitalize on its open society, English-language skills, and technologically sophisticated diaspora as a services exporter. Alan Blinder, an economist and Federal Reserve Governor, suggested early in 2006 that the telecommunications network might triple the number of jobs subject to international competition in a decade.

What we must ask is whether these challenges, in contrast to their predecessors, are impossible to meet. This is the basic question of trade policy—and the answer is much the same as the one Hamilton found in the 1790s, and Einstein suggested in the 1920s.

Neither China nor India is an invincible competitor. Both have weaknesses. China, with all its strengths, remains an authoritarian state with an obsession for control over information, censorship of financial and political news, and a rapidly aging population. India has weak infrastructure and a vast, poor, uneducated rural population. Both have enormous and growing environmental bills to pay. And the advice of Hamilton and Einstein on technology as the wealthy nation's way to meet low-cost competition remains very relevant.

By 2006, American factories were not declining, but in the midst of a little-noted boom. Far from losing industry, the United States was adding four new plants each day and factory production was at a new peak. Manufacturing exports rose by $100 billion in a single year—

fastest of all, incidentally, to China. And the American share of world manufacturing remains stable, even as those of Europe and Japan have slightly dropped.

Table 6: **U.S. Manufacturing In The World**
(measured by value-added)

1993	1998	2003
U.S.		
21.4%	23.2%	23.3%
China		
3.5%	5.1%	6.9%
Japan		
22.4%	19.8%	18.2%
EU		
29.3%	28.4%	26.1%
Other		
22.4%	23.5%	25.5%

[Sources: UN Industrial Development Organization, World Bank]

Table 7: **U.S. Manufacturing Exports, 1990–2006**
(in billions)

1990	1995	2000	2005	2006
$304	$474	$666	$748	$853

Evidently the machine remains cheaper than the man. American factories are meeting a challenge from low-cost competitors by substituting machines for labor, just as Hamilton suggested they would in 1790. Having shed three million of its workers during the last recession, American factories have hired none back. Instead they have bought robots and computers, and make more goods with fourteen million workers than they did with seventeen million. The loss of factory jobs is simply a portent of the workerless factory of the future, in which a few experts shift dials and mouse-pads while machines do the work. It is a very stressful adjustment, probably even more so than the adjustment to the Japanese challenge twenty years ago. But there is no good reason to think it will not succeed.

Table 8: **The Vanishing Factory Job**

1990	1995	2000	2005	2006
Private-sector jobs in millions				
90.7	98.7	111.7	112.5	113.8
Manufacturing jobs in millions				
16.4	17.2	17.2	14.2	14.1
Manufacturing as %				
18.1%	17.4%	15.4%	12.6%	12.4%

So much for the first charge. There is little reason to think the Whig theories are any more valid today than in the past. Trade is not eviscerating the economy. High labor and environmental standards have not become disadvantages. If businesses make the adjustments they must, and the country retains the quality-of-life policies, higher education system, and scientific research base it needs to attract the most sophisticated industries, the United States will remain strong.

But there is abundant ground for accepting that the human stress of adjustment is high. National strength is no consolation for a man, or three million men and women, suddenly shifted out of factories. In the United States, with its weak safety net, the stress is higher than it might be elsewhere. It should be no surprise that the public, even aware of the value of trade liberalization for the country as a whole, is ambivalent. A first step in developing a modern agenda, therefore, must be to close the rents in the net.

Trade & Environment: Interlude with Turtles & Fish

WE CAN NOW MOVE to a second set of charges: those of lost sovereignty and environmental degradation.

One form of this critique is simply a variant of the "pauper labor" fear. Briefly put, it is that an open global economy encourages pollution, by allowing rich-country businesses to flee to countries with poor environmental laws or else giving poor-country businesses an advantage. It can be addressed swiftly and easily: the same statistics that show no large-scale drift of American businesses to poor countries apply to weak environmental policy as well as labor standards and wages. Fully half of American business investment is in Europe. Therefore, a government (in the United States or elsewhere) hoping to attract lots of American business money would do well to emulate Europe by offering well-educated workers, guaranteeing a high quality of life, and bringing nearby customers. Bad environmental laws might draw a few unscrupulous businesses, but presumably they are not really wanted in the United States anyway.

More interesting environmental charges come in two forms. One is that trade policy, in particular the WTO, is an enemy of environmental policy which threatens to block wise new policies or even strike down existing laws. The other is that that trade policy is not a friend of the environment, and does not help reduce pollution or protect natural resources when it could. The first is mistaken; the second has some foundation.

Enduring Relevance of Mencius

An old Chinese book again provides a good introduction to a modern debate: *Mencius.* Its opening chapter recounts a visit by Mencius, to the little principality of Wei and its aged King Hui in 320 BC. Located near today's Hunan province, Wei then lay between three predatory giants: Chu to the south; Chi to the northeast; terrifying Qin, destined for conquest and empire, on the west. King Hui feared, with reason, for his country's future.

At a formal reception, and then during a walk through the flowers and artificial ponds outside the palace, Hui pours out his frustration to the visiting sage. Why had he failed to attract talented immigrants to the kingdom? Had he not relieved famine in Ho Nei? Had he not labored more diligently and seriously than his neighbors? How could he protect his kingdom? Mencius had traveled a thousand *li* to Liang; he must, the king insists, have brought something the court could hear with profit.

Mencius becomes angry. Why, he asks, did Hui speak of profit? Conceding that Hui ruled more virtuously than his neighbors, Mencius says this was no reason to boast; the king of Wei was simply the least bad in a collection of greedy villains. "There is fat meat in your kitchen," he insisted, "and well-fed horses in your stables—yet the people look hungry, and on the outskirts of cities men drop dead from starvation."

Hui, Mencius says, must turn to benevolence. He should ease taxes and relax the criminal law. He should work with farmers to introduce more advanced agricultural technology. And he should launch an environmental program to protect the kingdom's natural wealth:

> If you ban nets with fine mesh from ponds, there will be more fish and turtles than the people can eat. If you ban axes from the forests on the hillsides except in the proper season, there will be more timber than the people can use.

Mencius then gets carried away, insisting that his program for good government and domestic reform would not just help the people of Wei but make the kingdom an impregnable fortress:

> If your Majesty practices benevolent government . . . then the people can be made to inflict defeat on the strong armour and weapons of Ch'in and Ch'u armed with nothing but sticks.[108]

The book does not record King Hui's response to this. If he agreed, Wei came to regret it; the Ch'in army wiped Wei off the map a few decades later. But though weak on military matters, Mencius' advice on domestic policy is absolutely right. If King Hui took it, Wei must have become a nicer place in which to live. His thoughts on turtles are as modern as one could wish—so modern as to be the principles which launched the most important of all WTO disputes.

Turtles, Trade and the WTO

The sea turtle is an ancient armored reptile. Scientists trace its ancestors 150 million years into the past. Tough enough to survive the end-of-Cretaceous asteroid and seven subsequent ice ages, an adult leatherback turtle reaches eight feet in length and weighs a ton. It is as big and heavy as a swimming golf cart, free from natural predators, and as close to invulnerable as an animal can be.

But big, old, and tough are no longer enough. Each of the world's six sea turtles—the leatherback, the Ridley, the green, the black, the loggerhead, and the hawksbill—is endangered or threatened. Human threats born in the century may soon do what the asteroid, the ice, and the great white shark never could.

One threat is trade itself. The turtle's shell is popular as cheap jewelry, and its meat supposedly makes tasty soup. Tourists in Mexico and Southeast Asia buy turtle-shell bracelets and eat turtle soups and steaks. This threat has been handled simply and rather effectively: a treaty signed in 1973 and known as the Convention on International Trade in Endangered Species, bans turtle trade altogether. The convention, CITES for short, controls a trade in wildlife thought to be worth

$12 or $15 billion a year—more than coffee, and almost half the value of the weapons trade. The principal attempt to manage wildlife trade and stop it from extinguishing wildlife altogether, it divides rare plants and animals into two types, banning trade in one and regulating it in the other.

One list, Appendix II, covers 1,400 animals and 25,000 plants. These are thought rare but not actually endangered. Pet and handicraft dealers can buy animals on this list, but only with an official permit from local environmental agencies, and only in numbers CITES-sponsored scientists consider too small to threaten the survival of a species. In 2002, for example, CITES gave Benin the right to export 2,700 rock pythons and Russia 2,000 lynx pelts. The theory, or forlorn hope, is that the governments and trappers of Benin and Siberia understand that they can make money by selling pythons and lynx pelts. For the sake of their livelihoods, they will protect the lands in which snakes and cats breed, and avoid shooting and trapping too many.

Appendix I is the red list. It covers three hundred animals and six hundred plants, all approaching the edge of the cliff. Here, no trade is permitted. The South American macaw, threatened by the enthusiasm of American exotic-pet fanciers, is an example. So are the Caspian sturgeon, which produces beluga caviar, the four species of rhinoceros, and all six sea turtles.

The CITES treaty breaches no trade rules. No one need worry that the WTO will strike it down. Its main problems are practical. Through bad luck, or some strange fact about climates and human development, most rare animals live in poor countries with small, low-budget environmental ministries. Papua New Guinea's National Fisheries Authority has sixty employees and owns two boats. With these rather meager resources it must enforce bans on trade in seven marine Appendix I species—five sea turtles, along with a dolphin and a dugong—and monitor permits for dozens of fish, coral, and giant clams mentioned in Appendix II. The difficulty is obvious. If rich-country governments and environmentalists want the treaty to work, they will need to spend the money to ensure that the Papuans have the scientific expertise and Coast Guard personnel to enforce the laws banning turtle-product exports.

But trade in canned soup and bracelets is the least of the turtles' concerns. Only a few turtles wind up in pots or find their shells turned into cheap jewelry. Many more end as the accidental victims of the fishery industry, sucked into bag-shaped trawl nets and drowned as shrimp and fishing fleets pass above them. A late-1980s examination by the National Academy of Sciences suggested that shrimp nets were killing at lest ten thousand turtles a year, and perhaps forty thousand.

Congress responded admirably in 1987, with a law requiring American shrimp boats to use nets equipped with a small metal grille known as a "Turtle Excluder Device." This TED, which sells for $200 or $300, blocks entry to the purse-shaped net, keeping wide-bodied animals out while small shrimp and fish flow through. It is not precisely Mencius' "wide mesh"—the law actually requires a narrow mesh—but the concept is very similar.

It works quite well. A case in point is the most threatened of all the turtles, the Kemp's Ridley: smooth and grey, about two feet in length and a hundred pounds in weight. Turtle-watchers found eight hundred Kemp's Ridley nests on the Gulf in the egg-laying seasons of the 1980s. They now find six thousand.

But the law also spawned international controversy. Shrimp-boat owners complained loudly—and reasonably—when they found rival boats steaming out of Honduras, Mexico, Jamaica, and Guatemala without the TEDS. Congress then changed the law, telling Mexican and Caribbean boats to fit their nets with the devices within three years or find their shrimp banned from the United States.

An environmental group, the Earth Island Institute, then went to court—also reasonably, at least from an American or turtle point of view—insisting that the law should apply not only to Latin and Caribbean boats, but all foreign boats selling warm-water shrimp to the United States. In practice these were the shrimp fleets of India, Malaysia, Thailand, and the Philippines. In 1996 a judge found the Institute to be correct. The Department of Commerce accordingly warned Asian shrimpers to outfit their boats with TEDs within five months, or stop selling shrimp in the United States.

Their governments angrily protested, claiming that their boats could never comply in time and TEDS would be too expensive anyway. They also raised a more fundamental objection, insisting that while the United States could do as it pleased with its own fishing boats, Congress had no right to ask anything of an Asian boat. To them, the TED law was a wealthy government's attempt to force expensive capital investments upon ships that could not afford them, doubtless in hopes of sealing off the American shrimp market. It represented, therefore, the sort of bullying the WTO exists in part to stop. The four governments filed a case with the WTO's Dispute Settlement Body, asking it to declare the TED law a violation of WTO rules.

American environmentalists saw the case as a deadly threat. The law asked nothing of Asian shrimpers that it did not require of Americans. It protected an attractive and troubled animal, and, at least in the Caribbean, was visibly helping it recover. It was, therefore, an effort to protect a vulnerable animal when foreigners would not. The Asians' ability to bring the case, they believed, showed that the WTO rules and dispute panels were standing threats to the integrity of environmental law.

WTO agreements are not oblivious to environmental concerns. A legal exception to the GATT—one of its oldest features, drafted in 1947—ensures that WTO members can impose environmental restrictions on trade, so long as they do not arbitrarily discriminate against foreign products, and trim trade back as little as possible to achieve the environmental goal. The actual text reads:

> [N]othing in this Agreement shall be construed to prevent the adoption or enforcement by any contracting party of measures necessary to protect human, animal or plant life or health; or relating to the conservation of exhaustible natural resources if such measures are made effective in conjunction with restrictions on domestic production or consumption.

The agreements, therefore, envision exceptions to the rules for environmentally sensitive matters. But they also leave definitions of these exceptions to national laws and international agreements, and national laws can conflict. CITES' ban on turtleshell bracelets is clearly reasonable and nobody challenges it. So are bans on trade in radioactive metals or chlorofluorocarbons. But opinions might differ over a purely American rule requiring foreign boats to adopt the grilles.

WTO panels hear about thirty trade disputes a year. The debate over turtles, the 58th in the series, is still the most important of them all. The panels and Appellate Body spent two years on the case, and eventually ruled almost entirely in favor of the United States. The appellate judges observed that the law was non-discriminatory, addressed a genuine environmental concern, and applied to American as well as Asian boats. It did say the American law had unfairly given the Asians only five months to adopt the TEDS, while the Latin and American boats had three years. The panel therefore asked the U.S. government to grant the Asians some extra time.

The outcome, though an example of calm and good sense in an emotional and politically charged matter, may have been chancy. The actual panel did not rule on the basis of any WTO agreement on endangered species trade, or a WTO declaration on environmental principles generally, because no such things exist. It simply felt its way through the dark. A different WTO panel, or one which heard from incompetent American lawyers, might have decided the law a violation of American commitments. If it had, the consequence would not have been constitutional crisis or infringement of sovereignty. The U.S., like other countries found in violation on lesser matters, could have chose to redraft the law, or accept a tariff penalty from the Asian states equivalent to their loss of roughly $1.2 billion in exports. But it raised the potential of a long-term conflict between environmental policies and trade institutions.

But chancy and groping as their deliberations may have been, the panels reached the right decision. The TED rule remains in effect ten years later, and Asian boats use the TEDs when they steam out to their shrimping grounds. The larger principle, that a country can restrict imports to protect the environment, if it does so fairly and on scientific grounds, not only remained intact, but is more secure now than it was before the case.

The ruling earned the WTO few thanks. Instead it damaged the group's image, less among the Asians who lost than among environmentalists who did not wholly grasp their victory. But it created an international legitimacy for the TED rule that purely American, purely coercive laws never could achieve. In this sense, the American law and the WTO combined to bring some lasting environmental improvement to shrimping.

The turtle law, though, is an unusual case. Congress' extension of the TED rule to Latin countries (and the court's extension of it to Asia) were measures meant to bring foreign trade partners to heel through the threat of a sanction. The threat worked, but for reasons that apply only rarely. America is the world's largest shrimp market; the TED requirement and the ban on foreign shrimp directly targeted a threat to turtles; TEDs are technically simple and cheap enough for Latin and Asian boats to install.

Most environmental matters are tougher. Few revolve, as the shrimping issue did, around trade per se. More often—whether the question at hand is habitat conservation, river pollution, urban air quality, or climate change—they are either matters of weak domestic policy or problems that affect the whole world simultaneously. Threats and sanctions cannot easily solve them.

In domestic matters, poor countries often fail because their institutions are weak. Like Papua New Guinea's fishery agency, they lack the scientists to manage sophisticated environmental programs, and the police and prosecutors capable of standing up to wealth. Some environmental agencies in poor countries are corrupt, most are weak in relation to large employers, and many lack trained scientists and lawyers. Using coercion as a substitute for training and technical assistance risks leaving everything worse off than before.

Were the United States to try to coerce Cambodia, for example, into managing a modern clean water program by threatening to cut off clothing imports, Srei and her friends would simply lose their jobs. Cambodia lacks the scientists it needs to monitor and enforce water quality throughout the country.

Even in relationships with stronger and wealthier countries, the right choice is not always obvious. Should the workers of a clean and well-managed computer factory in Shanghai, for example, be punished for the sins of a mismanaged computer factory somewhere else? For those of a paper mill two hundred miles up the Yangtze, which makes paper not for export but for Chinese newspaper chains? For the corruption of forestry officials in Sichuan? For all China's environmental sins simultaneously?

In such matters, trade per se is rarely the main problem. Correspondingly, trade measures—even well-designed ones like the TED rule—are partial solutions at best. The greatest threat to turtles, for example, is neither trade in soup and bracelets nor by-catch, but loss of habitat. If people continue to build homes and hotels on nesting beaches, mother turtles do not lay eggs. With no eggs there are no turtles, and so turtle counts continue to fall. To paraphrase Mencius, when fishermen use nets with a wide mesh, turtles and fish will thrive in the ponds—but if the ponds themselves are drained?

Governments must face such matters directly, through international agreements like CITES or the Kyoto Protocol, and technical assistance to developing-world agencies which cannot handle scientific analysis and law enforcement alone. The world may need an environmental institution comparable to the WTO or the UN, which could create agreements to manage global problems and to define minimum national standards. An attempt to substitute trade sanctions for these structural improvements will simply cause trade to collapse. Trade policy would then fail in its primary mission—to create growth, reduce poverty and strengthen peace—and the effect on the environment would be nil.

The Right Role for Trade

Neither the WTO nor trade policy generally, then, are enemies of environmental protection. Nor can threats of trade restriction replace actual clean air and water laws, durable conservation programs, scientific expertise, and effective law enforcement. The better approach—easy to imagine, with an inventive American government interested in environmental quality and some thought from environmental groups—is to harness the existing system for environmental goals.

American fuel is a simple and small example. Ethanol, the pure form of alcohol, burns clean and hot. It can power a car with less smoke and carbon dioxide fumes than gasoline. It remains more expensive to distill ethanol from corn or sugar cane corn than to refine gasoline from crude oil, but the gap is shrinking. Brazil, the world's largest ethanol producer, uses sugar cane to make ethanol for a dollar per gallon. Half its cars now run on the stuff.

America's more expensive ethanol is brewed from corn, and few cars use it. The sorry fact demonstrates the difficulties with real-life "infant-industry" tariff programs.

Just as Hamilton hoped to use tariffs to create hatmakers and glue factories, Congress in 1980 used a tariff of 54 cents per gallon of ethanol to midwife an "infant" American ethanol-distilling industry. Twenty-five years later, the American ethanol-business is still an infant, and American ethanol costs $2 a gallon. If it cannot be brewed more cheaply, the best choice is to buy the less costly Brazilian product. The tariff makes this more costly than gasoline, and therefore unattractive to drivers. Thus a hope for cleaner air and lower emissions fades into the future.

Were WTO members to agree to abolish ethanol tariffs, the United States and the world generally could buy a cleaner fuel that puts less smoke into city air and less carbon into the sky. Alternatively, Congress could simply give American ethanol brewers a deadline: five years from now the tariff will be scrapped, so make an affordable fuel, or let the environmentally conscious public buy from Brazil. In such cases, a very traditional use of trade policy could mean better American environmental quality, and could contribute a bit to the world's effort to slow climate change.

Fishery subsidies offer the same opportunity on a much larger scale. Think of the Grand Banks off Newfoundland, John Adams' obsession in the Paris peace talks of 1783 and even then a 200-year-old source of fish for the Atlantic world. In 1583, a quarter-century before the Pilgrim landing, an English sailor named Haye found an army of birds there, a hundred miles from shore, hovering above a small floating city. The birds had arrived, as they did each spring, to feast on fish-guts thrown from the decks of European fishing boats arriving in the spring to catch cod. He describes the sight:

> The Portuguese and French, chiefly, have a notable trade of fishing upon this Bank, where there are sometime a hundred or more sail of ships: who commonly begin the fishing in April, and have ended by July. During the time of fishing, a man shall know without sounding when is upon the Bank, by the incredible multitude of sea fowl hovering over the same, to prey upon the offals and garbage of fish thrown out by fishermen.[109]

Adams' negotiations kept American boats on the bank for another two hundred years. Today they are gone. The Bank is home to no birds, few boats, and fewer fish. Factory ships invented and built after 1950 netted the cod into insignificance. The birds then vanished. And the Bank is simply a spectacular example of a phenomenon affecting every sea. The yellowtail flounder is following the cod, as are the Pacific perch, the Atlantic bluefin tuna, and the sharks whose fins are go into gluey Chinese soup. In all, two-thirds of the world's fishing grounds are fully exploited, or fished heavily enough to cause permanent damage, and scientists' count of genuinely big fish has plummeted by 90 percent.

The cause is simple. With more people and richer countries, almost everyone eats more fish. The miserable Shanghainese of 1976 might sneak a carp from a canal; today's wealthy Pudong condo owner visits a luxury restaurant to sample the oversized "geoduck" clam, hand-plucked from the depths of Puget Sound, and the "Patagonian toothfish" netted a mile below the Chilean sea. In all, the world's fishing catch has grown four-fold, from twenty million tons of fish in 1950 to more than eighty million tons a year today; and even this excludes seven million tons of doomed but commercially useless "bycatch," including the turtles netted by shrimping boats[110].

To catch more fish, fishermen first build more boats, then better boats. The world fishing fleet doubled in size between 1970 to 1990, to 1.3 million large "decked" ships and three million more smaller craft. Since then it has stopped growing, but has grown continuously more efficient. Satellites track their prey from miles above the ocean, hull-mounted radar arrays bring boats to the largest shoals, deep trawls catch fish older nets could not reach.

Fish no longer keep up. As their catches drop, boats lose money and desperate fishermen appeal for help. Sympathetic governments respond all over the world. The World Wildlife Fund reports that fishing bureaucracies in North America, Europe and Asia spend 14 to 20 billion dollars each year to keep boats on the sea and catch levels up. Japan's Ministry of Agriculture, Forestry and Fisheries spends two or three billion dollars a year. The European Union's Common Fisheries Policy accounts for 1.4 billion euros, with the U.S. and Russia close behind.[111]

The money comes in many forms, most of them making the existing problems worse. Tax credits allow boats to buy better radar and deep-sea netting gear more cheaply. The European Union is notorious for thinly disguised bribes, known as "access payments" and applied through the Common Fisheries Policy, to poor countries to open up their fishing grounds. The largest agreement, with Mauritania,[112] pays $109 million a year in exchange for exclusive and unlimited rights to hake and tuna caught off Africa's Atlantic coast.[113]

The problem is a simple logical puzzle, described in the 1950s by the inventors of "game theory." Everyone would win with shared sacrifice of subsidies. Each individual player would lose, however, by abandoning his own—and any single player would lose disastrously by surrendering subsidies if the rest won't. Thus all governments and fishermen share an interest in healthy ocean fisheries, but no government can keep them healthy by ending its own tax writeoffs and access payments. If the American fleet—or that of Japan, Europe, Russia, or China—gives up its payments while the others keep them, the consequence will simply be that the virtuous fishermen will lose their catch to unscrupulous rivals. Therefore governments continue to spend and boat owners catch what they can.

Trade restrictions like those used to help the turtles are unlikely to help. Latin and Asian shrimpers were sensitive to American pressures (even if they resented the pressures) because they sold most of their catch to American restaurants and seafood markets. Exports are much less important to fishing boats. Japan's fleet carriers its catch to the Tsukiji market in Tokyo, not to New York. Korea's boats take their fish to Seoul and Pusan. Spain's go to Bilbao, Santiago and Barcelona. Eighty million of the 132 million tons of fish sold in a year go to domestic markets, and trade sanctions would bother their boat owners not at all.

A WTO agreement, though, has great promise. As early as 1994, the group's members agreed to stop subsidizing factories. They could easily do the same for boats. An agreement limiting subsidies to payments meant to get fishermen out of the business and scrap their boats would cover all the major fishing nations but Russia—and Russia's likely entry to the WTO next year would bring its Arctic factory ships under the agreement as well. With fewer boats on the water, fish would get a bit of relief. The World Wildlife Fund proposed precisely such an agreement in 1999. The Clinton administration adopted it, the Bush administration to its credit did the same, and the WTO members placed on their negotiating agenda in 2001. For now the idea is in a negotiating limbo, generally accepted but on hold unless the Doha Round revives. Completing the work would not restore fisheries by itself—that would require more direct agreements to limit fish takes—but would make the task a bit easier.

Here we come to the second step in our agenda. Environmental protection and trade are not enemies, and are not likely to become enemies. But neither have they been allies. Instead they have been strangers. The task is to unite them, taking the specific cases of ethanol and fish and using them as guidelines for a systematic and comprehensive approach.

Poverty: Why Trade Policies Are Toughest on the Poor

THE NEXT CHARGE is unfairness to the poor. This has a very strong foundation. It needs qualifications—it is tempting and easy, for example, to exaggerate the culpability of rich countries and avoid the failings of poorer countries—but it is fundamentally correct. Almost every major country (the honorable exceptions are Chile, Hong Kong, and Singapore) imposes its highest tariff rates on the products most important in the budgets of its own low-income families. All likewise impose their toughest policies on the things the world's poorest countries make and grow. And though the United States is not the world's worst offender, the inequities of American trade policy, hidden away in the tariff system, should be among the easiest to solve.

Battle of Steel vs. Lingerie

With the exception of Prohibition, the Smoot-Hawley Act is the last of the Jazz Age policies to hold a place in the American political imagination. Each President, sooner or later, invokes it to ridicule opponents of trade agreements. Al Gore famously did so in 1993, pointing to a large black-and-white photograph of Smoot and Hawley to embarrass the eccentric billionaire Ross Perot during a debate on NAFTA. But tariff debates went out of fashion long ago. As early as 1956, Woodrow Wilson's biographer had to add a small apology to his chapter on tariff reform: "So largely has the tariff been eliminated from present-day partisan debates, that it would be easy for the reader to fail to understand the significance of the issue in Wilson's day."

Half a century later, few even realize that it still exists. Congress held its last hearing on the topic in 1974. The Treasury Department wrote its last tariff report sometime in the Johnson or Kennedy administration. Even the experts—academic economists, activists, Congressional aides, and trade journalists alike—abandoned the topic decades ago, thinking it boring and hard to understand as well as unimportant.

But the tariff system is not unimportant and it is easy to understand. With the right products, it need not even be boring. A mildly sensational comparison, between the permanent tariffs on underwear and the last tariffs that reached the media illustrates how little even the best-informed people know about the system.

These were the temporary steel tariffs President Bush imposed in 2002. To recap the matter briefly, steel mills appealed to Mr. Bush for help shortly after his inauguration in 2001. Their grievance was a large increase in steel imports during the Asian financial crisis of 1997-1999. (Steel mills in Europe, Asia, and Latin America had redirected their output, at low prices, away from failing Southeast Asian and Korean construction firms and auto plants to American customers.) By 2001 the import boom was over and the argument for limit questionable. Nonetheless, Robert Zoellick—the Bush administration's first chief trade negotiator and Barshefsky's successor—thought steel tariffs would earn gratitude from Ohio and Pennsylvania Representatives, whose votes would help to pass the big trade agreements he envisioned for the coming years. White House officials made a similar calculation about the Electoral College.

The administration therefore agreed. In March, a year after his inauguration, Mr. Bush arrived at the White House press room in person, to announce tariffs on about ten million tons of imported steel. This was roughly a quarter of American steel imports, and the tariffs would begin at 8 percent and peak at 30 percent.

By September they had cut imports by seven thousand tons a day. Construction firms, auto plants and makers of metal drums which continued buying foreign steel paid an additional $20 million in tariff revenue each month. Steel executives were pleased, construction firms angry, and influential foreigners enraged. Tony Blair called the tariff scheme "unacceptable and wrong." Fernando Cardoso in Brazil said it made a joke of the administration's call for a western hemisphere free trade zone. Japan's cautious bureaucrats said little and plotted revenge.

A small litigation war began within a week of the decision. Brazil, the European Union, Japan, Korea, Norway, and Switzerland filed grievances at the WTO. China and Taiwan, united at least in this, joined them a month later. All eight won their cases. Europe, authorized by the WTO to "withdraw" concessions to the United States, threatened retaliatory tariffs against Florida orange juice, Harley-Davidson motorcycles, and South Carolina fabrics. The Administration then removed the steel tariffs in December 2003.

Dozens of TV outlets covered the tariffs and their removal. NKK in Japan, the BBC, O Globo in Brazil, China Central in Taiwan, even *al-Jazeerah* put it on television. The famous conservative columnist George Will termed the tariff decision the "worst day of Bush's Presidency," wisely adding the qualifier "so far."

During these twenty months, no government filed a WTO case on lingerie. No network ran video on the topic. But underwear tariffs, especially on brassieres, made the steel policy look modest. As $23 billion in steel raised $560 million in tariff fees, $10 billion worth of imported underwear brought in almost $800 million.

Table 9: **Steel Vs. Underwear, (2002–2003)**

Imports	Tariffs Collected	Average Rate
Total Steel		
$23.1 billion	$560 million	2.4%
Total Underwear		
$10.0 billion	$786 million	7.9%
Women's		
$8.1 billion	$670 million	8.3%
Brassieres		
$2.1 billion	$270 million	12.9%
Panties		
$2.3 billion	$150 million	6.7%
Garter belts, negligees, etc		
$3.5 billion	$250 million	7.1%
Men's		
$1.9 billion	$116 million	6.0%

Why? Each brassiere has a permanent 16.9 percent tariff, almost exactly the average of the administration's steel tariffs. A billion bras crossed the border during the steel experiment. They cost retailers $2.1 billion and raised $270 million in tariff money. Meanwhile, imported steel cost $23 billion and raised $540 million. The normal bra tariff, therefore, was five times as high as the extraordinary and temporary steel tariff.

The $270 million in brassiere tariff revenue alone, spread across 140 million American women, amounts to a "breast tax" of seventy cents per breast per year. The rest of the feminine gear added another $400 million. Men's underwear—taxed noticeably more lightly than women's, to add insult to injury—raised $100 million more. And unlike the steel tariffs, which were temporary and extraordinary, the underwear tariffs are permanent and normal. They remain in place today. They will remain in place forever, unless someone decides to change them.

Even the hundreds of millions of dollars in border payments vastly understate the cost. Retail chains pay their fee to the Customs Service when they pick up the underwear at the border. They then lump it in with their payments to the factories that make the bras, and to the shippers who ferried them across the Pacific in containers. This total is known as the "landed cost." The retailers add markup fees—usually a fixed percentage—to the landed cost, and state governments then impose sales taxes. Magnified twice, lingerie tariffs easily takes a billion dollars from women in stores every year. The money shows up on no sales receipt, so nobody knows.

U.S. Tariffs as Taxes on Clothes

Lingerie tariffs are sensational only because the product is sensational. Among clothing tariffs they are perfectly typical. Taken as a whole, the clothing tariffs show the steel tariffs as a very visible but essentially trivial matter—something like a comet in the sky, colorful but insignificant against the stars and planets. The heart of the tariff system remains, as it was in the 19th century, taxation of clothes and shoes. These goods account for only six percent of imports, but raise half of all tariff money.[114]

Table 10: **Tariff Collection (2004)**

Import Value	Tariff Collected	Tariff Rate
	(in billions)	(in billions)
Total		
$1,460	$21.3	1.4%
High-tariff goods		
$112	$11.2	10%
Clothes and shoes		
$88	$9.3	11%
Linens and Luggage		
$12	$1.2	9%
Silverware, Sports Gear, Plates, Watches, Drinking Glasses		
$9	$0.5	6%
Milk, Butter, Cheese, Juice		
$3	$0.2	7%
Everything Else		
$1,348	$10.1	0.7%

The tables illuminate something important and sad about American trade policy. The negotiators have labored and often achieved great things. Most of their efforts, though, have gone into reform of trade in products important to wealthy people and businesses. But their work on clothes and shoes, and also some kinds of food, has usually been an effort to prevent or delay reform. And with the illustrative case of underwear in mind, we can move on to a more systematic examination of the reasons for this contrast.

As early as Hoover's era, the tariff system lost its role in taxation. Roosevelt's launch of international trade negotiations removed it from domestic politics altogether. These were good things—but they inadvertently killed the Progressive era's interest in the domestic effects of tariff policy. Nobody picked up the thread again until development-oriented NGOs like Oxfam became interested in trade and poverty in the early 21st century.

By the 1970s, after the agreements concluded by Truman, Eisenhower, Kennedy, and Johnson, tariff rates in the big developed countries had fallen, at least on average, to low levels. The principal American goals in the Tokyo and Uruguay Rounds accordingly shifted away from tariffs to arcane newer issues—agricultural and manufacturing subsidies, import licensing and quotas; and, later, to electronic commerce, labor standards, and environmental policy.

But the system remained alive. Individual businesses and their lobby groups, though, remained interested in the tariffs applied to their own products, both in the United States and abroad. Throughout this series of agreements, from the 1950s to the early 1990s, business groups and trade unions filed their batteries of requests with the U.S. Trade Representative Office—just as they did in the China talks of the later 1990s. Sympathetic Senators and Congressmen sent letters and calls backing them up. Administrations, looking ahead to votes on approval of the agreements, did their best to grant the requests.

No administration since Nixon's, or perhaps even Kennedy's, has been interested in tariff policy in its own right. Anti-poverty lobbies barely knew the system existed. The consumer movement long since lost its interest in prices and living standards, at least as far as trade policy goes, and and focuses almost exclusively on safety. Therefore the tariff system evolved without any general plan throughout the

1970s, 1980s, and 1990s, as negotiators satisfied Congressional and interest-group demands. It now reflects, almost perfectly, the different preferences of the American businesses (and to a lesser extent the trade unions) of the 1970s and 1980s.

In general, American tariffs are low or zero on high-technology products and heavy-industry goods. They are zero or trivial on natural resources and industrial goods, and also low on luxury goods. But they are very high on a narrow but important set of products: the cheap and simple clothes, shoes, and food that poor people buy and poor countries make and grow.

More specifically, we have no tariffs on high-tech products, because computer firms, semiconductor fabricators, pharmaceutical firms, and manufacturers of airplanes, scientific instruments, and medical equipment, are confident and sell their products everywhere in the world. Their principal goal has been the elimination of foreign trade barriers that hamper exports. Tariffs on these products accordingly fell to very low levels during the Tokyo Round, and vanished altogether after the Uruguay Round in 1994 and the WTO's Information Technology Agreement in 1996.

Tariffs on natural resource products—oil, wood, metal ores—and tropical goods like coffee and tea are also usually minimal or zero. Most vanished when Hoover redesigned the system in the 1920s, and a few even earlier.

But tariffs on fabrics, cloth, shoes, and luggage remain all but untouched. Their makers, as they were in the 1920s, remained convinced that each penny a tariff adds to a competitor's cost is a key to the future. On their behalf, lobby groups like the American Textile Manufacturers Institute and the Association of Rubber and Plastic Footwear Manufacturers fought from the 1950s up to the Uruguay Round to exclude clothing and shoe tariffs from the agreements. A few smaller allies—in particular the makers of luggage, watches, silverware, dinner plates, drinking glasses, and costume jewelry—joined. So did the extremely powerful lobbies for dairy, sugar, and fruit juice. All more or less got what they requested. Ever since the 1960s trade agreements have been preserving tariffs on clothes, shoes, and food, while abolishing or driving them to minimal levels on high-tech goods and industrial inputs.

Skewing the system even more sharply, luxury goods firms joined high-tech businesses in their willingness to abolish tariffs. This is because they care little about price competition. Wealthy shoppers will buy a cashmere shawl, a pair of Italian leather shoes, or sets of sterling silver cutlery and cut crystal precisely because they are so costly. Thus the makers of these things never cared much about tariffs. Most are gone.

Underwear is again a sensational but utterly typical example of the consequences. The $270 million in bra tariff money mainly comes from the cheap polyester or cotton bras that carry the 16.9 percent tariff. But high-priced silk bras have tariffs of only 2.7 percent. Silk panties likewise have a tariff of 1.1 percent, cotton 11 percent, and polyester 16 percent.

Likewise, where a cashmere sweater has a 4 percent tariff, an acrylic version gets 32 percent. The Four Seasons hotel chain pays a 3 percent tariff on the French cut-crystal glass that holds champagne at New Year's, but a Salvadoran family running a store-front pupusa shop pays 28 percent for cheap drinking glasses from China or Turkey. Cheap sneakers get the highest tariffs in the whole manufacturing tariff schedule: 37, 48, and even 60 percent. The only products more heavily taxed are sticks of butter and glasses of orange juice.

Table 11: **Cheap Goods and Luxuries**

Product	Type	Tariff Rate
Men's Shirts:	Synthetic Fiber	32.5%
	Cotton	20.0%
	Silk	1.9%
Ladies' Underwear:	Polyester	16%
	Cotton	11.2%
	Silk	1.1%
Shoes:	Men's dress leather	8.5%
	Sneakers over $20/pair	20%
	Sneakers under $3/pair	48%
Drinking glasses:	Leaded crystal, over $5/apiece	3%
	Plain glass, $3–$5 apiece	7.5%
	Plain glass, 30¢ or less apiece	28.5%
Forks:	Silver-plated	0%
	Steel, above 25¢ apiece	8.5% + 0.5¢
	Steel, below 25¢ apiece	15.8% + 0.9¢

Consequences for the Poor Abroad

Without any particular intention, therefore, the United States has created a system that is open and kind to wealthy countries and rich people,
but wildly harsh for the poor.

The effects abroad are simple. Rich countries which make luxury
goods and sophisticated manufactures rarely face any significant tariffs.
Neither do oil producers. The steel tariffs accordingly came as a shock to
Europe, Japan, China, Korea, Taiwan and Brazil, whose goods generally
arrive in America with little trouble. Clinton's African Growth and Opportunity Act, and the string of preferences and free trade agreements
allotted to the western hemisphere since the 1980s, mean the tariff system also treats Africa and Latin America lightly. The poorest countries
of Asia and the Muslim world face something rather different.

A poor country enters the global economy by one of three gates.
If it has oil or gold, it invites extractive businesses in to dig wells and
mines. If it has a tie to the rich world's food businesses, it grows coffee
beans, cocoa pods, or tea. Otherwise it starves or sews clothes. Here
we return again to Cambodia. It has no oil or precious metal. Its farmers cannot compete with their Thai and Vietnamese neighbors even
in Phnom Penh. So like Bangladesh, Nepal, Pakistan, and Sri Lanka, it
sews clothes. And because tariffs remain so high on cheap and simple
clothes, American tariffs hit Cambodia harder than any other country
in the world.

The cotton blouses Srei made last year get a tariff of 16.5 percent.
Factories like hers compete for orders for low-cost cotton and polyester
pajamas, underwear, T-shirts, cotton pants and skirts, acrylic sweaters,
and baseball hats, all of which get tariffs between 6 and 32 percent.

Last year, therefore, as Cambodia sold Americans two billion
dollars worth of clothes, it faced a tariff penalty of about $370 mil-
lion. Cambodia's GDP being about $5 trillion, this penalty is nearly the
equivalent of a tenth of the country's national income. The old colonial
power, France, sells us about $37 billion worth of imported airplane
parts, perfumes, wines, and cognacs. Airplane tariffs are long gone. So
are perfume tariffs. Wines and spirits get small fees. French exporters
earn thirty times the money Cambodia's humble containers of clothing
bring, but their buyers pay less tax.

Nor is this a freakish exception. Cambodia's $370 million penalty is half again as much as the tariff penalty on $37 billion in Malaysian computers and TV sets. (Computer tariffs are gone, and TV tariffs vary from 2 to 6 percent.) It is nearly eight times the penalty on Saudi Arabia's $33 billion in crude oil exports. In effect, Cambodia's simple goods face a barrier almost twenty times higher than that confronting the sophisticated goods of Europe and Japan, and eighty times that for the natural resources of the Persian Gulf.

Table 12: **Imports And Tariffs, France, Cambodia, And Others (2006)**[115j]

Imports	Tariff Collection	Average Tarrif Rate	Per Capita Income (2005)
France $37.1 billion	$367 million	1.0%	$34,810
Saudi Arabia $32.6 billion	$50 million	0.2%	$11,770
Malaysia $37.0 billion	$244 million	0.7%	$4,960
Bangladesh $3.3 billion	$494 billion	15.0%	$470
Cambodia $2.2 billion	$370 million	16.7%	$380

Cambodia's treatment, though extreme, is not unique. A small, unlucky club of about twenty low-income countries in Asia and the Muslim world get the same treatment. Mongolians, who earn about three hundred dollars a year, lose $25 million on their $150 million worth of sweaters and wool exports. This is more than buyers of goods from Norway, whose people earn $40,000 a year, lose on $5 billion in oil and salmon. Bangladesh loses more than its old colonial ruler Britain; Pakistan loses five times as much as Russia.

A quick list, printed below, shows how it works. It is a simple list of the tariffs on the top hundred goods imported from the world at large, and then from twenty countries. In most cases, the top one hundred goods account for the bulk of American imports from a country—98 percent of goods from Cambodia, 70 percent from India, and so on. As the table shows, worldwide about two-thirds of American imports come in duty-free, and only thirteen of the top hundred face a very high tariff. For Cambodia, more than half of the top hundred get exceptionally high tariffs, and ninety-four of them are above 5 percent.

Table 13: **U.S. Tariffs On Top 100 Goods From 20 Countries, 2003**[116]

	Duty-free Products	Tariffs 0.1%–4.9%	Tariffs 5%–15%	Tariffs >15%
WORLD	63	24	8	5
Cambodia	5	1	42	52
Bangladesh	6	5	48	41
Mongolia	9	9	43	39
Pakistan	10	7	66	17
Oman	30	8	31	31
Nepal	30	10	36	24
Syria	35	17	22	26
Egypt	37	17	31	15
Turkey	49	9	27	15
Indonesia	54	11	14	19
India	48	15	25	12
China	56	20	20	4
Brazil	64	18	15	3
EU	65	24	11	0
South Africa	83	7	9	1
U.K.	69	23	7	1
Japan	57	37	6	0
Saudi Arabia	69	22	9	0
Norway	77	17	6	0
Germany	60	38	2	0

The countries at the top of the list face discriminatory as well as ungenerous treatment. With good intentions and sometimes good results, Congress has used preference programs to excuse seventy African and Latin countries from the tariff system. The Bush administration's more controversial FTAs have done the same for fourteen more countries. Nothing of the sort has been done for Cambodia, Bangladesh, Mongolia, and the rest.

Pakistan is another example. Its specialty is "textile products": bedsheets, pillowcases and carpets join shirts and pajamas in accounting for 90 percent of Pakistan's exports to the United States. The textile businesses support about half of the seven million Pakistani industrial jobs. An American buyer can purchase cotton bedsheets sewn in Karachi or China, with a tax of 15.5 percent; or from South Africa or Honduras with no tariff. The cases of Egypt and Bangladesh are identical. Afghanistan and Turkey—Indonesia too—are just slightly less vulnerable.[117]

Or examine the low-cost drinking glasses you might find in a Salvadoran restaurant. Half of America's cheap drinking glasses come from China, and a quarter from Mexico. The rest—about ten million— are from Turkey and Indonesia. The 25-cent drinking glass made in the Turkish glass factories along the Bosporus face a tariff penalty of 7 cents. Mexico's version is exempt from the tariff. A restaurant can buy Mexican glass and avoid the tariff, or buy from Guangdong and Shanghai in bulk. Factory-managers in Istanbul and Jakarta must make a powerful case to get the order.

Lacking influential supporters in the United States, Srei's factory—and it is no different from thousands more in Bangladesh, Pakistan, Mongolia, Laos, Nepal, Sri Lanka, Turkey, Egypt—is caught between daunting rivals. Giant China and India loom up on one side, with their vast reservoirs of workers, their economies of scale and their wealthy diaspora investors. Eighty other countries whose shirts face no tariff squeeze from the other side. The vise has grown tighter every year.

Table 14: **in a Vise**[118]

Product	Acrylic Sweater	Printed Bedsheet	Leather Suitcase	Drinking Glass
China	32%	15.5%	22%	28.5%
India	32%	15.5	22%	28.5%
Afghanistan	32%	15.5%	22%	28.5%
Bangladesh	32%	15.5%	22%	28.5%
Cambodia	32%	15.5%	22%	28.5%
Egypt	32%	15.5%	22%	28.5%
Turkey	32%	15.5%	22%	28.5%

Table 14: **in a Vise** (*continued*)

Acrylic Product	Printed Sweater	Leather Bedsheet	Drinking Suitcase	Glass
Honduras	0%	0%	0%	0%
South Africa	0%	0%	0%	0%
Mexico	0%	0%	0%	0%
Peru	0%	0%	0%	0%

This is all by default, rather than intention. None of it was intended at all.

Roland Eng, Cambodia's Ambassador to the United States in the 1990s, is a slight, slender man with a crewcut. In 2002 I brought a sheet of paper to his Embassy—it is a big, thinly populated brick building on Washington's 16th Street, with a five-foot stone cobra on the lawn recalling the statuary of Angkor—and explained the system to him. Learning for the first time of Cambodia's sorry treatment, he looked intently at the figures and asked whose idea they were. What Senator or lobby group was responsible? What were their complaints about Cambodia? Could the Cambodian government mollify them by fixing the problems? Or might there be a way to outmaneuver the critics?

The sad answer is that nobody is responsible and there are no critics to mollify. Cambodia has simply collided with the vestiges of Hoover's system, designed to meet a supposed threat from Europe, China, and Japan in the 1930s and preserved by all-but-defunct business lobbies in the 1970s and 1980s. The system, purely by accident, has been designed to encourage Cambodia to fail and to direct retailers whose orders preserve the jobs of 300,000 young Cambodian women to go elsewhere.

Srei's job is secure only temporarily, and perhaps only through yet another accident. The American textile industry lobbied for a limit on clothes imports from China in 2005, as they did for Cambodia in 1998. Once again (through a small loophole in the Chinese WTO accession agreement, allowing a final extension of clothing quotas until 2009), they got it. The limit has done little for the America industry, and has temporarily eased pressure on factories in Cambodia and Bangladesh, as Chinese investors spread out to new countries.

Cham Prasidh, the Minister, glumly points to this as the reason for the industry's growth in 2005 and 2006. Worrying about looming competition from Vietnam and the 2009 expiry of the quota on Chinese clothing, he can do little but plead for help. He cannot complain to the WTO as Japan, Europe, and China complained about steel tariffs. The clothing tariffs were preserved through the Uruguay Round in 1994, and all are entirely legal under the WTO rules. The system may be strange and unfair, but it violates no rule.

Cambodia's businesses and Commerce Ministry officials can only hope Congress will help. If not, their future is full of lowering clouds. If Cambodia cannot make clothes as efficiently as Vietnam and China, and if it gets no tariff benefit, the owners may simply move. Even a big factory like Srei's takes barely two weeks to dismantle. If so, there is no net to catch the employees as they fall. Cambodia's government, barely able to collect taxes, has no money to spend on unemployment insurance or job training. They will fend for themselves. They will sell their earrings and bracelets to pay for room and food, as they try to find jobs as maids, waitresses, or hostesses at karaoke bars. If they fail, they go home or to a massage parlor.

A small change could make their lives secure. At any time it chooses, Congress can abolish tariffs. The cost of this would be essentially nothing. The fifteen least-developed countries not already enrolled in a trade preference program account for about $6 billion of America's $2 trillion in imports, or a third of a cent in each dollar. Nobody would notice—except for some retailers, a few million young women hoping to keep their jobs, and the tens of million rural families their salaries support.

Consequences for the Poor At Home

The tariff system's domestic effect is very similar. Though trivial for rich people and businesses, a minor matter for middle-class families, it strikes one particular group of Americans with special force. These are single mothers.

The reason is intuitively simple. Single moms earn less money than other Americans, spend more of their income on life necessities, and buy cheap goods rather than luxuries. The tariff system reserves almost all of its high penalties for cheap life necessities: cheap clothes, shoes, food, and a few types of household goods. Therefore, single mothers feel its effects more than anyone else.

A reasonable estimate is that America's seven million single-parent families earn about $210 billion a year, and lose a bit more than two billion of it—roughly three days' pay each year—to the tariff system. The calculation runs along the following lines.

1. Americans spend $320 billion on shoes and clothes each year. Imports made up about 90 percent of this total, or roughly $290 billion.
2. The border cost of shoes and clothes was $85 billion, and tariffs added $9.3 billion. Markups and state sales taxes therefore roughly triple the cost of imported shoes and clothes between the border and the store.Americans spend $320 billion on shoes and clothes each year. Imports made up about 90 percent of this total, or roughly $290 billion.
3. Tariffs make up about a tenth of the price of clothes in stores, or about $28 billion in consumer costs. The calculation is a bit conservative, but close enough.

A final table illustrates the general effect through its extreme case, cheap-sneakers. Tariffs inflate the price of a pair of cheap sneakers by slightly less than half. Then the retailer's markup magnifies the cost again, and the state sales tax magnifies it a third time.

Table 15: **Tariffs On Cheap Sneakers**

	Cheap Sneakers With Current Tariff	Cheap Sneakers if Tariff Were Removed
manufacturing/transport cost	$2.20[119]	$2.20
tariff	+ $1.06	+ $0.00
landed cost	= $3.26	= $2.20
notional 100% retail markup	× $2.00	× $2.00
retail price	= $6.52	= $4.40
state sales tax	× $1.05 (5%)	× $1.05 (5%)
final consumer cost	= $6.85	= $4.62

Tariff loss to shopper = $2.23

The general calculation is much the same. Tariffs account for about 10 percent of the landed cost of shoes and clothes; the cost of imported shoes and clothes in stores is $290 million. Therefore, tariffs account for a store "tax" of $28 billion on clothes and shoes on the public in general, though the government earns much less than this figure. Smaller high-tariff household goods—a set of forks and spoons here, a suitcase there, a watch, a bicycle—add a few billion more.

We can also calculate the cost of tariffs to single-parent families. According to the Bureau of Labor Statistics, a typical single-parent family earned about $31,000 in 2004. The family spent about $2,000 of it buying shoes and clothes. Across seven million single-mother families, the shoe and clothing bill is therefore about $14 billion.

Third, poorer families buy cheaper goods than wealthy and middle-class families buy. Cheaper goods, as we have seen, face much higher tariffs than luxuries. A conservative estimate might make the tariff an eighth of the store cost rather than a tenth. Single-mother families, therefore, would lose $1.5 billion to shoe and clothing tariffs each year. Another 1.5 billion would go to tariffs on food, luggage, household textiles, silverware, and other minor goods. Per family, this would mean a loss of about $300 a year; families with two or three children would lose $400 or $450.

The sums are not unbearable. Neither are they trivial. After Social Security and Medicare taxes, a single mom usually earns about $25,000 a year. A $250 tariff bill amounts to three days' pay. The tariff system might cost a recent welfare system graduate, who earns $15,000 a year as a maid in a hotel, a week's salary to the tariff system. Adding a bit of insult to injury, the hotel manager, earning a hundred thousand or so, would lose two or three hours' pay.

Compare this inequity to the Bush administration's tax cuts. Liberals and Democrats generally denounce them as rewards to wealth. Rightly so. But a policy designed to reward wealth, as misguided as it might be, is far less offensive than a policy designed to punish want.

Failure to Protect Jobs

To fix the tariff system for Cambodia and Bangladesh would be easy and painless. One need only poke a small hole in it. To fix it for low-income

Americans would be more ambitious—it would require abolishing almost all the clothing and shoe tariffs.

This sounds like an ethical dilemma with no easy answer. America has seven million single-parent families. About four hundred thousand Americans work in high-tariff consumer industries.[120] Should seven million single moms and their children pay to preserve four hundred thousand clothing and shoe jobs? Should the four hundred thousand workers give up their jobs to ease life for seven million single mothers?

The question has no easy answer—but in reality it is meaningless. The tariff system is really a bit of black comedy: it no longer protects jobs at all. The sacrifice imposed upon seven million unwitting single mothers, and twice as many poor-country garment workers, is pointless.

The shoe industry is again a simple illustration. In the 1950s, about 260,000 Americans worked in shoe factories. Shoe lobbyists managed to exempt shoes from the trade agreements of the 1960s, 1970s, 1980s, and 1990s. The industry all but vanished anyway. Today shoe companies employ only 17,000 Americans. Five thousand work in sales and design, and many of the rest make exotic protective gear for soldiers, workers in chemical plants and people in other hazardous jobs. The sneakers come from Taiwanese and Korean companies that make their shoes in China, Indonesia and Vietnam, regardless of the tariff. Though the Customs Service continues to collect $1 for every pair of $2 sneakers that arrives in a port, the last pair of American-made cheap sneakers came off the line thirty years ago.

Here the tariff, losing its character as trade policy entirely, has reverted to its 19th-century origins as a federal tax. Clothing is a decade or two behind. Garment factories employed 1.2 million Americans in 1974, and are now below 240,000. And where 300,000 Americans made watches, luggage and silverware in 1980; now there are fewer than 20,000. The reality seems to be that container shipping, the Internet and the China boom have cut transport and production costs so sharply that even a 30 or 40 percent tariff no longer works. Unable to protect jobs, it simply raises the price of cheap shoes and clothes at home, while tilting jobs and investment away from Cambodia, Bangladesh, and a few other disfavored countries.

The price for helping the poor, in fact, is essentially nothing. A study by the ITC, released in the spring of 2007, suggests that eliminating all the U.S.' remaining trade barriers—not simply for poor countries and poor people but for Europe, Japan, China and all the rest; not just in clothes and shoes but in sugar, milk and cheese, orange juice, watches, and every other product—would move about 60,000 people from one sort of job to another over five years. This is about eight hours' worth of routine job turnover in modern America: a few thousand fewer sugar-cane cutting jobs, and a few thousand more candy-making jobs; a few thousand fewer garment-factory jobs and a few thousand more warehousing and trucking jobs. A reform in favor of the poor alone would likely have no cost at all.[121]

Like Royalty: European Agriculture

The other great tilt against the poor is in agricultural policy. This cannot be solved purely through reform in the United States, as the web of farm tariffs, quotas, and subsidies extends throughout the rich world. American systems, though no cause for pride, are much smaller than those of Europe and Japan. Like the smaller question of fish subsidies, farm policy requires an international effort to fix.

Consider, for example, the "notifications" of farm subsidy payments the European Commission sent to the WTO two years ago. A notification is a list, required by the WTO's Agriculture Agreement, in which each WTO member itemizes its most recent farm subsidy payments. The EU's report $47 billion spread across forty-nine commodities. European cucumber-growers got 535 million euros, the equivalent of $700 million. Converting euros into dollars, European cattle ranchers and slaughterhouses got $13 billion. Sugar-beet farms received $5.7 billion, and cherry orchards 472 million euros. Wheat received 1.2 billion euros, wineries 892 million, and a few hundred thousand euros went to beekeepers and silkworm cocoon managers.[122]

The count is partial. WTO rules require Europe to account for only the "trade-distorting" subsidies, which are two-thirds of Europe's farm programs. A more comprehensive list, compiled each year by the OECD, places farm subsidies worldwide at about $300 billion a year. Europe accounts for half the total at $150 billion, followed by the United

States at $45 billion and Japan at $30 billion; the Swiss, Norwegian, and Korean programs appear smaller only because their economies and populations are smaller.

Only rarely are the recipients small farmers struggling to preserve village tradition and rural life. A British newspaper, the Guardian, found a list of British and Irish beneficiaries in 2005 through the Freedom of Information Act. This found Britain's largest subsidy recipient to be a sugar refining company called Tate & Lyle, which got 98 million pounds sterling in 2004 and 130 million pounds the year before. The British royal family made off with only a bit less.

Queen Elizabeth's Sandringham Farm received 399,440 pounds "and sixpence" in 2005, to grow apples, wheat, rye, barley, and fruit. The Prince of Wales received almost 135,000 pounds for a battery of farms in the Duchy of Cornwall and 90,000 for an organic farm in Gloucestershire. [123] Asked by the *Guardian* about the matter, a Palace press officer blandly replied:

> The Queen is a landowner and a farmer. She receives subsidy, just as any other farmer would do.[124]

Ireland's winners are the same sort. Larry Goodman, the largest Irish subsidy winner, lives in a castle in County Louth and owns a beef processing company. He rides a personal helicopter to work and gets half a million euros in subsidy payments each year.

Were this simply a matter of European choices about how to use tax money, an American could dismiss it as comedy. But its effects reach everywhere on earth. Tariffs and quotas accompany the subsidies—examples are a 26.5 percent tariff on apricots, a fee of 13 euros per hundred kilograms of olives, and another fee of 122.6 euros per hundred kilograms of olive oil. The combination is effective enough to seal Europe and even the United States off from swaths of the world's farmers, and depress prices in poor countries as well.

Olive oil is an interesting example. Here, the European subsidies and specific duties weigh mainly upon the Arab world. Greeks, Italians, and Andalucians grow olives on the Mediterranean's northern shore; Moroccans and Tunisians manage olive trees on the south shore, where the climate and soil are much the same. Lebanese, Syrians, and Turks tend orchards in the east.

Lower-cost orchards in the Levant and the Arab world lack the fame of their northern neighbors, but nonetheless win prizes for quality and authenticity. But despite its low cost and high quality, Tunisian oil almost never shows up in an American market. Each bottle sold abroad simply rids the owner of a surplus, at a loss of about a dollar. This is because every year, the European Commission writes 2.5 billion euros in subsidy checks—at the current exchange rate, roughly $3 billion a year—to growers in Italy, Spain, and Greece. And all the olive oil trade in the world outside Europe comes to only about a billion dollars.

The subsidy is three times the value of world trade in olive oil, and more half the value of the world's $5.7 billion in olive oil production. The money means cheaper European oil and more of it—six years ago, an investigative report found Spanish farmers and landowners planting 50,000 more hectares with olive trees every year to qualify for subsidy payments.[125] And with all the extra trees, Spain and Italy satisfy not only Europe's appetite but America's.

Our supermarkets sold almost 240,000 tons of oil last year, nearly triple the hundred thousand tons of 1990. California's twenty-seven mills press only enough olives to produce two thousand tons, and the rest comes in tanks and casks from the Mediterranean. With a dollar of subsidies in each quart, Italy and Spain divide 90 percent of the American market. Greece takes most of the rest. Moroccans, Tunisians, Turks, Syrians, and Lebanese are left to fight for ten or fifteen thousand tons a year. Moroccan orchards usually send us three thousand tons or so, and Tunisia six thousand.

Sad little Lebanon manages only five hundred. Nor are the Lebanese farmers much more successful with their near neighbors. Europe's 2000 trade agreement with Lebanon reads rather painfully: it carefully excises everything that might help a Lebanese farmer, from olives and olive oil to table grapes, wine, potatoes, pears, apples, garlic and tomatoes, buttermilk, cream yoghurt, sweet corn, margarine and fructose, malt, flour, pasta, tapioca; to even ice cream, cocoa, and chocolate.[126]

Europe is the largest subsidizer, but not the only one. The OECD's $300 billion farm subsidy figure comes to nearly half the $750 billion in agricultural trade, and three times the value of all the world's foreign aid programs combined. In combination with webs of quotas and specific-duty tariffs like those of the Smoot-Hawley Act—gone long ago in manufacturing trade, still routine in farming—it reshapes life for tens of millions of people.

Some webs of tariffs and subsidies, like the American sugar program or the orange juice tariff, keep markets closed and raise prices. Others, like the cotton program, force prices down abroad. An American example works as well as European oil. In 2002, the Bush administration and Congress raised America's cotton payments by a billion dollars a year. The money went to about 25,000 people, and cut the price of cotton by about a third. Within months, cotton from the Sahel, where ten million farmers grow the crop,[127] vanished from textile mills in Pakistan and China. As I toured a big mill in Karachi in the spring of 2003, the manager regretfully picked up a fistful of raw cotton from a bin, saying it was Pima from Arizona; and that he had had to drop his earlier suppliers in Benin. His competitors having done the same, he had no choice. Farmers in Benin and its neighbors Mali and Niger—where rural families are even poorer than those in Cambodia—lost sales and livelihoods. The World Bank predicts that an end to the cotton subsidy would raise their incomes by 40 percent.[128]

Yoweri Museveni, the President of Uganda, speaks of dairy subsidies with detached bitterness. His country, a mountainous place with mild summers and temperate winters, might easily send cheese and butter around the world. But $11 billion in American, Swiss, EU, and Norwegian dairy subsidies—nearly twice his country's $7 billion GDP—combine with nets and webs of tariffs and subsidies to keep it all off the market. Uganda's dairy farmers sell none of their produce abroad. Museveni's observation is scholarly, not passionate, but very bitter:

> By blocking value-added products, our partners in the world kill the following opportunities: ability to earn more foreign currency, employment, enhancing the purchasing power of the population, expanding the tax base for the governments of Africa, and the chance to transform African societies from the backward, pre-industrial states—in which they are now—to modern ones by building a middle class and a skilled working class.

This is the challenge trade negotiators have failed to meet for twenty years. The Doha Round, whose collapse in 2006 reflected above all the refusal of rich countries to change farm policy, is only the most recent example.

Their recalcitrance is not impossible to understand. It is not limited to rich countries either. (Though because their governments can afford subsidy programs, their failings are the greatest.) Throughout the world, farming and food lie close to national identity. A Thai may live in a Bangkok high-rise and follow American celebrity culture, but his vision of "Thai-ness" remains the emerald rice paddy, the farmer in his rough blue shirt and conical bamboo hat, the brown buffalo, and the rural monk in the clean orange robe. The slightly different images that farming evokes in Japan or in France have the same emotional charge: a sense of place, a connection with history, a definition of self.

But for the poor abroad, reformed agricultural policies could mean more than clothing-tariff reform. And it is not impossible to preserve the images even in a world driven more by computers and factories than by farms. Only a third of American farmers get subsidies and tariff protection; most growers of fruit and vegetables do well without them. Government might, for example, pay people to live on the land rather than pay them to produce larger crops. Europe has in fact begun this, in a few products. Tariff reform could start with shifts from specific duties to percentage-based ad valorem tariffs, which at least do not punish the most efficient producers. To preserve the arrangements of today, though, is surely foolish and can be cruel.

India as Bad Neighbor

Rich countries are not uniquely villainous. Almost every country, and each genuinely big economy, reserves its toughest policies for the countries least able to defend themselves.

India's trade negotiators, for example, denounce the rich countries for discrimination against the poor in every speech they make. Often they do so with reason. Occasionally they should look at themselves. Their own tariff system uses specific duties—the flat fees which made the Smoot-Hawley Act so damaging, and which today survive in rich countries almost exclusively in agriculture—to keep out the low-cost products of Bangladesh, Nepal, and Sri Lanka. An illustrative case, from the "knitted clothing" chapter of India's 2006 tariff schedule, reads:

> Women's or girls' blouses, shirt and shirt-blouses, knitted or cro-
> cheted, of cotton: 12.5% or Rs. 90 apiece, whichever is higher.[129]

In standard English, this means India will apply a 12.5 percent tariff, or else a 90 rupee flat fee, to a knitted cotton blouse. When an expensive blouse arrives at a port, the Indian Customs officer applies the 12.5 percent charge. An expensive skirt from a fashion house in New York or Milan, for example, may cost a hundred dollars, and a 12.5 percent tariff brings twelve dollars and fifty cents, while a ninety-rupee fee is the equivalent of two dollars. Therefore the inspector collects 15 percent and sends the skirt off to its shop, perhaps at New Delhi's big shopping roundabout in Connaught Place. The rate is not low, but the designers and society shoppers can afford it.

A cheap cotton blouse made in Bangladesh or Nepal, by contrast, usually costs a dollar or so. Here a 12.5 percent tariff is a dime and two pennies, or the equivalent of five rupees. The ninety-rupee fee, worth two dollars, is obviously higher. The inspector applies the fee. The equivalent of a 200 percent tariff, it is high enough to keep low-cost cotton shirts out of India altogether. Despite America's stingy system, Bangladesh exports $3 billion worth of clothes to America each year. It manages only $100 million to its giant neighbor.

Anecdotes like this pile up in every continent. Huge Nigeria, its population rising toward 150 million, buys $40 million worth of fish from faraway Iceland. The same country buys only $25 million in goods of all kinds from nearby Mali, Niger, Togo, Burkina Faso, Benin, and Cameroon combined. So too, Brazil keeps out Colombian flowers and Paraguayan shoes. In these simplest and cheapest of products, big developing countries are usually stingier than the rich.

The strange thing in all this is how little it would take to ease life for the poor. A small reform of Indian specific duties; a shift in the way Europe pays people to live on the land; a change in the American tariff laws and cotton programs. A simple story, picked from East Africa, illuminates what it might be.

Ethiopia's Bird-Seed Coup

Picture a range of sepia hills, a field of bright yellow flowers punctuating its light-brown earth. A few coffee-skinned farmers in white gauze robes move, deliberate and unhurried, among the flowers and the warm dry air. Occasionally one bends to examine the ground. As truck moves slowly up a dirt road between the fields, a cloud of beige dust rises, eddies, and settles.

The farmers are Ethiopian peasants. The yellow flower is known to botanists as *Guizotia abyssinica*, or "niger seed." To the farmers it is "noug." They have grown it for centuries on the high Abyssinian plateau. Blossoming each spring, the flowers produce a harvest of tiny black cylinder-shaped seedlets, something like caraway seeds. In the *tukul* homes of up-country Gondar—beehive huts, with adobe walls and forty-foot ceilings thatched with a cone of straw—the seed is a staple of the rural Ethiopian diet. Matrons press the seeds between flat boards, and then use the oil to fry their spongy bread.

Noug is also a favorite for songbirds, and especially attractive to the American finch. Trademarked as Nyjer, it costs more than two dollars a pound and is the most expensive bird-food on the American market. Professionals in the birdseed business are said to call it "black gold." Second-rate noug from India and Nepal began trickling into American feeders a decade ago. The genuine Ethiopian stuff showed up only in 2001. Mr. Tewodros Yilma, Managing Director of Alpha Trading Partners in Addis Ababa, exports noug, along with chickpeas, spices, and Ethiopia's famous coffee. He learned of the seed's appeal a few years ago from Singapore-based commodity traders, and explains—by e-mail from Addis—in the best English he can muster:

> We hear that Niger seed goes to the USA market for bird feed, which really amazes us because we know the product as for human consumption only. Ethiopia uses the Niger seed for oil extraction for human consumption/cooking oil. A few years back some traders from Singapore, USA, and Europe discovered the availability of this product and started to buy from Ethiopian exporters and ship it to the USA buyers. These USA buyers are major traders, by number not more than eleven. They have become the target for whomever wants

to sell the Niger seed . . . USA is a major market for Niger seed and buys almost 60% of the world production.

Stunned to find people ready to buy expensive seed simply to throw it at birds, Mr. Yilma is happy to sell. He now employs a team of collectors to drive tough German trucks around Gondar's roadless plateau in the spring, pay the gauze-clad farmers cash, and bring it to one of twenty small factories in the Addis Ababa suburbs to clean. There it goes into 50-kilogram bags for a trek to the United States.

The bag's route recalls that of Srei's shirt. It takes a twelve-hour run by truck, four hundred miles down one of Ethiopia's four paved highways to Djibouti to a shipping container at the Port. Then it travels up the Red Sea along Solomon's incense trail, through the Suez Canal and the Strait of Gibraltar; then across the Atlantic to the ports of Baltimore and New York. There the noug meets a friendly reception. It faces no American tariff and no quota. No European subsidy drives down the price or keeps the Ethiopian seed off the market. The noug chain runs smoothly from farmers to exporting firms, shippers and truckers, pet-shop managers, and finally bird-feeders. Six years after the trade began, it brings 54 million bags of Ethiopian noug a year to the United States. The bags raise $14 million a year—more than Ethiopia's famous coffee, more than coffee, clothes, and spices combined—and accounts for a third of Ethiopian exports to the United States.

Twenty years ago Gondar's farmers were helpless petitioners for famine relief. Today they are still among the world's poorest people. The noug sales give them a few dollars to pay school fees and buy metal hoes; they become participants and modest winners in the global economy. Mr. Yilma, their agent in the capital, ends his note with a optimistic request for advice: "Ethiopia [has no] chance to get a direct sale to the USA traders and get a better price for the product. Rather we are pressed by the traders outside the USA." Mr. Yilma is doing well. He simply wants to know how to bypass the Singapore traders and go straight to the birdseed men.

It is purely serendipity. An Ethiopian staple grown for centuries or millennia, American suburbanites fond of songbirds, a clever group of Singapore shippers—suddenly it is a blessing for the poor. Sima Qian would recognize this: with no apparent effort, things appear unsought and people produce them without being asked.

It is also far rarer than it ought to be. The activist charge of WTO bias against the poor finds the wrong target—it should be directed against the members rather than the organization—but is fundamentally correct. It cannot be right to find tariffs twenty times as high on Cambodia's clothing factories as on French airplanes and wineries. Lebanese farmers ought not find their onions and olives impossible to sell. And to tax poor women's underwear is to offend decency. A remarkably small reform—new tariff policies for 1 or 2 percent of American trade, redirecting a few billion dollars of government spending in a $15 trillion European economy—could cure the problems. To paraphrase Churchill, rarely could so little accomplish so much for so many.

War and Peace: Middle East as the Blank Spot on the Trade Map

NOW WE COME TO THE LAST CHARGE—one that, though rarely made, returns to the origins of trade policy in the hope of freedom from want, and freedom from fear. Shakespeare's unlucky Richard II, of all people, explains it as he compares himself to his newly crowned rival Bolingbroke:

> Two buckets: the emptier ever dancing in the air, the other down, unseen, and full of water. That bucket down and full of tears am I, drinking my griefs, whilst you mount up on high.

China is a kind of Bolingbroke of the trading world. Its economic ascent gets everyone's attention. The China boom brings endowed chairs to universities, arouses complaints about unfair trade or demands for market access from business lobbies and unions to Congress, evokes speeches from senators and reports about currency rates from think-tanks.

Richard's counterpart, a great civilization fallen on dismal times, was for most of recent history almost a blank spot on the trade policy map. This, not low-income competition, environmental policy or even mistreatment of the poor, is trade policy's most dangerous failure.

We are speaking of the Muslim heartland. This region—the space of land from Morocco across the Middle East to Central Asia, as large as North America—joins thirty countries and an eighth of the world's people. It is almost precisely the land ruled a thousand years ago by the old Abbasid empire; the modern term "Middle East" is a bit too narrow, but close enough.

Even to mention the name is to call up sad and sinister mental images: the billowing grey and black smoke of a car bomb, the blind-folded and doomed victim of a kidnapping, a videotaped appearance by a masked man with a rifle, the wailing family on a sunlit street. It has continued so long that it seems normal.

Why? Wars, assassinations and terrorist movements seemed just as normal in the Europe of the 1930s and the East Asia of the 1950s and 1960s. Not a generation ago, scholars spoke wisely of "ancient hatreds" and "long histories of conflict" in Central America and Southeast Asia of the 1980s. All have faded into history. Why is the Middle East so different?

American and European liberals use secular political grievances to explain: the occupation of the West Bank and the Gaza Strip, the Iraq war, in the extreme case the creation of Israel. Muslim-world commentary published in English-language papers and western translation often backs up this line of thought, and explains hostility to the United States by claiming a consistent prejudice against Muslim causes.

There is no doubt of the anger, and no reason to believe the sense of grievance some sort of insincere pose. But the theory holds up less well than its supporters think. From 1992-2003 there was no Iraq war. As the PLO took up offices in Jerusalem and Bill Clinton moderated talks between Yitzhak Rabin, Ehud Barak, and Yasser Arafat, the Arab-Israeli dispute seemed to be fading. The R.A.F. and the U.S. Air Force rescued the Muslims of Bosnia from annihilation in 1995, and stopped a second genocide in Muslim Kosovo before it began in 1999. Neither American foreign policy nor western policy generally tilted against Muslims. But these were precisely the years in which al-Qaeda was born.

More conservative thinkers find fault within the Middle East. The region's oil ministers and Presidents-for-Life, intent upon keeping un-earned wealth, divert public anger onto western surrogates. Ordinary people, unable to influence their own governments, store up resentment over old and utterly insoluble grievances; and the rulers encourage them to do so. The influential essay *The Roots of Muslim Rage*, by Bernard Lewis, traces the region's troubles to the abolition of the Ottoman Empire.

But this explanation is even less convincing. Corrupt and undemocratic governments are far from unique to the Muslim world. None elsewhere are producing al-Qaedas. And every country in the world can dig up a hundred-year-old grievance if it wants an excuse to be angry. Few bother. Cambodia, with more historical grievances than many nations—very recent ones at that—produces garment-workers rather than terrorists.

Neither explanation is self-evidently wrong. But neither satisfies— and more important, neither gives much reason for hope that anything will ever get any better. Writers on the Arab-Israeli conflict disagree over almost everything, except that it is hard to solve. And grievances rooted in long-past history have no solution at all.

Like China, the Middle East looks back upon a golden past. As Athens was the "globalizing" state of the classical western world, the Abbasid world was the "globalizing" culture of the medieval world. The facts are almost as remarkable as the candy-colored haze of *Arabian Nights* legend. A geography named Yakut, for example, describes old Baghdad in a passage as surprising as it is painful to a modern reader:

> A veritable City of Palaces, not made of stucco and mortar, but of marble. The buildings were usually of several stories. The palaces and mansions were lavishly gilded and decorated, and hung with beautiful tapestry and hangings of brocade or silk. The rooms were lightly and tastefully furnished with luxurious divans, costly tables, unique Chinese vases and gold and silver ornaments. Both sides of the river were for miles fronted by the palaces, kiosks, gardens and parks of the grandees and nobles, marble steps led down to the water's edge, and the scene on the river was animated by thousands of gondolas, decked with little flags, dancing like sunbeams on the water and carrying the pleasure-seeking Baghdad citizens from one part of the city to the other. Along the wide-stretching quays lay whole fleets at anchor, sea and river craft of all kinds, from the Chinese junk to the old Assyrian raft resting on inflated skins. The mosques of the city

were at once vast in size and remarkably beautiful. There were also in Baghdad numerous colleges of learning, hospitals, infirmaries for both sexes, and lunatic asylums.

Arab merchants carried "pepper and other spices" from Java, pepper and gems from India, cloth and porcelain from Tang dynasty capital Chang'an, furs from the Viking kingdom in Russia. In return they sent out textiles, crafted metal, military gear, and worked ivory, and minted silver coins used as far away as Oxford and Sweden. Tunisian historian ibn Khaldun, a few centuries later, suggested that the boldest of them dealt in goods from exotic lands, but the cleverest in simple, medium-quality products more attractive to the general public than to emirs:

The merchant who knows his business will travel only with such goods as are generally needed by rich and poor, rulers and commoners alike. [General need] makes for a large demand for goods. If the merchant restricts his goods to those only needed by a few, it may be impossible for him to sell them, since these few may for some reason find it difficult to buy them. The best quality of any type of goods is restricted to wealthy people, and the entourage of the ruler. They are very few in number. As is well known, the medium quality of anything is what suits most people. This should by all means be kept in mind by the merchant, because it makes the difference between selling his goods and not selling them.[130]

European medievals, despite their reputation as violent louts, learned from their neighbors as often as they warred with them: of the fifteen books of medical lore Geoffrey Chaucer's Physician committed to memory, five are by Arab or Persian doctors—al-Razi, al-Sarabina, Avicenna, Averroes, and "Haly," or Khalil—and four more are by Greek authors available only in translations via the Arabic. Even now, shreds of medieval Arab science and commerce remain embedded in the American vocabulary: chemistry and algebra, the tariff itself and the bank-check, algorithms, jars, admirals and arsenals, lemons and limes, coffee and cotton and candy.

But all this is today nothing but curious fact, taught perfunctorily in seventh-grade history. Like China and its neighbors, the Middle East buckled before western technology and organization two centuries ago. Unlike them, it has not recovered. Today, as China makes television sets, India writes software programs, and Vietnam farms catfish and makes semiconductor chips, and as all of them churn out engineers and business executives, the Middle East pumps oil and produces extremists—and its experience over the past quarter-century is the modern world's closest parallel to that of the Depression.

The region is in the midst of a population explosion. Home to 400 million people in 1980, it now has 650 million.[131] Pakistan's Karachi, already a giant of six million in 1980, is now a grey dusty monster of twelve million—punctuated, pleasingly, by women wearing brilliant robes in lime green, crimson, purple, rose, and black—as big as Los Angeles. At the other end of the Abbasid world, Morocco was a medium-sized state in 1980 and now has a population as large as Canada.[132]

And as its population soared, the region's economy has crumbled. After the oil bubble burst in 1982, its share of trade dropped from above 13 percent of world exports to below 5 percent.[133] Its share of investment fell just as fast. In 2004, the twenty-two Arab states, Iran, Pakistan, Afghanistan, Bangladesh and Central Asia together received $14.5 billion in foreign direct investment—barely more than Ireland and less than Singapore.[134] Economically, the region has probably never been so isolated and so effectively pushed to the margin as it is today.

Table 16: **Invisible Depression: The Muslim Middle East and South Asia, (1980-2000)**[135]

	1980	2000
Total population	400 million	650 million
Share of World Population	10.4%	12.4%
Share of World GDP	5.4%	5.2%
Share of World Exports	13.6%	4.7%
Share of World Direct Investment	4.8%	1.6%

As in the western and Asian world of the 1930s, when population rises while trade and investment contract, living standards must fall. Per capita income in the Arab world fell from $2,300 to $1,650[136]—adjusting for inflation, a drop comparable to America's loss of income between

1929 and 1935. By 2000, the Middle East was the only part of the world poorer than it had been in 1980. Unemployment in the Middle East is above 13.2 percent, twice the world average; and at 25 percent, youth unemployment is the highest anywhere in the world.[137] By 2000, the Middle East was the only part of the world poorer than it had been in 1980.

Such a disaster is almost never confined to lost jobs and profits. It spreads into the individual mind, and then into politics. Jobless men become depressed, angry at themselves for failure to marry or to provide for families, prone to conspiracy theories and revolutionary cures. Political opposition movements shift from criticism to millennialism, or searches for foreign villains, or both. Like the Atlantic world of the 1930s, the Middle East of the 1990s was a world of contracting economies, rising population, frustrated publics, political repression, and angry or pathological politics.

A high civilization, conscious of past glory, had fallen upon grim and embarrassing times. Young people, unable to find work, were getting by on handouts from families and welfare agencies, or trying to get to Europe. Frustration in personal life makes anger over autocratic government, or perceptions of national political humiliation, grow intense. To such people, Al-Qaeda offered a narrative something like the totalitarians of the 1930s offered Europe, and those of the 1950s offered Asia: an idealized past, foreign intrusion, a purification of society, and a restoration of pride. The western world missed it.

Perhaps this was normal. Even casual observers have no difficulty seeing success in trade. They react with admiration, envy, or fear, but never indifference, as a China rises. But decline is very hard to see. Stagnant textile imports from Egypt in the 1990s made no impression upon Congress. The collapse of oil prices aroused mainly relief. No anti-globalization NGO demanded a response to the lack of manufacturing investment in Oman and Bangladesh. No journalist wrote an alarmed article about the lack of "offshoring" to Pakistan. No union president testified before the Ways and Means Committee about the region's falling market share. And no government anywhere in the world acted upon the Muslim world's economic crisis.

Economic analysis does not make explanations drawn from history and politics irrelevant. The policies it suggests are no substitute for new efforts to solve the Arab-Israeli dispute or to settle the Iraq war.

But it does offer some new perspectives and untried ideas. Two very different people, in the autumn of 2001, suggested a place to start.

One was an unemployed young Moroccan named Karim, introduced by Fatima Mernissi in her book *Islam and Democracy*. A 25-year-old economics graduate from the university, he had failed to find a permanent job or get a Spanish visa, and was making a bleak living as a part-time cashier in an Internet café what the Moroccans call a *diplome-chomeur*, an unemployed university graduate. As the Afghanistan war approached, Karim had a wistful thought:

> I wish I could advise Mr. Colin Powell. . . . A good military leader is one who can imagine turning a conflict into equal opportunities for both adversaries. In a situation where people can make a living trading peacefully, violence becomes an absurdly costly choice.[138]

A more influential man four thousand miles east—Abdul Razak Dawood, Pakistan's Minister of Commerce—had the same thought. Asked by a journalist about the appeal of fundamentalism in Karachi and Peshawar, Dawood responded with the converse of Karim's hope: "If you want Pakistan to be a liberal and modern state, you are not going to get that unless you've got people employed."[139]

Where Karim had a wish, Dawood had a request. He wanted the Bush administration to grant Pakistan a tariff concession on bedsheets, pillowcases, leather jackets, and clothes. At minimum, it might stem a flow of scared businesses out of the country. If it was very successful, it might take a few young people out of madrassas or off the streets.

At the opposite ends of the old Abbasid world, both men pointed to something western analysis has missed. That is, al-Qaeda and its allies emerged during a profound and prolonged economic crisis. During the 1980s and 1990s—as Europe united, Asia began to boom, and Central America shifted from guerrilla warfare to garment factories—the Muslim world conducted a twenty-year experiment in "de-globalization." Its countries walled each other off, some of its major governments stayed out of the WTO, and its share of world trade and investment collapsed.

Most of the region's governments retained trade barriers adopted between the 1930s and the early independence period, while Europe,

Asia, and Latin America were abandoning them. To use a simple illustration, the World Bank has a list of tariff rates covering two hundred
countries. Only twenty-one have manufacturing tariffs averaging above
15 percent; and twelve are Muslim states in the Middle East; south Asia
and Central Asia make up more than half.

Boycotts and sanctions imposed on political grounds have been
proliferating through the region since the mid-1970s. The Arab League's
boycott isolates Israel from its neighbors. The Kashmir dispute blocks
trade between India and Pakistan. Sanctions imposed by the United Nations and United States cut Iraq, Afghanistan, and Libya out of the regional economy for nearly twenty years. Where the medieval traveler
ibn Battuta could travel on foot and by donkey from Morocco to India,
his modern descendant would have trouble getting across the Algerian
border. If he managed the trick, he would be blocked again crossing
from Libya to Egypt, and from Egypt to Israel. He might succeed at the
edges of Iraq, Iran, and Afghanistan, at the risk of his life; then the Paki-
stan-India line would block him again.

Some of the region's biggest countries remain outside the WTO.
Even today, ten of the Arab League's twenty-two members—Algeria,
Iraq, Lebanon, Libya, Syria, Yemen, and others—are outside the group,
along with Iran, Afghanistan, and three of Central Asia's five republics.
They cannot use dispute settlement to defend their manufactures and
farm products against arbitrary discrimination, negotiations and trade
agreements to open new markets for their goods, or the WTO's services
and intellectual property agreements to develop the regulatory transparency, intellectual property laws, and services markets that bring
jobs and technology.

Oil itself is a barrier to change. Saudi Arabia's $125 billion in oil
exports is a big figure. But it is little more than Malaysia earns by selling
TV sets, computers, clothes, and telecom gear, and much less helpful
for development. The petrodollars flow through the accounts of a few
thousand Saudi princes and oil-ministry officials while Malaysia's electronics receipts employ millions of young Malay men and women; the
prices of oil gyrate up and down every year, causing inflation and corruption when they are high, and sudden crises when they are low.

Once the most integrated and open part of the world, the Abbasid
lands are now the most divided and isolated. Its countries barely trade

with one another at all.[140] Egypt, for example, usually buys twice as much from Australia as from its neighbors Lebanon, Israel, Syria, Jordan, and Libya combined.[141] The Gulf monarchies pump oil for China, Europe, and Japan, and sometimes for Americans, but produce little else. The entire region's businesses and farms, losing out daily to Asian and Latin rivals in the rich-world markets, produce a hundredth of the world's agricultural and manufacturing exports with a tenth of its people; Abdullah II, the King of Jordan, suggests that the entire region resembles "a series of isolated islands of production," something like the Atlantic world of the 1930s.

And the policies of the big western economies make matters worse rather than better. American tariffs treat Egypt, Pakistan, Turkey, and other big Muslim states almost as harshly as they treat Cambodia. European farm policies do the same for the farmers of the Maghreb and Levant.

Here, paradoxically, is cause for optimism. Purely political or cultural diagnoses of the region's problems lead to deadlock or despair. Violence arising solely from the Arab-Israeli dispute and the Iraq war will be exceptionally difficult to solve; violence flooding out of an underground well of culture or history has no end. But economic problems are technical matters. They can be fixed with changes of policy—as Europe and Asia have done, and as Central American and Southeast Asia have done—and success has at least a chance to ease the tasks of peacemakers and democratic reformers.

It is easier, of course, to advise foreign governments to improve their policies than to tell them how. And the region's problems go well beyond isolation from trade and foreign investment. In 2002, only half the young women of Pakistan, Yemen, and Egypt knew how to read. Its governments spend twice as much on weapons and soldiers as their counterparts in Latin America and East Asia. They spend less of their income on health than the African governments.[142] Trade is only one element of economic policy; and economic policy is only one element of development. A thorough reform would cover universal education, effective schools, internal markets, and much else, and would have to come from within. But foreigners can contribute quite a lot to trade policy—and we now may have a unique chance.

The UN Development Program's remarkable *Arab Human Development Reports* series illustrates the rethinking underway among Muslim economists and intellectuals. Dr. Rima Khalaf, the principal author of the series, noted the obvious in 2002: the region is "richer than it is developed."[143] She suggested internal reform to put its cash to better use, plus development of foreign markets for its farmers and urban workers:

> Domestic markets are too small to provide the basis for sustainable growth based on manufacturing and services. For this reason, the most viable response to globalization is openness and constructive engagement, in which Arab countries both contribute to and benefit from globalization.[144]

Within Muslim governments too, ideas have shifted and policies begun to change. Pakistan and Egypt, where economic success is both crucial in its own right and likely to lift neighboring states as well, have reshaped their approach to the global economy. Starting earlier and further along, Pakistan is enjoying an unlikely boom, although a fragile and quiet one. Its economy grew nearly as fast as those of China and India in 2005, and its businesses created a million and a half new jobs.[145] King Abdullah, as the intifada and the Iraq war make tourism a very difficult sell, has overseen a national effort to open the economy and attract manufacturing investment, and suggests that the experience of Europe and Asia has lessons for the Middle East as a whole:

> In Europe, North America, and Southeast Asia, regional cooperation and free trade areas allowed for private enterprise to invest, prosper, and sustain the growth of national and regional economies. . . . We in the Middle East are still in need of an explicit and clear political decision to pursue this path of collaboration. As the circle of peace widens to become comprehensive and more inclusive, we must venture and collectively agree on the importance of its priority.[146]

In some cases, events have helped accelerate and amplify domestic economic reform. In particular, some of the sanctions and boycotts of the 18970s and 1990s are now gone. War ended the sanctions on Afghanistan and Iraq four years ago. Diplomacy lifted the sanctions on Libya in 2004. The WTO has been bringing in Muslim governments since the turn of the century—Jordan, Kyrgyzstan, Oman, most recently Saudi Arabia. More are on the way, as the WTO's list of thirty-two applicants include thirteen Muslim states: six Arab League members, four Central Asian states, Bosnia, Azerbaijan and Iran.

Help from America and Europe would be welcome, perhaps decisive. One should be cautious, of course. As 2008 approaches the skies are full of baleful stars—the still free al-Qaeda leaders, the deadlock in Israeli-Palestinian talks, the daily violence in Iraq, the menace of a reviving Taliban in Afghanistan, the Iranian bomb, the volatility of Pakistan—and an economic initiative might easily prove the modern counterpart of Roosevelt's Reciprocal Trade Agreements program in the 1930: too little, too late. But it should at least be tried, and soon. If diplomacy can revive, if there is any path to calm in Iraq, an economic effort ambitious enough to change lives in Cairo's alleys and Karachi's dusty squares might be the necessary complement.

Karim and Dawood suggested this six years ago. Barshefsky's Clinton-era agreement with Jordan showed that in the right circumstances it can work. A small tariff benefit in 1997 let Jordan attract dozens of new factories, lift exports to America from $16 million to $400 million—now, after a Free Trade Agreement, to $1 billion—and create nearly 50,000 jobs.

Barshefsky's successor Zoellick seemed to hint at a similar idea in 2001, in a newspaper article arguing that trade policy could help fight terrorist groups by promoting growth and job creation.[147] But his superiors at the White House, rejected each attempt to implement the idea. Minister Dawood never got his tariff benefit. The Bush administration offered him nothing of any value, pointing to opposition from Congress. A year later, it publicly ignored and quietly killed a congressional plan for a tariff relief bill for eighteen countries in the Middle East and South Asia, which Senators John McCain and Max Baucus, joined by two House Democrats, had offered them.

In its place, the administration has pursued a series of bilateral agreements with little obvious value or strategy. (The first was with Morocco, a large and influential country that needs the help; the rest have been simply diversionary efforts with four small Persian Gulf monarchies which, awash in oil, need less help than any other countries in the region.) Afghanistan has gotten nothing but a small tariff break on rugs.

In relations with the five big countries in which half the Muslim world's people live and the struggle with jihadism will succeed or fail—Egypt, Pakistan, Turkey, Bangladesh, Indonesia—there is silence. Europe has done little better.

Here we have the last element of a new agenda. Experiences in Central America and Southeast Asia carry lessons. El Salvador, Nicaragua and Guatemala, once rising or falling with the world coffee markets, now make clothes. With more jobs and more reliable export markets, their economies have stabilized since the 1980s. With the waning of economic turbulence, national reconciliation after the wars has had a chance to take hold. Likewise in Cambodia and Vietnam, weariness with conflicts, urban industrial development, and economic growth has offered employment to rural young people and a period of political calm.

The Muslim world needs no aid program on the scale of the Marshall Plan. Instead it needs a western policy suited to a region with lots of cash but little industry, few jobs, and too much oil. Though some help for Pakistan's schools and Egypt's roads and ports would be welcome, the region's real need is to attract investment, create jobs, and restore a sense of hope to the public—and for this, trade is far more effective than aid. To scrap American textile and leather tariffs, and convert some European farm subsidies to simple cash payments rather than production bonuses, would be a step covering about two pennies in every dollar of imports. As in the related question of trade and poverty, it is really a small matter.

II.
PROGRAM

A BOOK ON POLICY MATTERS normally ends with a set of recommendations. The tradition is a good one—and relevant today, as liberals move on from delighted blinking over the end of the conservative ascendancy to speculation over a presidency—but often dull and long. In trade, though, there is no need to make this section very long. The main points are to remember the early rationale for trade policy, understand the costs of success, grasp the flaws of the modern system, and act so as to preserve the first, heal the second, and fix the last.

More specifically, an updated version of the liberal global-economy project ought to begin with some observations:

1. After sixty years, trade policy has fulfilled many of its founders' hopes for broadly shared growth, higher living standards, and a stronger peace.

2. The achievements have brought powerful competitive stresses, and with them anxieties that are real and deserve response.

3. Stress and anxiety over low-income competition are not new. They have emerged many times in the American past—and in

the deeper pasts of Europe and Asia too—and history is a good general guide to the right and wrong ways to respond.

4. The system has gaps, and they should be especially embarrassing and troubling to liberals. It tilts steeply against the poor, misses opportunities to ease environmental stress, and does much less than it should to ease the world's most dangerous threat to peace.

From these points, they would build a program. It would start by resolutely facing some happy facts. The global economy brings some stress and raises some questions that need answers. But it has neither cost jobs and weakened American industry, nor brought exploitation to other countries. There is no need to begin a new liberal program with seventies nostalgia, party-of-gloom thinking, and unwitting revival of the theories of vanished Whigs and Hooverites. As Roosevelt predicted in the 1940s, and Clinton predicted again in the 1990s, the trading system has proven itself as a way to strengthen peace, promote rule of law, reduce poverty, and accelerate growth.

Therefore, 21st-century liberals can instead use the high ground of freedom from want and freedom from fear as the point of departure. They can draw inspiration, if not blueprints, from earlier eras as they mend the flaws in policy and ease the price of success. The insights of Einstein and (stretching a definition of "liberal," but not so far that it breaks) Hamilton on technological innovation remain the appropriate and honorable response for rich nations worried about fast-moving poorer rivals. Wilson's Progressive-era tariff reform is relevant as we seek to relieve the burden of poverty in American inner cities and reservations, and to encourage growth and job-creation in the world's poorest states. The optimistic internationalism of Roosevelt and Clinton remains the best guide to peace and shared prosperity. And the basic qualities liberalism brings to government—international law, special concern for the poor, active and energetic government—remain the principles which can build upon and improve their work. In their spirit we can imagine the next liberal president devising a program in three parts.

At Home

THE CHALLENGES COME IN TWO CATEGORIES, the first being the problems that come with success: the stresses and anxieties of the open world market, the evolving American economy, and the revival of China and India. Here a response would begin by recognizing that the success of these new powers is real, irreversible, and desirable—just as, sometime in the future, the revival of Africa and the Muslim world will be real and desirable. But it would be optimistic about America's ability to succeed in any case: with the world's best universities, the deepest pools of capital, intellectual property laws, and environmental quality, all helping attract high-quality investment and create good jobs, we should do well. And it would accept that their success means a transition, in which American businesses, unions, and policies will need to adapt and improve, both to keep the national economy inventive and successful and to ease the transitions of workers from one career to the next.

Businesses are already adapting—as Einstein and Hamilton suggested they would in the 1790s and 1920s—by substituting machines for human workers. This is natural and appropriate, if ruthless. Modern American liberals should not emulate Harding and Hoover by shielding them from competition. To mention only the most direct consequences, ignoring economic stability and world politics, new tariffs, or labor-linked import limits would help a few factories but hurt many more. Government and unions instead should complement business' adaptation and ease its social cost with their own new approaches.

The essential problem to solve is the fraying of America's unusual social contract. Since the 1940s, businesses rather than governments have been the guarantors of family security, through health insurance and pensions often negotiated by trade unions. American governments, in contrast to those of other rich countries, simply filled the gaps with help for the very, the disabled, and the old.

Even for people with reliable jobs, these sources of security are becoming outdated, as businesses pull back from their older roles. For people on the edge it is much worse, because job loss in the United States is so extraordinarily painful. A European or Japanese worker replaced by a computer need not fear loss of health insurance and pension. In most cases, a family need not fear losing the chance to send a teenager to college, thanks to extensive access to free university. Americans have no national health care system, no pension guarantees beyond Social Security, and only modest supports for college.

In these circumstances, the loss of a job can be the equivalent of a fall from a cliff. Living standards can suddenly drop, health insurance can go, and 401(k) contributions can end. A family may be forced to send a high-school graduate to work rather than school. Even with unemployment rates low by historical standards, and several years of strong economic growth, the American public has good reasons to be worried—and a business retreat from health insurance and pension guarantees makes the anxiety all the higher, and all the more justified.

Government must fill the space businesses are abandoning, with guaranteed and portable health and pension programs, and some form of tuition insurance for families with teenagers expecting college. Here there is no shortage of ideas piled up during eight years in the wilderness. But a manageable first step would be a much more generous program of help for dislocated workers.

The Trade Adjustment Assistance program, invented under Kennedy and bolstered three times since, is now the only unemployment program which offers a two-year option for federally funded job training, assistance in finding a new job, and a tax credit to preserve health insurance.[148] Only a few hundred thousand people a year receive TAA, though, among the fifteen to twenty million Americans laid off each year. The appropriate step, especially as the Internet spreads international competition to offices as well as factories, farms and mines, is to make TAA-style health insurance support and job training available to all dislocated workers. Congressman Rangel's 2007 outline for the next year or so of trade policy has already proposed such a program, under the title "Strategic Workers' Assistance and Training;" Baucus has a similar plan. This might mean spending additional $4 billion a year, in a budget now near $3 trillion.

Here is also an opportunity for renewal of the labor movement. Its traditional services are visibly losing appeal and seem unlikely to recover it. Bargaining with employers on behalf of a pool of career employees is less relevant today—when retail clerks and construction workers expect to work a few years at one company, build a resume, and then return to school or leave for a better job elsewhere—than it was in the 1950s. As modern workers find seniority-based raises and job tenure of less value, dues payments become financial sacrifices with little return. Therefore young workers are less and less likely to join unions. They might happily, though, join unions that offer skill development programs, help keep pension and health care secure during periods of job transition, and alert their members to new and higher-paying job opportunities nearby.

At the same time, the national public services that support competitiveness should get a review and an upgrade. The Bush administration's tax program should go, replaced with a different approach that offers less reward to wealth, and does more to encourage family savings. Energy policy should find the tax incentives and research spending necessary to make energy use more efficient in general, and reduce reliance on oil in particular. Government support for scientific research in fields where it has been slowly retreating for decades—physics, computer science, chemistry, materials—should be restored. To pinch money on the investment that in the past helped create the semiconductor chip and the Internet, as Hamilton would remind us, is to narrow the future. And immigration policies, both for foreign students and workers, ought to be more ambitious: the National Science Foundation finds a third of

America's science and engineering Ph.D.'s were born abroad, and visa policies should allow us to attract the world's best.

This is simply a sketch or outline. But there is not much need for more. Congress, universities, and think-tanks are full of ideas for a Democratic President on all these topics. Bruce Reed and Rahm Emanuel offer dozens in their book *The Plan,* as does Gene Sperling in *The Pragmatic Progressive*; after the 2006 election, Barney Frank was suggesting a sort of "grand bargain" between business and liberals to mesh economic security with economic growth policies. The point is simply that an open world economy is demanding, but that the demands are not impossible to meet. With a stronger safety net and better public services, workers will be more confident in moving from one job or career to a better one, the public will feel more confident, and the foundation for internationalism will be stronger.

Abroad

If the domestic challenge is responding to the cost of success, the international challenges are more often responses to some sort of failure: the completion of work abandoned too soon, its extension into new fields, even the refocusing of activism and idealism. The institutions and agreements in social and environmental fields are far behind those of economics. Trade regimes remain weighted against the poor, and in the Muslim world they are sometimes at odds with security. And liberal activism itself has at times alienated the low-income workers and developing-country governments it means to help.

The beginning of a successful new approach, then, can be a change of emphasis in liberal activism, toward incentives and rewards for reform abroad rather than sanctions and punishments.

A decade of speeches and Congressional debates about "desperate Chinese workers" and 30-cent or 10-cent factory jobs, and insistence on trade sanctions and limits to address labor and environmental problems abroad, have blurred the line between hope for labor reform abroad (and sometimes environmental progress too) from pauper-labor arguments against trade with the poor. Most developing-country governments—and almost all with intellectual influence, from South Africa and Brazil to China, India, and Vietnam—have concluded that the two cannot be separated, using the insistence on "enforceability" and sanctions as proof. They now believe calls for labor standards are meant less to promote humanitarian values and ethical reforms than to block imports and the reduction of poverty, and the resulting gap between liberal America and poor-country governments has grown very wide.

In extreme cases, of course, sanctions and punishments are appropriate. To ban Burmese teak, or carpets from Taliban-era Afghanistan, or "conflict diamonds" from West Africa may not overturn a dictatorship or end a war. Even so, it can make a moral point. At least in a general way, sanctions like these can target people responsible for grave human rights abuses, rather than using factory workers as proxies. But extreme situations need to be defined narrowly. Praise, rewards and moral support for businesses and poor-country governments which are trying to set high standards, perhaps not with total success but in good faith, will usually achieve much more.

For example, a report last year by the International Labor Organization found Mexico and Brazil quietly approaching the elimination of child labor. Each government has a program—Brazil's is *Bolsa Familia,* Mexico's is *Oportunidades*—of small cash payments to low-income families who keep their children in school. The ILO's report suggests that the programs are startlingly successful: both have cut child labor rates by two-thirds between 2000 and 2004.[149] Yet no trade-labor activist group or trade union has suggested a campaign to buy Mexican or Brazilian goods, to reward their governments and encourage others to follow them. Few have done so even for Cambodia, despite its unique status as the only country in the world to link exports and trade to ILO standards.

The approach taken by a number of development organizations and anti-poverty NGOs is much healthier. One of the encouraging recent developments of trade politics is the emergence of groups in Europe and the United States willing to criticize rich-country trade policies for discrimination against the poor, and more generally to use trade policy to achieve liberal ends. Several of them are famous—the anti-poverty group Oxfam and the rock star Bono's DATA organization are examples—and of course the World Wildlife Fund almost by itself convinced the WTO to take up fishery subsidy reform.

Another group, Women's EDGE in Washington, has taken up the

mission of designing economic policies to help low-income women in poor countries. Its trade project, run by former USTR negotiator Katrin Kuhlmann, helped in 2006 to win passage of tariff exemptions for Africa and Haiti and now hopes for a much larger program, designed to exempt the poorest countries from tariffs and agricultural trade restrictions. In accord with the Grameen Bank's Dr. Yunus, Kuhlmann suggests that "such a program could provide potential life-changing benefits for the world's poorest, including impoverished women in the developing world."[150]

This sort of activism revives the Progressive tradition of critical examination of U.S. trade policy by domestic activists, for the first time since the 1920s. Its spread to other issues—if, for example, groups like United Students Against Sweatshops searched for well-run factories whose workers are fairly paid and whose shop floors are safe, and urged their college bookstores to buy their sweaters, rather than constantly urging sanctions and boycotts—would do far more for labor and environmental reform than any number of threats and sanctions.

Meanwhile, a new liberal presidency could reshape trade policy— not completely, but in ways small enough to manage and ambitious enough to fix the worst flaws.

As a purely commercial matter, it should start by demoting the free trade agreements central to the last six years of policy to a proper subordinate place. They can be appropriate when an ally in a difficult situation needs unique economic support, as Jordan did in the late 1990s; or, in a variant of the Clinton administration's clothing agreement with Cambodia, they can help to encourage countries interested in experimenting with very high labor standards. But as the central element of trade policy, they are a bad combination of large controversy and small consequence.

About two-thirds of all American trade is with five big partners: Canada, Mexico, the European Union, Japan, and China. Most of the basic American commercial interests, whether in promoting exports or reducing the world's trade and financial imbalances, need to be worked out with them, along with India, Brazil, and a few other big developing countries. None of these, perhaps with the exception of Japan, are current or likely future FTA partners. Therefore the next president should replace the FTA program with fewer agreements that require fewer Congressional votes but have greater economic consequence. These would include an effort to revive the WTO's Doha Round, perhaps larger regional initiatives in Asia and Latin America, and an end to the trade embargo on Cuba.

These would be negotiated bargains, similar to the earlier links in the chain of postwar trade policy: In essence, attempts to open other markets in exchange for some more incremental change in American policies. The distinctive liberal addition would be to add to the agenda three more items.

One would be a comprehensive environmental agreement, concluded either through the Doha Round, or a separate WTO accord if the Doha talks cannot be finished. This would broaden the representative cases of ethanol tariffs and fishery subsidies into a systematic elimination of tariffs on environmentally beneficial goods, promotion of trade in environmental services, and elimination of environmentally destructive subsidies.

As it happens, the WTO already has two lists of environmentally misguided tariffs. One, compiled in the late 1990s by the usually ineffective Pacific trade discussion group APEC, included about a hundred manufactured goods where tariffs raised the cost of pollution control—things like catalytic converters for automobiles, power plant scrubbers, scientific instruments for monitoring water quality, and so on. Another, developed by the OECD, ran to 164 products and included some agricultural goods.[151] The two could easily be combined and broadened to include new inventions and semi-agricultural fuels like ethanol. The WTO's services talks have created a similar list of environmentally beneficial services. A similar approach to environmental services damaging natural-resource subsidies is more complicated—no list seems ever to have been compiled—but in general terms would cover fishery subsidies, tax breaks for logging and mining, and farm payments that encourage conversion of forest and grassland into croplands.

The result, not in the remote future but within five years, would be a twenty-first WTO agreement on trade and the environment. The shift would not be millennial—it could never replace good national environmental laws, and is no substitute for international agreements to address climate change or cross-border pollution directly. But it would be large enough to matter, and give trade policy the useful position it should.

The next would be a reform of America's least attractive trade policies. With or without a WTO agreement, the United States ought to voluntarily eliminate half its tariff system. This would begin with a new tariff exemption along the lines of a very recent proposal by Senators Dianne Feinstein and Gordon Smith, along with Congressman Joe Crowley, comparable to the African Growth and Opportunity Act, for the least-developed countries in Asia, the major Muslim-world states. An especially generous version could include the eight larger low- or middle-income countries—Indonesia, Thailand, Sri Lanka, the Philippines and Paraguay; Armenia, Georgia, and Azerbaijan—still excluded from American tariff preferences. Again excluding oil, this would cover $70 billion in imports. This is still less than a twentieth of American trade, and barely three months' worth of imports from Canada. Either way, benefits would be immediate and conditions minimal, limited to cooperation in anti-terrorism efforts and the absence of genuinely grave violations of human rights.

This initiative would proceed whether or not other countries joined, though other big economies would be asked to contribute their share. Canada, Japan, and Europe could lift tariffs on fruit and vegetables, grains, olive oil, and dairy products from Africa, low-income Asia, and the Muslim world. India would abolish the specific duties that block goods from Bangladesh, Sri Lanka, and Nepal, and perhaps also the limits on its neighbors' farm products. China would be expected to contribute as well. The American contribution alone would cover only about $25 billion in imports—less than 2 percent of American trade—but would instantly make the livelihoods of Cambodia's garment workers secure, along with those of their sisters in Bangladesh, Pakistan, Nepal, and a few more Asian and Muslim countries. If all the major economies participated, it could double farm and factory exports in the Middle East and Muslim South Asia, filtering $40 billion a year through factories out to poor city neighborhoods, and creating few million new jobs for the young women and *diplome-chomeurs* of the Arab world and Muslim Asia.

Finally, over a longer period—perhaps five years, at most ten—this benefit for low-income foreigners would broaden into full elimination of tariffs that hurt America's poor most. Tariffs on cheap shoes, clothes, luggage, and silverware no longer made in the United States would go immediately. Tariffs on clothes, leather, household textiles, silverware, plates, and other life necessities should go in the later stages.

And so the worst flaws of our own policies would be gone. The effect on jobs in the rich countries would be small, possibly nil. Recall that the International Trade Commission's a far more hypothetical—eliminating all American tariffs, quotas, and trade-related subsidies—would mean only the equivalent of one day's normal layoffs and hire. The policies it would scrap are not worth keeping; all either funnel wealth to people who are already wealthy, tax the poor, or are proven failures in protecting jobs. Though the result would not be the vision of Paine or Cobden, it would be something significant for environmental quality, for people in the U.S. and abroad whose lives are very difficult, and for the hope of better times in the Muslim world.

A Concluding Thought

Such a plan is never as easy to execute as it is to imagine, even with the most willing government possible. And of course trade and the global economy have no special claim to attention. Long-frustrated hopes for national health insurance, newer demands for energy efficiency, and a response to climate change will contend for priority, along with education, election reform, and many other issues. Two legacies of the Bush presidency—a chronic budget crisis and the awful dilemmas of Iraq—will press upon the next administration regardless of its own hopes. And the trade policy breach within the Democratic party is as fresh as it was ten years ago, with even Charles Rangel and Nancy Pelosi drawing angry blasts from activists and leftist Representatives over their trade accord with the Bush administration.

Supporters should also concede that after sixty years, much of the work of trade policy is complete. The open world destroyed between 1914 and 1930 has been rebuilt on a steadier foundation. The trade rules and agreements have helped, at each great test, to prevent a panic and unraveling like that of the early 1930s. Though still tougher on the poor than on the rich, the system can still help nations as poor and troubled as Ethiopia and Cambodia to find their place. And peace among the great nations grows more stable by the year.

There is, therefore, a reasonable case for leaving the matter alone.

But it is a case based upon prudence, not ideals. Both the trading system and American trade policies are flawed—and their flaws should be especially troublesome and embarrassing to the American liberals whose ancestors and heroes created them. Policies and institutions that should take special care for the poor instead make poverty, within the United States and overseas, harder to escape. Agreements that could assist in conservation and pollution control remain ideas rather than law. A system of open trade and mutual benefit, designed above all to secure peace, all but misses the most violent and dangerous part of the modern world.

And to fix the flaws requires so little—only, in fact, the qualities that are typical of liberalism at its best. The work requires good-government virtues—careful attention to the details of policy, and willingness to drop ideas that empirical facts and evidence show mistaken—informed by signature ideals: special concern for the poor, a commitment to broadly shared prosperity, the rule of law, foreign policy with a base broader than military power alone.

These qualities served well in the past. As the "grandchildren" Roosevelt imagined in his letter to Congress, we live in a world which has moved a long way toward unity. As it has done so, it has also moved toward shared prosperity and peace. Roosevelt's trade project deserves some of the credit, and its work is not yet done.

NOTES

1   *The Nation*, June 4, 2007; Senator Russ Feingold in Congressional Record, May 17, 2007, page S6261.
2   Skipping the task of accounting for both inflation and the falling price of consumer goods. A British historian, Angus Maddison, estimates a "real" seven-fold expansion of world GDP in the last fifty years.
3   Zhou Daguan, "The Customs of Cambodia," 1305 AD; translated J. Gilman D'Arcy Paul, Social Science Association Press, Bangkok, 1967.
4   Dr. Muhammud Yunus, testimony to Senate Committee on Finance, May 16, 2007.
5   ILO website: www.betterfactories.org
6   Statistics provided by Mr. Norng Sayeth, Marketing Manager of Sihanoukville Autonomous Port.
7   Information from betterfactories.org, the ILO's Cambodia labor monitoring project.
8   Scott Carrier, "In A Brothel Atop Street 63," *Mother Jones*, March–April 2006, http://www.motherjones.com/news/feature/2006/03/brothel_cambodia.html
9   Srei does make about 30 cents an hour, discounting overtime and attendance bonuses. Her Chinese competitors, according to a 2002 survey by the International Trade Commission, make a dollar or so.
10 From Rep. Sanders' website, at http://bernie.house.gov/trade.asp, viewed 5/15/2006
11 Brown Sherrod, *Myths of Free Trade: Why American Trade Policy Has Failed*, W.W. Norton & Co., 2004, pp. 61–62.
12 Sweeney, John, Remarks at Jones Day Speakers Series, Cleveland OH, November 2005, at http://www.aflcio.org/mediacenter/prsptm/sp11212005.cfm?RenderForPrint=1
13 Quotes from *Alternatives to Economic Globalization: A Better World is Possible International Forum on Gobalization*, Berrett-Koehler Publishers Inc., San Francisco, 2002.,
14 John Halpin and Ruy Teixeira, "The Politics of Definition, Part IV," *The American Prospect*, April 27, 2006.
15 John Sweeney.
16 Franklin Roosevelt, "The President Urges the Congress to Strengthen the Trade Agreements Ad." March 26, 1945, in Public Papers of the President, 1945.
17 Xenophon, *Ways and Means*.

18 The Emperor ordered Sima Qian castrated, after his public defense of an unfairly disgraced general.

19 General Meng. Unjustly condemned to death, he reflected that his fate was necessary; in building the Wall, he had cut the sinews and arteries of the Earth. Quite a different general from the one mentioned in footnote 9, whose name was Li Ling.

20 A shekel was not a coin but a specific amount of silver. It weighed about fifteen grams. Sixty shekels would be the equivalent of a pound of silver.

21 On Sheba and frankincense, the 1th-century Roman writer Pliny described a caravan which delivered the frankincense crop from Yemen via Gaza, on an annual trip taking sixty-five days. In 66 A.D., he says, Nero bought the whole crop and burnt it to show his grief for the loss of his wife Poppaea Sabina, whom he had kicked to death. Ophir is traditionally thought to be Ethiopia or Somalia; much earlier, the Egyptian Queen Hatchepsut sent a merchant fleet to this region looking for incense. Her sailors found villages with huts built on poles and roofed with palm leaves, ruled by a dwarfish and very fat queen. They returned after six months with a cargo much like that of Solomon's later fleet: a few pet monkeys, a boatload of ebony, bags of cinnamon, incense, gold and ivory.

22 "Of all those expensive and uncertain projects which bring bankruptcy to the greater part of the people who engage in them, there is none perhaps more perfectly ruinous than the search after new gold and silver mines . . . when any person undertakes to work a new mine in Peru, he is universally looked upon as a man destined to bankruptcy and ruin, and is upon that account shunned and avoided by everybody." Adam Smith, *An Inquiry into the Nature and Causes of the Wealth of Nations.* 1776, Chapter XI, Part 2. (Modern Library Edition, 1937) p. 170. See page 529 for more abuse of gold-mining ventures.

23 Smith, Adam, T*he Wealth of Nations*, Modern Library, 620–621.

24 *Ibid.*, page 462.

25 *Ibid.*, page 424

26 *Ibid.*, 613.

27 Romila Thapar, the historian of ancient India, suggests a figure of 550 million sesterces for the India trade alone. This would imply a deficit of 10 percent of GDP, larger than America's today.

28 Smith, John, *Memoirs of the Wool Trade*, Chapter lxvii, "Debates Over the East India Company in Parliament," London, 1815.

29 Earle, Peter, *The World of Defoe*, Weidenfeld & Nicholson, 1976, page 124.

30 Bureau of Labor Statistics, "Earnings By Industry" survey, at http://stats.bls.gov/ces/home.htm

31 U.S. International Trade Commission, Textiles and Apparel: Assessment of the Competitiveness of Certain Foreign Suppliers to the U.S. Market, Volume II, Investigation 332–448, June 2003, at http://hotdocs.usitc.gov/pub3671/profiles.html

32 Across the Channel, the French wool-spinners faced the same questions. Their sly response, according to Fernand Braudel, was to appeal for a law requiring prostitutes to wear cotton clothes. The effect, presumably, would be a stigma on cotton which deterred respectable women from buying the stuff.

33 Pliny thought the Chinese were blond and spoke in loud voices.

34 *Phaedo*, Plato, in The Last Days of Socrates, (Penguin, 1954) p. 111.

35 Plato, *Laws*, Book iii.
36 *Ibid.*, Book xi.
37 Sima Qian, *Records of the Historian*, (Trans. Burton Watson, Columbia University Press, 1958) pp. 333-334.
38 Economic History Net. See http://eh.net/hmit/gdp/
39 Early trade data from the Historical Almanac of American Statistical Abstracts, vol 2, page 902 http://www2.census.gov/prod2/statcomp/documents/CT1970p2-08.pdf All tea came from China until 1839, when India opened its first commercial tea plantation.
40 Thomas Jefferson, "Report on the Privileges and Restrictions on the Commerce of the United States in Foreign Countries." 1793.
41 Thomas Paine, *The Rights of Man*, 1790, Chapter 5, Part 1.
42 He was, however, a little soft on book importes, suggesting that the sort of books "which usually fill the libraries of the wealthier classes and professional men" should get a tariff of 5 percent, and books meant for libraries and universities should be exempt altogether.
43 Alexander Hamilton, Report on the Subject of Manufactures, reprinted in F.W. Taussig, *State Papers and Speeches on the Tariff*, Harvard University, 1892; reprinted by August Kelley, 1972, page 35.
44 William Mckinley, "The Triumph of Protection," Address to Nebraska Chetaque Association, August 2, 1892.
45 United States Magazine and Democratic Review, 1846
46 *State Papers and Speeches on the Tariff*, F.W. Taussig ed., Harvard University, 1892; reprinted by August Kelley, 1972, page 202.
47 William Walker, "Report from the Secretary of the treasury, on the state of the Finances, etc." Washington DC, 1846.
48 Richard Cobden, "Free Trade II" Address at Manchester, January 15, 1846.
49 Weightman, Gavin, *The Frozen Water Trade*, Hyperion, 2003.
50 J. M. Keynes, *Economic Consequences of the Peace*, (Harcourt, Bruce and Row, NY, 1920) pp. 11-12
51 Benton McMillin, "The Income Tax," *Saturday Evening Post*, May 17, 1913.
52 Warren G. Harding, Inaugural Address, March 4th, 1921.
53 *Ibid.*
54 Interview with Nieuwe Rotterdamsche Courant, 1921; reprinted in Einstein, Albert, *Ideas and Opinions*, Crown Publishers, 1954; 1982 reprint, pp. 4–5.
55 Herbert Hoover, Cleveland campaign speech, October 15, 1932.
56 House Committee on Ways and Means, Hearings on Tariff Act of 1930.
57 *Ibid.*
58 *Ibid.*, page 3580.
59 *Ibid.*, page 1253.
60 *Ibid.* page 1677
61 House Committee on Ways and Means, Hearings on Tariff Act of 1930.
62 Eckes, Alfred, *Opening America's market: U.S. Foreign Trade Policy Since 1776*, University of North Carolina Press, 1995, Chapter 4 passim; Brown, Sherrod, op. cit., pp. 178–179.
63 Egg price data from U.S. Department of Agriculture, at http://usda.mannlib.cornell.edu/data-sets/livestock/89007/table002.xls
64 See Charles Kindleberger, *The World in Depression*, second edition, 1986.
65 Statistical Yearbook of the League of Nations for 1926–1935, available online at http://www.library.northwestern.edu/govinfo/collections/league/stat.html

66   League of Nations annual statistical reports, 1929–1933: http://www.
      library.northwestern.edu/govpub/collections/league/stat.html#1930
67   Herbert Hoover, speech at Des Moines, Oct. 4, 1932.
68   Wyatt, David, *History of Thailand*, 1982, page
69   Kobkua Suwannat-Piam, T*hailand's Durable Premier: Luang Pibul Through
      Three Decades*, Oxford University Press, 1995.
70   Siam is thought to be originally a Cambodian name. "Thailand," used
      since the 1930s. translates the local "Prathet Thai" or "Muang Thai" into
      English.
71   Storrey, Richard, *History of Modern Japan*, Penguin, U.K., 1979.
72   Franklin Roosevelt, "Remarks at the Inter-American Conference of the
      Maintenance of Peace. Dec. 1, 1936.
73   Cordell Hull, *Memoirs of Cordell Hull, Vol. 1*, MacMillan, NY, 1948,
      page 364.
74   *Ibid.*, page 364.
75   Though the third of Woodrow Wilson's Fourteen Points suggests some
      kind of attempt at an international open-trade agreement.
76   The Havana Charter remains available, through the WTO at
      http://www.wto.org/english/docs_e/legal_e/havana_e.pdf
77   The first three are named for the sites of conferences opening the talks;
      the last for an American Secretary of State, Douglas Dillon.
78   Eckes, op. cit., page 188.
79   "Remarks to National Association of Manufactures"," John F. Kennedy,
      Washington, DC, December 6, 1961.
80   The American selling price required Customs officials to assume that
      chemicals should sell at the existing price found in the United States,
      even though a German or British alternative might be cheaper than the
      American version. For example, a 20 percent tariff on a $5 can of green
      British paint would normally be $1 If the American paint industry was
      charging $10 for the paint, though, the Customs officer would assume a
      $10 price for the British paint and charge a $2 tariff.
81   Maddison, Angus, *The World Economy: Historical Statistics*, OECD
      Development Centre Studies, 2003, Table 8b on page 261.
82   Disclosure note: and brought me to the agency
83   This simply meant the end of an annual review of MFN status, which
      had proceeded each year because of China's inclusion in a 1974 law,
      conditioning trade with communist countries on freedom of emigration.
      Known as the Jackson-Vanik Amendment for its sponsors Henry Jackson
      and Charles Vanik, this law was meant to pressure the Soviet Union to
      grant Jews freedom to leave for Israel and the United States. The law was
      written loosely in the early 1970s, long before trade with China became a
      controversial or even interesting subject, and seems to have applied only
      by accident to China.
84   Bureau of Labor Statistics, 100 Years of Consumer Spending, August
      2006.
85   See World Health Organization, World Health Report 1998 and succeeding
      years, at http://www.who.int/whr/1998/en/index.html
86   ILO, The End of Child Labor: Within Reach, at http://www.ilo.org/dyn/
      declaris/DECLARATIONWEB.DOWNLOAD_BLOB?Var_DocumentID=6233
87   Human Security Report 2005, http://www.humansecurityreport.info/
      HSR2005/Part1.pdf

88   Though to this day, partly by accidents of the calendar, no Republican
      President since Dwight Eisenhower has finished a GATT or WTO
      agreement. 89   Destler, I.M., *American Trade Politics, Third Edition*,
      Institute for International Economics/The Century Fund, Washington, DC,
      1995, page 49.

89   Destler, I.M., *American Trade Politics, Third Edition*, Institute for
      International Economics/The Century Fund, Washington, DC, 1995,
      page 49.

90   Gephardt, Richard, 1988 Presidential announcement address, March
      1987.

91   Job data from Bureau of Labor Statistics; import figures from Bureau of
      the Census; GDP figures from Bureau of Economic Analysis.

92   From the Commerce Department's Survey of Current Business, August
      1987, and August 2006.

93   Direct investment data from Bureau of Economic Analysis for 2005;
      October 1986 Survey of Current Business for 1985; Historical Statistics of
      the United States, Colonial Times to 1970, for 1965.

94   Bureau of Economic Analysis, Current Population Survey, available at
      http://stats.bls.gov/cps/home.htm

95   Bureau of Economic Analysis, GDP by Industry survey, "Real Value Added
      By Industry" series, available at http://www.bea.gov/bea/industry/
      gpotables/gpo_action.cfm?anon=173&table_id=18891&format_type=0

96   U.S. International Trade Commission, "Assessment of the Economic
      Effects on the United States of China's Accession to the WTO,"
      Investigation 332–403, September 1999, http://hotdocs.usitc.gov/docs/
      pubs/332/PUB3229.PDF

97   Historical Statistics of Japan

98   AFL-CIO, petition to U.S. Trade Representative under Section 301 of 1974
      Trade Act relating to China labor policy, Page 1 http://www.aflcio.org/
      issues/Jobseconomy/globaleconomy/upload/china_
      petition.pdf

99   *Ibid.*, page 61

100   U.S. International Trade Commission, Textiles and Apparel: Assessment
      of the Competitiveness of Certain Foreign Suppliers to the U.S. Market,
      Volume II, Investigation 332–448, June 2003, at
      http://hotdocs.usitc.gov/pub3671/profiles.html

101   Yomiuri Shimbun, June 20, 2006.

102   U.S. Department of Agriculture, "State Laws Child Labor Laws Applicable
      to Agricultural Employment, January 1, 2006," at
      http://www.dol.gov/esa/programs/whd/state/agriemp2.htm,
      viewed December 21, 2006.

103   Rivoli, Pietra, *The Travels of a T-Shirt in the Global Economy: An Economist
      Examines the Markets, Power and the Politics of World Trade*, John Wiley &
      Sons, NY, 2005, pp. 92–93.

104   Lee, Ching Kwan, *Gender and the South China Miracle: Two Worlds of
      Factory Women*, University of California Press, 1998, pp. 5–8.

105   Kwan, op. cit, page 78.

106   Rivoli, op. cit,, page 94.

107   Lee, op. cit., page 39.

108   Mencius, D.C. Lau trans., Penguin 1970, Part 1A.

109   From Hakluyt, Richard, Voyages and Navigations, Penguin, London, 1978. The title of Haye's report gives an interesting flavor of the time and the risks of these trips: "A report of the voyage attempted in the year of our Lord 1583 by Sir Humphrey Gilbert intended to discover and to place Christian inhabitants in a place convenient, upon those large and ample countries extended northward from the cape of Florida, lying in very temperate climes, esteemed fertile and rich in minerals, yet not in the possession of any Christian prince, written by Mr Edward Haye who alone continued unto the end, and by God's assistance returned home."

110   The State of World Fisheries 2004, UN Food and Agricultural Organization, at http://www.fao.org/DOCREP/007/y5600e/ y5600e00.htm

111   See World Wildlife Fund, at http://www.panda.org/about_wwf/what_we_ do/marine/problems/problems_fishing/subsidies/index.cfm

112   A study of the consequences in Ghana, by Justin Brashares of the University of California, showed that access payments not only opened new waters for Europeans and swept up fish, but made fishing unprofitable for Ghanaians and forced them to turn to "bush meat." This in turn threatened land animals as well as marine species. Brashares found Ghanaian populations of forty-one big animals—lions, hyenas, bongos, giant hogs, colobus monkeys—falling by 76 percent after the access payments began. ://news.nationalgeographic.com/ news/2004/11/1111_041111_bushmeat_fishing.html

113   Reuters, "EU, Mauritania Agree on Fish Fisheries Partnership Pact," July 24, 2006.

114   The tariff system raised $23 billion in 2005. Over a third of this money— $8.3 billion—came from clothes. Shoes added $1.8 billion, food nearly a billion, and minor home necessities like spoons and towels another half billion.

115   Tariff and trade data from International Trade Commission dataweb; per capita income from World Bank, World Development Indicators 2006, Table 1.1.

116   HTS classification, 8-digit level, full-year 2003. All tariff data is from the U.S. International Trade Commission, and treats goods imported through the Generalized System of Preferences, Free Trade Agreements, the African Growth and Opportunity Act, or the Caribbean Basin Initiative as duty-free.

117   Trade data from the U.S. International Trade Commission, available at dataweb.usitc.gov, show textiles and clothing accounting for 37 percent of Turkish exports to the U.S., 42 percent of Egyptian exports and 40 percent of Afghanistan's infant export trade.

118   U.S. International Trade Commission

119   Average cost of cheap sneakers imported in 2002.

120   Bureau of Labor Statistics, Employment, Hours and Earning survey, at http://stats.bls.gov/ces/home.htm

121   U.S. International Trade Commission, The Economic Effects of Significant U.S. Import Restraints, Fifth Update 2007, March 2007, page 113.

122   EU AMS (Aggregate Measure of Support) notification to WTO, marketing year 2001–2002.

123   Report from freedomofinfo.org, at http://www.freedominfo.org/ features/20050407.htm

124 Guardian, "Royal Farms Get 1 Million Pounds From Taxpayers," March 23, 2005.

125 Guy Beaufoy, The Environmental Impact of Olive Oil Production in the European Union, published by European Commission, 2000 at http://www.europa.eu.int/comm/environment/agriculture/pdf/oliveoil.pdf, page 27

126 "The EU's Relations With Lebanon," Office of External Relations, European Commission, December 2005, http://europa.eu.int/comm/external_relations/lebanon/intro/

127 UN Food and Agricultural Organization, at [http://www.fao.org/newsroom/en/focus/2005/89746/article_89759en.html

128 Kym Anderson and Ernesto Valenzuela, WTO's Doha Cotton Initiative: How Will It Affect Developing Countries, The World Bank, March 2006, at http://siteresources.worldbank.org/INTRANETTRADE/Resources/239054-1126812419270/TradeNote27_Anderson&Valenzuela.pdf

129 Indian tariff schedule 2006, Chapter 61 (knitted clothes), published in 2006 at http://www.cbec.gov.in/cae/customs/cs-tariff/cus-tariff-2005/chapters-2k5/chap-61.pdf

130 Ibn Khaldun, The Muqaddimah: An Introduction to History, trans. Franz Rosenthal and edited by N.J. Dawood, Princeton University Press, 1967, pp. 310–313.

131 World Bank, World Development Indicators 2005, Table 2.1, pp. 48–50.

132 United Nations, World Urbanization Prospect: the 2003 Revision, Department of Economic and Social Affairs, Population Division, pp. 271–272; http://www.un.org/esa/population/publications/wup2003/WUP2003Report.pdf

133 See IMF annual Direction of Trade Statistics, for example the 1984 and 2004 editions.

134 http://www.unctad.org/Templates/WebFlyer.asp?intItemID=3489&lang=1

135 Sources: IMF Direction of Trade Statistics yearbooks 1982 and 2003 for export data; World Bank World Development Indicators 2002 for population figures. More detailed figures for the world population, GDP, and exports for Arab states, Iran, Turkey and Muslim South Asia are as follows:

	1980	2000	Change
World population	4.43 billion	6.04 billion	+36%
Muslim Middle East/ South Asia	469 million	770 million	+64%
World GDP	$12.9 trillion	$45.2 trillion	+250%
Muslim Middle East/ South Asia	$0.7	$2.4 trillion	+142%
World GDP Per Capita	$2900	$7485	+160%
Muslim GDP Per Capita	$1492	$3120	+109%
World Exports	$1.88 trillion	$6.36 trillion	+230%
Muslim Middle East/ South Asia	$256 billion	$310 billion	+20%

136 UN Development Program, Arab Human Development Report 2002, page 88, available at http://www.undp.org/rbas/ahdr/bychapter.html

137   "Youth Employment Trends," International Labor Organization, August
       2005, at http://www.ilo.org/public/english/employment/strat/
       download/getyen.pdf
138   Mernissi, Fatima, Islam and Democracy, Mary Jo Lakeland trans., Second
       Edition (Cambridge: Perseus Publishing), 2002, xi–xv.
139   "Pakistan Looks for Better Deal on Textile Exports," Financial Times,
       September 29, 2001.
140   World Trade Organization, World Trade Statistics 2005, at http://www.
       wto.org/english/res_e/statis_e/its2005_e/its05_toc_e.htm In 2004, only 6
       percent of the Middle East's trade was internal—Latin America's rate was
       17 percent, Africa's 8 and East Asia's 40—while the rate for Muslim South
       Asia was even lower.
141   IMF, Direction of Trade Statistic, 2005. See also Barshefsky, Charlene,
       "Bridges to Peace: The U.S.-Jordan Free Trade Agreement and U.S. Trade
       Policy in the Middle East," Amman, Jordan, July 2000.
142   World Bank, World Development Indicators 2006, Table 5.13; UNDP,
       Technology and Diffusion Indicator, at http://hdr.undp.org/statistics/
       data/indicators.cfm?x=129&y=2&z=1; Transparency International,
       Corruption Perceptions Indexes, at http:/www.transparency.org/
       policy_research/surveys_indices/cpi/2005http://www.transparency.
       org/policy_research/surveys_indices/cpi
143   Khalaf, Rima, "Arab Human Development Report," United Nations
       Development Program, 2002, at http://www.rbas.undp.or/ahdr2.
       cfm?menu=10
144   "UNDP Releases the First Arab Human Development Report," Executive
       Summary, United Nations Development Program, http://www.undp.org/
       rbas/ahdr/ahdr1/presskit1/PARExecSummary.pdf
145   Economic Survey of Pakistan 2005–2006, at http://www.finance.gov.pk/
       survey/home.htm
146   King Abdullah II, Speech to Los Angeles World Affairs Council, June 5th,
       2000, at http://www.lawac.org/speech/pre%20sept%2004%20speeches/
       abdullah.html
147   Zoellick, Robert, "Fighting Terror with Trade," Washington Post,
       September 20, 2001.
148   See Department of Labor, "Trade Adjustment Assistance (TAA) and
       Alternative Trade Adjustment Assistance (ATAA) Services and Benefits,"
       2005, at http://www.doleta.gov/tradeact/benefits.cfm
149   ILO, The End of Child Labor: Within Reach, May 2006, at http://www.ilo.
       org/public/english/standards/relm/ilc/ilc95/pdf/rep-i-b.pdf . See page 8
       for statistics, and page 14 for a discussion of Bolsa Familia in Brazil.
150   Kuhlmann, Katrin, "U.S. Trade Preference Programs: How Well Do They
       Work?," testimony to Senate Committee on Finance, May 16th, 2007.
151   Ronald Steenblike provides a good summary of the lists in a paper done
       for the OECD: Environmental Goods: A Comparison of the APEC and OECD
       Lists, published November 29, 2005 and available at http://www.oecd.
       org/dataoecd/44/3/35837840.pdf

INDEX

1970s, v, 19, 22, 91, 107, 117, 123, 125, 202
  oil crisis of, 22, 110
Abbasid empire, 188–189, 197
Abdullah II, King of Jordan, 194, 195
Addis Ababa, 183–184
Access payments, in fishery industry, 157–158
Adams, John, 49, 66, 156
Afghanistan, 190, 193, 195, 196. 207
AFL-CIO, 18, 99, 123, 131–133, 135
Petition for tariffs on Chinese goods, 132–133
Africa, 21, 94, 120, 194, 202
  African Growth and Opportunity Act (trade preference), vii, 94, 168
Agricultural lobbies, 72–73, 166, 177–180
AIDS, HIV, 13, 109
Airbus, 36
Albania, 43
Aldrich, Nelson, 56
Algeria, 193
Alpha Trading Partners, 183
American Iron and Steel Institute, 73
American Textile Manufacturers Institute, 99, 166
Angkor Wat, 6, 12, 172
Anti-globalization movement, 19–20, 47
APEC, 209
Arab Human Development Report series, 194
Arab League, 193, 196
Arab-Israeli conflict, 187, 194, 196
Arafat, Yasser, 187

Argentina, 43, 44, 79, 83
Arizona, as cotton exporter, 180
Armenia, 92
Arthur, Chester, 62
Asia, economic integration of, 130–131, 141–144
Asian financial crisis, 78–79, 161
Association of Rubber and Plastic Footwear Manufacturers, 166
Ataturk, Kemal, 81
Athens, classical, 30–31
Austria, 92
Australia, 77, 125
Azerbaijan, 196
Baghdad, 188–189
Bahrain, 29
Bangladesh, 140, 168, 169, 176, 182, 190, 196, 210
Bangkok, 7, 80, 81
Barak, Ehud, 187
Barenberg, Mark, 132, 135, 137
Barshefsky, Charlene, 95, 98, 100–101, 105, 161, 196
Bassett, John, 37
Baucus, Max, 104, 196, 205
BBC, 162
Belgium, 15, 70, 85
Benes, Edvard, 84
Benin, 150, 180
Biden, Joseph, 104
Blair, Tony, 162
Blinder, Alan, 144
Blue jeans, etymology, 62
Bono (rock star/activist), 286
Book publishing industry, American, Hamilton's tariff ideas, 51

Rejects tariff protection in Smoot-Hawley debate, 74
Bosnia, 187, 196
Brandeis, Louis, 65
Brassieres, 162–164
Bolivia, 80
Bolsa Familia (Brazilian anti-child labor program), 207
Brazil, 52, 62, 79, 85, 88, 94, 108, 129, 137, 156, 162, 168, 182, 206, 207
Britain, 48, 49, 50, 51, 57, 69, 70, 77, 78, 79, 84, 85, 110, 129, 169, 187
    17th-century, 36–37
    Low-wage competitor to US, 1791–1930, 52, 54, 56, 74
    Victorian, 61–64
Bronfenbrenner, Kate, 126
Brown, Sherrod, 18, 22, 75
Bryan, William Jennings, 57
Bruning, Heinrich, 82
Bulgaria, 79, 92
Bureau of Labor Statistics, 109, 175
Burkina Faso, 182
Burma, 43, 47, 73, 88, 96, 207
Bush, George W, v, vii, 161
Bush administration (second), 196, 205
Businessweek, 98
Cairo, 196
Calico Acts, 37–38
Cambodia, vii, 6–13, 87, 154, 167–169, 172, 176, 188, 196, 210, 211
    commerce ministry (also see Cham Prasidh), 139
    early history, 6
    garment industry, 6–14
    labor law, 7, 207
    sex industry, 13, 173
    rural conditions, 12
    textile agreement with US (1999), 138–139
    tourist business, 12
    U.S. tariffs on, 167–169
Cameroon, 182
Canada, 21,76, 77, 92, 110, 210
Cardoso, Fernando, 162
Carter, Jimmy, vii, 91, 97, 102
Cassidy, Bob, 99
Caviar, 35, 150
Center for American Progress, 21
Central America, 10, 17, 94, 187, 192, 194, 197

Central Asia, 187, 190, 193
Century Foundation, The, 21
Chaco War, 80, 83
Cham Prasidh (Cambodian Commerce Minister), 11, 139, 173
Chamberlain, Neville, 84
Chaucer, Geoffrey, 189
Cheney, Thomas (necktie lobbyist), 72, 81
Chevalier, Michel, 63
Chi-ying (Chinese electronics worker), 135–136, 140
Child labor, 19, 109, 134, 135, 139, 207
Chile, 4, 79, 109, 160
China, 7, 9, 15, 20, 49, 69, 79, 92, 95–103, 120, 126, 128–129, 140–144, 162, 168, 186, 203, 207
    Attacked by Japan, 1930s, 82
    As 21st-century importer, 130–131
    As competitor with poorer countries, 9, 10
    Dissidents, 105
    Industrial growth of, 21st century, 129–130
    Industrial workers, 131–137
    Modern history of, 95–98
    Economic trends compared to Muslim world, 191
    Permanent Normal Trade Relations (PNTR), vii
    Wage rates, 37
    Agreement on WTO membership, 92, 95, 100–102, 129, 134
China Central Television (Taiwanese network), 162
Chrysler Corporation, 22
CITES (See Convention on International Trade in Endangered Species)
Civil War, 54, 55
Clay, Henry, 56, 57, 63
Clean Air Act, 123
Clean Water Act, 123
Cleveland, Grover, 58, 65, 68, 70
Clinton, Bill, vi–vii, 95, 98, 115, 117, 138, 143, 168, 187, 202
Clinton administration, 98, 104, 106, 108, 119, 138, 158, 208
Clothing trade, 5, 9–10, 18, 138–139, 171–173
    In 17th century, 37–38

Cobden, Richard, 63, 77
Coca-Cola, origin and etymology, 62
Cochineal, 48
Coffee, 66, 79, 88
Colombia, 109, 182
Commerce Ministry, of Cambodia, 139, 173
Commerce Ministry, of China, 142
Common Agricultural Policy, 177–180
Common Fisheries Policy, 157–158
Competition among wealthy countries, 143–144
Competitiveness, 205–206
"Conflict diamonds", 207
Connaught Place (New Delhi shopping district), 182
Conservatism, American, vi–vii, ix, 20, 22, 36, 54–57, 67, 103, 117, 118, 187, 201
Consumer movement, U.S., 165
Container shipping, 5, 9–10
Convention on International Trade in Endangered Species, 149–150, 155
Coolidge, Calvin, 69
Cotton, U.S. subsidies for, 180
Cox, Samuel, 59
Cuba, 77, 85
Currency flows, 38, 79, 108
Currency, exchange rates, 130
Customs Service, 61, 163, 176
Dairy, subsidies for, 180
DATA (Debt, AIDS, Trade, Africa), 207
Dawud, Abdul Razak (Pakistani Commerce Minister), 192, 196
Dean, Howard, vi, vii, ix
Declaration of Independence, 49
Deep-Sea Otter Trawl Fisheries Association, 74
Defoe, Daniel, 37, 47, 51
DeLay, Tom, 125
Democratic Party, v, 54, 58–60, 117, 118–119, 175
Denim, etymology, 62
Depression, of 1930s, 75–82, 191
Destler, I.M., 118
Developing countries, 108, 120, 122, 125, 131, 137, 138, 182
Diplome-chomeurs, 192, 210
Dispute settlement (Also see WTO, Agreement on Dispute Settlement), 14, 91–92, 151–154, 162–163, 173

Djibouti, 184
Doha Round, 107, 117, 159, 181, 209
Dollfuss, Engelbert, 84
Drinking glasses, 167
Earth Island Institute, 153
Eckes, Alfred, 75
Economic theory, 31, 33–35
Eggs, tariff war between US and Canada, 77
Egypt, 29, 33, 191, 193, 194, 195, 196
Einstein, Albert, 68–69, 144, 202
Eisenhower, Dwight D., 90, 165
El Salvador, 7, 80, 85, 93, 197
Elizabeth II, Queen of England, 178
Emanuel, Rahm, 206
Endangered Species Act, 123
Eng, Roland, 172
Environment, links with trade, 108, 147–159
Environmental agreements, international, 143
Environmentalists, U.S., 108, 123, 150, 151–152
Ethanol, 155–157, 209
Ethiopia, 15, 183–185, 211
Europe, 48, 49, 52, 68, 80, 82, 83, 84, 97, 108, 119, 143, 168, 172, 177, 194
  As low-wage competitor to US, 1791–1930 , 53, 56, 57, 60, 83, 120
  Main destination for modern US overseas investment, 124–125, 147
European Commission, 177
European Economic Community, 89, 90
European Union, 14, 15, 36, 89, 93, 157, 168, 210
  Farm policies of, 177–180, 194
  Fishery policies of, 157–158
  Tariff preferences, 94
"Everything But Arms," (European tariff preference program), 94
Exports, worldwide, 3–5
Fall, Albert, 67
Fallows, James, 119
Farm Bureau Federation, 73, 76, 99
Fast-track trade negotiating authority, 117
Faux, Jeff, 18, 19, 21
Finance Committee, Senate, 9

Fish, 35, 156–158
  As export product, 35, 49
Fisheries, loss of, 35, 156–158
Fishing fleet, world, 157
Flowers, as Colombian export, 16, 109
Foley, Tom, 119
Ford administration, 91
Fordney, Joseph, 68
Fordney-McCumber Act (1922 tariff
  increase), 68
Foreign direct investment, 124–125,
  147
  Within Asia, 141–142
  Falling Muslim-world share, 190
Foreign Policy (magazine), 117
France, 15, 51, 54, 56, 62, 63, 69, 70,
  72, 74, 78, 84, 85, 88, 168, 169,
  181
Francia, Jose Gaspar de (dictator of
  Paraguay), 43–45
Frank, Barney, 18, 109, 206
Franklin, Benjamin, 49
Free trade agreements, 87, 92–93,
  170–171, 208
Gallatin, Albert, 58–59, 65
Game theory, 158
Gandhi, Mohandas, 59
Gap, The, 10, 91
Garment Manufacturers Association of
  Cambodia, 139
GATT (General Agreement on Tariffs
  and Trade; see also World Trade
  Organization), 14, 15
GATT rounds, 1945–1994, 88–92
Generalized System of Preferences, 93
George III, 49
Georgia, 92
Gephardt, Richard, 103, 118–120
Germany, 15, 35, 62, 63, 72, 74, 76,
  79, 82, 84, 92, 129, 170
Gerry, Elbridge, 49
Gilded Age, 61
Gingrich, Newt, 125
Global economy, 3–5
  And American liberals, v–vi
  Described in statistics, 4
  Ancient, 29-30
  Founders' era, 48-50
  Victorian era, 60–64
  Modern, 108–110
Globalization, 3–5, 61–62
Gondar, 183

Goodman, Larry, 178
Gore, Al, 160
Grameen Bank, 208
Grand Bank, 49, 156–157
Grant, Ulysses, 131
Gray, Chester, 73, 76
Greece, 178, 179
Guangdong Province, 96, 135, 138,
  141
Guangzhou, 5, 28
Guatemala, 48, 152
Guardian, The (British newspaper),
  178
Gutta-percha, 62
Hai'er (Chinese appliance company),
  125
Haiti, viii, 62, 64, 85
Hamburger, etymology of, 62
Hammurabi, 29
Hamilton, Alexander, 48, 51–53, 55,
  144, 145, 155, 202
  Report on Manufactures, 51–53
Hanna, Mark, 57
Haplin, John, 21
Harding, Warren G., 67, 68, 70, 203
Harrison, Benjamin, 56
Hawaii, kingdom of, 62
Hawley, Willis, 71–72, 160
Haye (British fisherman, 16th
  century), 156
He, Yuanzhi (Chinese garment
  worker), 135–136, 137, 140
Health insurance, 203
Helots, Spartan, 43
Honda, 125
Honduras, 5, 7, 10, 15, 19, 85, 151,
  171, 172
Hong Kong, 9, 10, 12, 15,47,64, 105,
  129–130, 135, 141, 142, 160,
Hoover, Herbert, 69, 70, 71, 75, 77,
  165, 166, 203
  As Progressive, 70
  manages emergency relief in World
    War I, 70
  and low-wage foreign competition,
    70
  Tariff theory of, 71
Hoxha, Enver, 43
Hoyer, Steny, 104
Hufbauer, Gary, 127
Hui, King of ancient Chinese state
  Wei, 148–149

Hukou system, 132, 133–134, 135
Hull, Cordell, 66, 79, 84, 85, 86
Hunter, Duncan, 103
Hyundai, automobile, 119
Ibanez, Carlos, 79
Ibn Battuta, 193
Ibn Khaldun, 189
Ice, as 19th-century Massachusetts
    export, 64
Iceland, 182
India, 6, 15, 20, 36, 64, 69, 78, 88,
    94, 120, 122, 123, 133, 137, 144,
    151, 170,171, 183, 189, 190,
    193, 195, 203, 206, 208, 210
  As low-wage competitor to 17th-
    century Britain, 36, 37
  Modern tariff system of, 108,
    181–183
Indigo, 48, 49
Indochina, French (Cambodia, Laos,
    Vietnam before independence),
    72–73
Indonesia, 36, 77, 133, 141, 171, 176,
    197, 210
Industrial revolution, 19, 38
Infant mortality, 109
Institute for International Economics,
    127
Intellectual property rights, 15, 62,
    91, 117, 193, 203
Internal Revenue Service, 65–66
International agreements, 19th-
    century, 62–63
International Conference on the
    Meridian (1884), 62
International Forum on Globalization,
    19–20
International Labor Organization, 7,
    85, 134, 138, 139, 140, 207
International Ladies Garment Workers
    Union, 117
International Monetary Fund, 3, 19,
    86, 87
International Trade Commission (ITC),
    71, 129–130, 134, 177, 211
International Trade Organization, 88
Internet, as services trade and
    offshoring vehicle, 14, 91, 118, 144
Iran, 15, 36, 78, 187, 190, 193, 196
Iraq, 187, 191, 193, 194, 195, 196, 211
Italy, 63, 81, 74, 87, 92, 179
Ireland, 124, 190

Isolationism, 1920s, 67–69
Israel –93, 125, 187, 193
Istanbul, 171
Italy, 178, 197
Jackson, Andrew, 56
Jackson, Jesse, 120
Jakarta, 171
Jamaica, 152
Japan, 15, 36, 62, 64, 92, 117, 119,
    130, 142, 143, 157, 162, 168,
    172, 177, 210
  adopts western time, 62
  as manufacturing competitor, 1970s
    and 1980s, 22, 117–118
  as goldfish and silk competitor,
    1920s, 72
  conditions during Depression, 81–82
  attacks China, 82
  al-Jazeera, 162
JC Penney, 10
Jefferson, Thomas, 49, 52, 53, 77, 78
  Report on the Privileges and
    Restrictions of the Commerce
    of the United States in Foreign
    Countries, 49–50
Johnson, Harry, 115
Johnson, Lyndon, vii, 165
Jordan, 93, 194, 196, 208
Kampong Cham, 6
Karachi, 190
Karim (unemployed Moroccan
    university graduate), 192
Kashmir, 193
Kelley, William "Pig Iron", 56, 77
Kennedy, John F., vii, 89–90, 116, 117,
    119, 124, 161, 204
Kennedy administration, 89, 165
Kennedy Round, of GATT, 90–91
Keynes, John Maynard, 64–65, 69, 81,
    108
  The Economic Consequences of the
    Peace (1919), 64–65
Khalaf, Rima, 194
Khmers Rouges, 9, 11
Kim Il-sung, 43
Kings, Biblical book of, 32–33, 47
Kipling, Rudyard, 64
Knapp, S.A. (rice lobbyist), 72–73, 80
Korea, 10, 14, 78, 98, 117, 119, 125,
    131, 141–142, 158, 162, 168,
    176, 178
Kosovo, 187

Kuhlmann, Katrin, 208
Kuwait, 15
Kyoto Convention, 155
Kyrgyzstan, 196
Labor standards, commercial benefit
    of adopting, 137–140
Lamy, Pascal, 108
Lao Tzu, 45–46
Laos, 92, 171
Latin America, 50, 79–80, 87, 92, 93,
    109, 110, 168, 193, 194, 209
Laws (Platonic dialogue), 38–41
League of Nations treaty, 67
Least-developed countries, 15, 94,
    173, 210
Lebanon, 179, 193, 194
Leguia, Augusto, 79
Lee, Ching-kwan, 135, 136, 141
    Gender and the South China
        Miracle, 135
Lemons, as U.S. export to China, 143
Lesotho, 5, 7
Levin, Sander, vii
Lewis, Bernard, 188
Liang, Ying (Chinese electronics
    worker), 136, 140
Liberal internationalism, ix, 85–86
Liberals, American, v–ix, 16, 47, 51,
    87, 116–118, 175, 187, 201–212
Libya, 193, 195
Lin, Willy, 129
Lingerie, imported, 81, 162–164
Link, Arthur, 161
Litvinov, Maxim, 84
Lobbying campaigns –
    For Smoot-Hawley Act,
    For PNTR for China, 2000,
    For tariff preservation, 1970s,
Lomen Reinder Association, 74
Long Beach, port of, 10
Low-wage foreign competition, vi, 17,
    20, 68–69, 134–135
    As 21st-century liberal concern, vi,
        17, 20, 120, 206–207
    As 17th-century British mercantilist
        concern, 36–37
    Hamilton's view of, 52–53
    Whig Party and 19th-century
        Republican theory -
    Rebutted by 19th-century
        Democrats, 59–60
    In 1920s America, 68

Lu, Xun, 97
Lund, Christina, 99
Luxembourg, 15
McCain, John, 9, 196
McCumber, Porter, 68
MacDonald, Ramsay, 84
McKinley, William, viii, 18, 56, 57, 58,
    67, 77, 115, 119, 120
McMillin, Benton, 59–60, 66
Macartney, Lord George, 96
Macau, 15
Madagascar, 7
Madison, James, 53
Maddison, Angus, 96, 97
Madrassas, in Pakistan, 197
Malaysia, 8, 9, 17, 141, 151, 168, 169,
    193
Mali, 180
Manufacturers of Surgical
    Instruments, U.S business
    association, 74
Manufacturing industry, American,
    126, 145
Mao, Zedong, 97, 98, 100, 140
Marshall Plan, 197
Maseru (capital of Lesotho), 5
Mauritania, EU fishing agreement
    with, 158
Meaney, George, 117
Mencius, 148–149
Mercantilism, 33–35
Mernissi, Fatima, 192
Mexico, 15, 20, 21, 48, 64, 78, 93,
    118, 120, 124, 152, 208
    Exempted from US tariffs by NAFTA,
        171, 172
    As recipient of US investment,
        124–125
    Successful against child labor, 207
    Sea turtles, 149, 151
Middle East (also see Muslim world),
    10, 107, 109, 143, 186–197, 207,
    208
Milan, 182
Mitchell, George, 119
Mongolia, 92, 169–171
Morocco, 178, 187, 190, 193
Murkowski, Frank, 9
Museveni, Yoweri, 180
Muslim world, 120, 186–197 passim,
    202, 210
    economic decline of, 190–191

Myths of Free Trade, by Sherrod
  Brown, 18
Nader, Ralph, 19
NAFTA, vi, vii, 9, 18, 19, 20, 21, 22,
  93, 116, 125, 126, 127, 160
Napoleon, 43, 54, 77
Nation magazine, vii
National Academy of Sciences, 151
National Association of
  Manufacturers, 90
National Science Foundation, 205
National Security Council, 98
National Trade Estimate (U.S.
  government publication), 50
NATO, 85, 92
Ne Win, 43
Nepal, 168, 182, 183, 210
New Deal, v
New York, 182
Nicaragua, 10, 85, 197
Nicholas II, Russian tsar, 69
Niger, 180
niger seed (see noug),
Nigeria, 182
Nixon, Richard, 97, 165
NKK (Japanese network), 162
Noug, 183–185
North Korea, 41, 43, 92, 108
Norway, 162, 169, 170
Novick, Bob, 99
O Globo (Brazilian TV network), 162
O'Neill, Tip, 119
Ocean Garments (Cambodia-based
  factory company), 7
Occupational Safety and Health Act,
  123
OECD, 179–180, 209
"Offshoring" in services, 144
Oil, 4, 5, 15, 20, 22, 79, 80, 110, 143,
  155, 166, 191
Oksenberg, Michel, 98
Olive oil, subsidies for, 178–179
Oman, 29, 191, 196
Oportunidades (Mexican anti-child
  labor program), 207
Oxfam, 165, 207
Oxford, 189
Paine, Thomas, 50–51, 63, 211
Pakistan, 168, 170–171, 190, 191,
  194, 195
Papua New Guinea, 150, 154
Paraguay, 15, 43–45, 80, 182

Parliament, British, 37–38
Parrots -
  In 19th-century American political
    campaigns, 53
  In 21st-century trade policy, 150
"Party of Gloom", 36–38
"Party of Hope", 30–36
"Party of Virtue", 39–41
"Pauper labor" theory (also see low-
  wage competition), viii, 56, 59,
  70, 120, 131, 137–138, 147, 206
Pelosi, Nancy, vii, 103–104
Perot, Ross, 160
Persian Gulf monarchies, 194, 196
Peru, vii, 7, 66, 79, 130, 172
Pew Research Center, 116
Phaedo (Socratic dialogue), 39
Philippines, 74, 94, 137, 141, 151,
  152, 210
Phnom Penh, viii, 6–7
Pibulsonggram, Field Marshal Plaek,
  81
Plato, as trade critic, 38–41
Playfair, Lyon, 35
Pliny, the Elder, 36, 38
PLO, 187
Plutarch, 42
PNTR (see China)
Poland, 79
Polling, public opinion, 116
Pollution, vi, 62, 120, 131, 147
Portugal, 33, 35, 78
Poverty, vi, 7, 11–12, 23, 160, 173–
  175
Powell, Colin, 192
Prajadhipok, King of Siam, 80
Prestowitz, Clyde, 119
Progressive era, 65–66, 165, 202
Pythons, as export product, 150
al-Qaeda, 188, 191
Quakers, 50
Qianlong, Chinese emperor, 96
Rabin, Yitzhak, 187
Race to the bottom (global economy
  theory; see also low-wage
  competition), 18
Rangel, Charles, vii, 205
Raspberries, as Chilean export, 4, 109
Reagan, Ronald, 20, 105
Reciprocal Trade Agreements Act, 85,
  87, 196
Reed, Bruce, 206

Reed, Thomas B. "Czar", 56
Republican Party, vi, viii, 18, 54, 55–57, 59, 63, 66, 67, 68, 70–71, 88
Retail industry, U.S., 134
Rhinoceros, 150
Ricardo, David, 35, 47
Richard II, Shakespearean play, 186
Rights of Man, (Thomas Paine), 50–51
Rivoli, Pietra, 135, 136
    Travels of a T-shirt in the Global Economy, 135, 138
Robertson brothers, 44
Robespierre, Maximilien, 41
Roosevelt, Franklin, vii, 22–23, 27, 75, 86, 95, 110, 115, 143, 165, 202, 212
    1944 State of the Union address, on war and trade, 22–23
    as founder of WTO system, 87
    As critic of Smoot-Hawley Act, 75
    On tariff retaliation as contributor to Depression and fascism, 83
    Good Neighbor Address,
Roosevelt, Theodore, 65, 66
Rousseau, Jean-Jacques, 43, 95
Rush, Benjamin, 50
Russia, 15, 35, 69, 70, 77, 92, 97, 107, 143, 150, 157, 158, 169, 189
Salmon, Norwegian, 4, 169
Sanders, Bernie, 17–18, 20, 21, 60, 131
Samurai orders, in traditional Japan, 131
San Pedro Sula, 5
Sandringham Farm, 178
Sanduk Watch Corporation, complaints about low Swiss wages in 1920s, 74
Saudi Arabia, 169
Schacht, Hjalmar, 94
Scientific Apparatus Makers Association, 73
Scotland, 33–34
Sea turtles, 149–154
Seaweed, edible, as topic in dispute settlement, 14
Semiconductors, vii, 4, 15, 92, 99, 119, 129, 143, 166
Senate, U.S., 10, 56, 67, 88, 134
Shanghai, 134, 154, 157, 171
Shi ji (see Sima, Qian)
Shireman, E.C. (goldfish entrepreneur), 72

Shoe industry, 166, 174, 175
Shrimp, as export product, 4, 109, 151–152
Sihanoukville port, 9–10
Siam (also see Thailand), 73. 78, 80–81
Silk, 6, 36, 37, 38, 64, 72, 81
Sima, Qian, 3, 31–32, 45–46, 47
    Historical Records of, 31–32
Sinclair, Upton, 18
Singapore, 10, 64, 125, 141, 160, 183–184, 190
Single-parent families, U.S., 173–176, 210–211
Slavery,
    In Athens and Sparta, 43
    U.S. and Caribbean, 47, 48,
Solomon, biblical king, 32–33
Smith, Adam, 33–35, 47, 54
    As liberal thinker, 33–34
    Disagrees with French over Chinese cultural superiority, 96
    On Elizabethan trade laws, 34
Smith, Al, 70
Smithsonian Institution, 48
Social contract, American, 204
Social Security system, 204
Smoot, Reed, 160
Smoot-Hawley Act, 71–77, 81, 83
    Exceptions to (black pepper, chewing gum, cocoa, spices, ant eggs, Gobelin tapestries, platinum bars, turtles, etc), 76
    Specific duties in, 76–77, 180
Soong, T.V., 84
Spice trade, ancient and medieval, 36
South Africa, 79, 88, 108, 130, 137, 143, 170, 171, 172, 206
South Carolina, 48, 49, 124
South Korea (see Korea),
Spain, 37, 48, 49, 78, 51, 158, 179
Sparta, 41–43
    As economically isolationist state, 41–42
    As totalitarian aristocracy, 42–43
Sperling, Gene, 206
Srei (Cambodian garment worker), 6–11, 138–139, 154, 168
    factory, 7–8
    pay and holidays, 11
    as competitor to U.S. workers, 17
Sri Lanka, 10, 168, 210

Star-Spangled Banner (actual flag), 48
State Department, 88, 89, 138
Steel industry, US, 22, 57, 65, 66, 72, 73, 99, 117, 119, 162
Steel, Bush tariffs on, 161–162, 168
Storrey, Richard, 81
Sturgeon, 35
Submarine cables, 4, 62
Subsidies, agricultural, 177–180
Sweden, 50, 78, 85, 110, 189
Sweeney, John, 19, 21, 22
Switzerland, 78, 85, 162
Syria, 170, 179, 193, 194
Taiwan, 9, 15, 117, 141–142, 162, 168
Takahashi, Korekiyo, 81–82
Taliban, 196, 207
Tarbell, Ida, 57, 59, 119
    The Tariff in Our Times, 59
Tariffs, U.S., 10, 161–176
    Failing to protect jobs, 175–176
    On brassieres, 162–163
    On shoes, 174–175
    On clothing and textiles, 10, 14, 192
    On drinking glasses, 167
    On eggs, 77, 92
    On ethanol, 155–157, 209
    On high-tech products, absence of, 166
    On low-income country products, 10
    On luxury goods, absence of, 166–167
    Preferences, 93, 210
    Hamilton's ideas, 52–53
    19th-century, 53–57
    As part of tax system, 55, 65–66
    As taxation of poor, 58–59, 173–176, 210–211
Tariff retaliation, 1930s,
Tate & Lyle (British sugar company), 178
Tax policy, of Bush administration, 175
Tea trade, colonial and early republic, 49
Teapot Dome scandal, 67
Technology, as solution to low-cost competition, 53, 68, 145–146
TEDs (Turtle Excluder Devices), 151–153
Teixeira, Ruy, 21
Tennessee, 59, 66
Terrorism, 188
Thailand (also see Siam), 7, 12, 78, 80, 81, 94, 141, 151, 181, 210
Togo, 180
Tokyo Round, of GATT, 91, 166
Tonga, 15
Toyota, 124
Trade Adjustment Assistance program (TAA), 204, 205
Trade agreements (also see free trade agreements), 92–93, 170–171, 208
    WTO, 88–90
    19th-century, 62–63
    In 1930s, 85, 87
Trade, as contributor to peace, 22–23, 50–51
Trade deficits, 129
    In Roman Empire, 36
    After Napoleonic war, 54
    Current U.S., 54, 130
Trade limits, 35–36
    For environmental purposes, 35, 149–152
    For humanitarian purposes, 50
Trade negotiations,
Trade preference programs, vii, 93, 94, 168, 210
Trade protection,
    For infant industries, 35, 36, 155–156
    For industries important to national security, 35
Trade unions, v, 22, 139
Treaty of Rome, 89
Truman, Harry, vii, 27, 87, 88, 165
Tsukiji fish market, Tokyo, 158
Tunisia, 178, 189
Turkey, 130, 171, 194
Turtle Excluder Devices (see TEDs),
Turtles, conservation policies, 148–155
Tycoon, etymology, 62
Uganda, 180
Underwear, trade policy respecting, 162–164
Unemployment, 22, 124, 126
United Nations, ix, 85, 87
UN Development Program, 194
United Students Against Sweatshops, 208

Universal Declaration of Human
    Rights, 85
University of British Columbia, 110
Uruguay Round, of GATT, 91–92, 165,
    166, 173
U.S.-Cambodia Textile Agreement
    (1999), 138, 208
U.S.-China Economic and Security
    Commission, 130
U.S. Trade Representative, 89–90,
    99–100, 104–105, 165
Victoria, Queen, 5
Victorian globalization, 61–64, 108
Vietnam, 9, 12, 79, 92, 190, 196, 207
Voltaire, 95
Wal-Mart, 10
Walden Pond, 64
Walker, Robert J., 59
War, declining frequency of, 110
Ways and Means Committee, 59, 72–
    74, 76, 191
Wealth of Nations, 33–35
Webster, Daniel, viii, 55–56, 58, 63,
    120
Wei kingdom (classical China), 148–
    149
Whig Party, viii, 54, 55–56, 57, 58, 60,
    65, 67, 70, 118, 131, 137, 146,
    202
Will, George, 162
Wilson, Woodrow, vii, 58, 59, 65–66,
    67, 68, 70, 76, 84, 87, 92, 134,
    161, 202
    Progressive program,
    Tariff legislation –
Women's EDGE (activist NGO), 207

World Bank, 86, 87, 108, 193
World Economic and Monetary
    Conference, 1933, 84–85, 86
World Health Organization, 109
World Trade Organization (WTO), vi,
    vii, 5, 13–17, 18 ,107, 108, 118
    And environment, 147–159, 209
    General Agreement on Tariffs and
        Trade, 14, 15, 152
    GATT rounds, 88–92, 165–166
    Doha Round, 209
    Agreement on Agriculture, 14
    Agreement on Customs Valuation,
        14
    Agreement on Dispute Settlement
        (see dispute settlement), 14,
        91–92, 151–154, 193
    Agreement on Rules of Origin, 14
    Agreement on Subsidies, 14
    Members, 15–16, 92–93, 99–100,
        193
    and Muslim world, 193, 195
World War I, 67, 87
World War II, 85
World Wildlife Fund, 157, 158, 207
WTO (see World Trade Organization)
Xenophon, 30–31, 41–42, 47
Yakut, 188
Yemen, 33, 193, 194
Yunus, Mohammad, 7, 208
Yilma, Tewodros (Ethiopian noug
    dealer), 183–184
Yuan Dynasty, 6
Zhou, Daguan, 6
Zhu, Rongji, 98, 106
Zoellick, Robert, 161, 196